THE *Bigger* PICTURE

THE
Bigger
PICTURE

A HISTORY OF
SCOTTISH ART

Andrew Gibbon Williams
AND
Andrew Brown

BBC BOOKS

NOTE All the measurements for paintings
are given in centimetres.
Height precedes width.

FRONTISPIECE Detail of Plate 54,
David Wilkie, *Pitlessie Fair*, 1804
National Galleries of Scotland, Edinburgh

ISBN 0 563 36948 5

DESIGNED BY HARRY GREEN
PICTURE RESEARCH BY DEIRDRE O'DAY

First published in 1993 by
BBC Books, a division of BBC Enterprises Limited
Woodlands, 80 Wood Lane, London W12 0TT

Set in 11/15 pt Monophoto Baskerville
by Selwood Systems, Midsomer Norton
Printed and bound in Great Britain
by Butler & Tanner Limited, Frome and London
Colour separations by Radstock Reproductions,
Midsomer Norton
Jacket printed by Belmont Press Limited, Northampton

Contents

Foreword
PAGE 7

Introduction
PAGE 9

CHAPTER ONE
A TRUE *Likeness*
PAGE 15

CHAPTER TWO
Enlightened TASTE
PAGE 53

CHAPTER THREE
Victorian VALUES
PAGE 83

CHAPTER FOUR
Land OF THE *Mountain* AND THE *Flood*
PAGE 117

CHAPTER FIVE
Modern MOVEMENTS
PAGE 147

CHAPTER SIX
Contemporary TRENDS
PAGE 181

Further Reading
PAGE 218

Picture Credits
PAGE 219

Index
PAGE 220

By far the greatest number of important Scottish pictures are in the collections of the National Galleries of Scotland in Edinburgh. The galleries comprise three separate institutions: the National Gallery of Scotland itself, the Scottish National Portrait Gallery and the Scottish National Gallery of Modern Art. In the first of the three galleries, the majority of paintings by Scottish artists from the eighteenth and nineteenth centuries (predominantly pictures depicting historical and genre subjects) can be found, but the gallery also contains a good number of very fine portraits by artists such as Henry Raeburn. The National Gallery also houses the Department of Prints and Drawings. The Scottish National Portrait Gallery holds a vast number of portraits of Scots and portraits which relate to Scotland's history by Scots. At the Scottish National Gallery of Modern Art, works by twentieth-century Scottish artists hang alongside a fine international collection of modern art. At time of writing plans are afoot to establish a National Gallery of Scottish Art in a separate building in either Edinburgh or Glasgow. Here the work of Scottish artists presently dispersed among the three institutions would be gathered to allow the visitor to gain a more rounded and thorough impression of Scotland's artistic achievements.

The Glasgow Art Galleries and Museums house the best collection of works by the Glasgow Boys and by Charles Rennie Mackintosh and his circle. Less numerous though excellent collections of Scottish paintings are also to be found in the public art galleries of Aberdeen, Dundee, Paisley and Perth.

Foreword

Over the past ten years interest in Scottish art has increased considerably, and this has been reflected in the ever growing number of publications devoted to the subject. There have been several excellent exhibitions focusing on distinct periods in the history of Scottish art, and on individual artists, and, of course, the scholarly research which has helped to bring about this happy situation is now far greater than it ever has been.

This book is not intended to satisfy the specialist, nor is it intended to cater for the needs of the enthusiastic student. Rather it is aimed at the many people both within Scotland and abroad who wish to discover and know more about Scottish painting, and thereby to obtain a general overview. It also provides a detailed companion to the BBC television series *The Bigger Picture* which offers an informative and entertaining introduction to the subject.

No such book, of course, could be written without the groundwork of scholars too numerous to mention, nor – since the bulk of Scotland's rich artistic heritage luckily still resides in Scotland – without the help of the National Galleries of Scotland and the Glasgow Museums and Art Galleries. We would therefore like to thank the curatorial staff at both institutions and, in particular, the Keeper of the Scottish National Portrait Gallery, Duncan Thomson, the Assistant Keeper, James Holloway, and, of course, the Director of the National Galleries of Scotland, Timothy Clifford, without whose help the tri-partite project of this book, the television series and the exhibition mounted at Glasgow's McLellan Galleries would not have been possible.

Thanks also to the Director of the Glasgow Art Galleries and Museums, Julian Spalding, and his Senior Curator of Art, Stefan van Raay, for facilitating the exhibition; to John Archer, Head of Music and Arts Television, BBC Scotland, for having the imagination to commission the television series; and to the private owners who have agreed to allow their pictures to be reproduced in this book.

ANDREW GIBBON WILLIAMS
ANDREW BROWN

Introduction

1 HENRY RAEBURN
Sir Walter Scott 1822
Oil on canvas 76.2 × 63.5
National Galleries of Scotland
Scotland's most famous artist first
painted her most famous man of
letters in 1808 at the behest of the
Duke of Buccleuch. This, his last
portrait of Scott, was painted in the
year before the artist's death for his
personal 'hall of fame'. In spite of
their position in the vanguard of
Scotland's cultural life, the two men
were not naturally in sympathy
with one another and Scott
disapproved of Raeburn's 'sketchy'
style. Nevertheless, the intellect of
a sitter whose features did not easily
lend themselves to the portraitist's
craft comes across vividly in this
splendid picture.

In what remains the most popular general history of Western culture, *Civilisation*, Lord Clark rightly asserts the undeniable fact that 'any survey of civilization cannot possibly omit Scotland'. One of the most erudite art historians of our century, the author – himself a Scot – was well aware of his own country's unique contribution to the visual arts, even if he had no room to explore it in any depth in his most wide-ranging work.

Nevertheless, skating over Scotland's artistic achievement has become something of a hallmark of general books on British art written outside Scotland. Perhaps because of the universal image of the Scots as an intensely practical people, and the pre-eminence of the country's scientists and men of letters, Scotland's artists have tended to be under-appreciated; this, in spite of an immense amount of study and attention devoted to them within Scotland over the past fifty years.

More than that of any comparable country, Scotland's art reflects the country's history to an extraordinary extent. It is a complicated history full of drama and extremes, yet it revolves around two momentous events. The first was the sixteenth-century Scottish Reformation, spearheaded by that narrow and unyielding firebrand John Knox; the second, the integration of Scotland into a greater English-dominated state, first with the Union of Crowns of 1603 and then, after a tumultuously unstable century, with the Act of Union in 1707.

The Reformation in Scotland was as thorough as any of the contemporaneous Protestant revolutions on the Continent and it excelled them in one particular respect – to the everlasting horror of all those who value the country's heritage. The northern iconoclasts – those who obeyed Knox's entreaties to rid Scotland's religious establishments of 'idolatry' – did their job especially well. Thanks to them, Scottish art prior to the seventeenth century is, sadly, thin on the ground; apart from royal portraits and decorative work – silver and illuminated manuscripts, for example – scarcely any first-rate Scottish art has survived from the medieval period.

By good fortune, however, a single great item of the highest quality was miraculously spared. This work, although more likely than not a 'one-off' in terms of its creator's output for Scotland, implies that the art which at one time decorated Scotland's churches and monasteries was as remarkable as that anywhere else in Europe. The so-called Trinity Altarpiece (Plates 2a and b) – probably spared destruction because of its regal content – is a major work by one of the greatest Flemish artists of the fifteenth century, Hugo van der Goes. It was commissioned by Sir Edward Bonkil, Provost of the Collegiate Church of the Holy Trinity in Edinburgh, and included portraits of King James III of Scotland, Queen Margaret of Denmark and their son, the future James IV. Although the royal portraits were probably inserted by the clumsy hand of a local artist after the altarpiece had been returned to Scotland, that of Bonkil was painted from the life in Bruges and is the first masterly portrait of a Scot in the history of art.

After Mary Queen of Scots' son, James VI, inherited the crown of England in 1603, conditions for the encouragement of the arts in Scotland were, if anything, poorer than ever before. With the permanent removal of the Scottish court to London, the pool of noble patrons upon which artists depended for commissions immediately dried up; and art, of course, was low on the list of priorities of the Presbyterian Church. Nevertheless, Scotland still managed to produce one native artist of note. The fascinating George Jamesone flourished in his homeland during the years preceding the English Civil War, producing some peculiarly effective portraits; he is the first really approachable personality in the history of Scottish art.

It is not, however, until after the controversial Act of Union of 1707 that any real sign of confidence among Scottish-born artists can be detected again. Due in part, no doubt, to a general feeling amongst Scotland's intellectual elite that the English market was now formally there for the picking, artists with ambitions beyond their own borders begin to emerge. One such was the aristocratic portrait painter, William Aikman. Schooled at home under the shadow of the sophisticated immigrant artist Sir John de Medina, and polished by the experience of a long sojourn on the Continent, Aikman removed to London and scored notable success by painting members of George I's court. The long tradition of Scottish artists achieving fame and fortune south of the Border had commenced.

In spite of Aikman's extended studies abroad, however, his talent was not individual enough to allow him to forge an original art from the combination of his Scottish character and the sophistication of the painting with which he came into contact in Italy. That honour was to fall to Allan Ramsay, a formidable genius whose major contribution to British art has only recently been fully appreciated.

Ramsay's love affair with Italy and his position at the forefront of the cultural movement known as the Scottish Enlightenment set a pattern which many Scottish artists attempted to emulate for the rest of the eighteenth century and a good part of the nineteenth. Painters such as the extraordinary Neo-Classicists Gavin Hamilton and Jacob More became absorbed by the artistic life of Rome, and the many younger Scottish artists who learned from them a love of the Antique and a dedication to 'serious' art helped to foster the atmosphere in which the Neo-Classical revival flourished to an exceptional extent back in Scotland.

In view of subsequent developments, however, it has to be said that this relatively short though fascinating period in the history of Scottish art now looks like something of a cul-de-sac. The ambitions of Scottish Neo-Classical artists to adorn the great buildings of their homeland with cycles of pictures depicting morally ennobling historical subjects were scarcely realized; and in any case, by the 1800s the aesthetic they subscribed to had radically changed, largely due to the activities of one man.

Sir Walter Scott towers over nineteenth-century Scottish cultural life and his influence dominates the work of Scottish artists during that entire period. Scott's prolific writing spun a Romantic web around the imaginations of Scottish artists which it took nearly a century for them to shake off. When a painter of histories such as William Allan needed a historical subject he turned to Scott; when a landscapist like Horatio McCulloch decided upon a view he could only see it through the eyes of Scott.

Conveniently, the author was painted a number of times by the artist generally acknowledged to have been the father of what was recognized in the Victorian period as the Scottish School of painting, Henry Raeburn (Plate 1). Although Raeburn came from the generation preceding Scott's and was exclusively a portrait painter, the Romantic spirit of Scott permeates almost all of his more important pictures. It is also, perhaps, more subtly present in the work of David Wilkie, the artist whose specialization in the depiction of subjects from ordinary life laid the foundation for the entire school of Victorian 'genre' painting.

By the end of the nineteenth century Scotland was, of course, a very different country from that inhabited by Raeburn. The most

2A AND B HUGO VAN DER GOES
Trinity Altarpiece: King James III
and *Sir Edward Bonkil panels*
c. 1478–9 Oil on panel
 Both 202 × 100.5
Royal Collection (on loan to
 the National Galleries of
 Scotland)

The *Trinity Altarpiece* was painted
for the Collegiate Church of the
Holy Trinity in Edinburgh by
one of the greatest Flemish
masters of the fifteenth century,
Hugo van der Goes. As a rare
survivor of Scotland's pre-
Reformation artistic heritage it
is evidence of the quality of art
which fell victim to John Knox's
Protestant Reformation. The
superbly realistic portrait of
Bonkil himself (the Scot
responsible for commissioning
the panels), painted from the life,
contrasts with the workaday
treatment of those of King
James III and his son, probably
painted by a local artist after the
van der Goes panels arrived
back in Scotland.

notable change in the landscape was the expansion of Glasgow. Although Scotland's capital, Edinburgh, retained its dominance as the focus of establishment art, the great industrial city in the west benefited from all the creative energy released by what was in effect a boomtown. It was therefore not entirely surprising that Glasgow produced the first groups of Scottish artists to recognize that radical artistic changes were occurring on the Continent. While, in the field of painting, the Glasgow Boys discarded the threadbare, sentimental myth of Scotland as a country of mists and mystery and, under French influence, began to look at their own country with a new objectivity, Charles Rennie Mackintosh and the several remarkable talents who gathered around him looked back to Scotland's ancient Celtic roots and devised an original version of the continental decorative style called Art Nouveau. For a brief period, Scottish artists were at the forefront of Europe's most progressive aesthetic developments.

The twentieth century presents a picture of Scottish artists swimming alongside their peers elsewhere in the West on the tide of modernism. To those outside Scotland, however, it may come as a surprise to find that the picture is – like the whole of Scottish art history – a bigger and more interesting one than they might have imagined. Following the turning point in the development of Western art marked by the experiments of Cézanne and the Post-Impressionists, Scottish artists, in particular J. D. Fergusson and his fellow Scottish Colourists, were to be found in France manning the avant-garde barricades next to heroes of the modern movement like Picasso.

Since 1945 artists trained in Scotland have continued the tradition, started by the Glasgow Boys, of looking directly at developments abroad. A succession of major artists – Joan Eardley, Alan Davie, Eduardo Paolozzi and John Bellany foremost among them – have achieved international reputations with work which, if not always classifiable as Scottish in any strict sense, is markedly different in tenor from that produced by artists coloured by the very different cultural climate south of the Border. In the 1980s this point was made forcibly with the phenomenal international success of a younger generation of Glaswegian artists, whose training as draughtsmen at the Glasgow School of Art allowed them to make technically skilful pictures which chimed in with the return to favour of figurative art abroad. This recent occurrence has encouraged a re-examination of the Scottish tradition upon which these artists have built and has confirmed the sense of national artistic identity which, in Scotland at least, has always been a positive inspiration.

CHAPTER ONE

A TRUE *Likeness*

The zeal with which Scotland's sixteenth-century religious reformers took it upon themselves to rid their country's churches of images they considered idolatrous means that virtually the only significant art to survive from the earliest chartable period of Scotland's art history is portraiture. Portraits were in continuous demand from the court and, even though most of them were painted by immigrant artists, this example encouraged a native tradition. From the early sixteenth century until well into the eighteenth, portraiture was the primary activity of both Scots-born and foreign artists working in Scotland.

In the sixteenth century, however, the religious and political turmoil which engulfed the country ensured that even the commissioning of portraits was rare, and in fact only a handful of continental artists managed to make a living in Scotland. Sadly, very little of their work survives and that which does appears strikingly feeble in comparison with the sophisticated work of their colleagues elsewhere in Renaissance Europe. The seventeenth century was scarcely more conducive; yet a small number of native painters did eventually manage to flourish alongside the foreign competition.

Although controversial in very many respects, from the point of view of Scottish artists the Act of Union with England of 1707 proved wholly beneficial. In its wake a new breed of wealthy, powerful Scottish aristocrats emerged and these new patrons began to actively encourage their compatriots. Consequently, during the course of the eighteenth century, several native portraitists of exceptional talent took advantage of the more sympathetic conditions and succeeded in forging solid reputations for themselves both at home and in England.

Of these, by far the greatest was Allan Ramsay, an artist now generally agreed to have made a major contribution to European portraiture. Ramsay, however, was more a cosmopolitan product of the Scottish Enlightenment than an artist of any marked Scottish characteristic, and it was not until Henry Raeburn began painting his penetrating studies of distinctive, Scottish types at the end of the eighteenth century that Scotland acquired an artist in whose work something intrinsically national can be identified. The Victorians dubbed him the Father of the Scottish School.

Raeburn died in 1823 and, not surprisingly in view of his artistic stature, in the course of the nineteenth century he had many successors: throughout the Victorian period, vast numbers of portraits were commissioned for both the stately home and boardroom, and this practice continued long after the camera had usurped the role of the brush and canvas. But by the time Glasgow's industrial magnates began collecting the work of Scottish artists the most interesting of them, like their counterparts abroad, were exerting themselves in different directions: the radical change in the artist's view of his role which occurred during the Romantic period meant that 'face-painting' was increasingly regarded by ambitious artists as a retrogressive activity.

George Jamesone AND THE IMMIGRANT TRADITION

The first Scottish portrait painter whose work is of sufficient merit to distinguish him as a distinct artistic personality is George Jamesone (1589/90–1644). Until his appearance the portrait demands of the Scottish court had been served almost exclusively by artists from the Low Countries. There was nothing unusual in this. Indeed, precisely the same practice was followed in England where the Gheeraert family of portrait painters served the court of Elizabeth I and where, in the next century, artists like Mytens, Van Dyck and Lely worked for the Stuart monarchs.

Only a few of Jamesone's foreign precursors in Scotland, however, can be identified with any degree of certainty. The Netherlandish artist Adrian Vanson (active 1581–1602) seems to have had a virtual monopoly of portraiture at the court of James VI before his accession to the English throne as James I in 1603. Vanson's pictures of this last ruler of Scotland as a separate nation are historically valuable depictions of a king who, it was reported, disliked sitting for his portrait. In the most revealing of them (Plate 3) Vanson has captured, in the hooded gaze, something of the cunning for which James was famous.

Nevertheless, in spite of his perspicacity, Vanson was certainly not in the same league as most of his great continental contemporaries. Nor does his work stand up well beside that of the English miniaturist

3 ADRIAN VANSON
James VI and I 1595
Oil on panel 72.9 × 62.3
National Galleries of Scotland
Vanson's portrait of the twenty-nine-year-old King James VI of Scotland is one of the finest sixteenth-century depictions of a Scottish monarch to have survived. The sureness of Vanson's Netherlandish technique has enabled him to convey the calculating personality of 'the wisest fool in Christendom'. No native artist of this period could have achieved such an accomplished portrait.

4 GEORGE JAMESONE
Self-portrait   Date uncertain
Oil on canvas 72 ×87·4
National Galleries of Scotland
In this work, the most impressive
of a number of self-portraits by
Jamesone, the artist has depicted
himself before a backdrop of his
own collection of small pictures.
The painting is a revealing
testament to the artist's social
standing and the sense of intimacy
is Jamesone's hallmark.

Nicholas Hilliard. Vanson's observation is incompetent and his technique crude. The backwardness of his style can be gauged by the fact that the great Baroque master Peter Paul Rubens was nearing maturity while Vanson was still painting.

The style of Adam de Colone (active 1622–8), Vanson's son, presents an aspect hardly more sophisticated than that of his father. Colone appears to have been Jamesone's chief rival in the 1620s but, in spite of his Scottish birth, it seems that he too trained in the Netherlands. Several of his portraits were formerly attributed to Jamesone yet they lack the charm which makes Jamesone's pictures so much easier to enjoy.

Born in Aberdeen, George Jamesone was apprenticed at an early age to the chief decorative painter working in Edinburgh in the early seventeenth century, John Anderson (active 1601–49). Anderson is a shadowy figure whose chief claim to fame is the now rather faded decoration of the small room in Edinburgh Castle where Mary Queen of Scots gave birth to the future James I of England.

5 GEORGE JAMESONE
Lady Mary Erskine, Countess Marischal
1626 Oil on canvas 67.3 × 54.6
National Galleries of Scotland
Jamesone's portrait of Lady Mary
Erskine is the best example of the
artist's work. Both in the refined
handling of the textures of the
sitter's costume and in the way that
light has been used to disclose form,
Jamesone reveals himself as an
artist who attempted to improve
upon the 'map-making' approach
to the delineation of features which
was the norm among those painters
who came to Scotland from the
Low Countries.

Jamesone, of course, was eventually to specialize in portraiture, but it seems that he remained involved in decorative activity for the greater part of his career. Proof of this is the fact that in 1633 he was summoned by Edinburgh's City Council to help with the preparations for Charles I's coronation visit.

As part of the festivities Jamesone organized a number of projects, the most important of which was the painting of a series of imaginary portraits of Charles's Scottish ancestors. These were used to decorate one of a number of triumphal arches erected in honour of the king's visit to his northern capital. Even more indicative of the artist's high standing, however, is the likelihood that he was permitted to paint the king from the life. Sadly, the portrait has not survived.

By this stage in his career, indeed, it seems that Jamesone had grown wealthy from his profession. In a fine self-portrait (Plate 4) he appears the image of the prosperous burgher, a Jacobean connoisseur-artist.

Most of Jamesone's surviving portraits are thinly but surprisingly spontaneously painted and this one, although in poor condition, is no exception. The wholly characteristic delicate use of glazes to create an atmospheric effect, however, can be seen to even better advantage in a very beautiful portrait of Lady Mary Erskine (Plate 5). Rather generously, though not without reason, the eighteenth-century critic Horace Walpole nicknamed Jamesone 'The Scottish Van Dyck'.

John Michael Wright AND THE *Catholic connection*

Jamesone's only pupil of note was John Michael Wright (1617–94). It is impossible to say for certain why this aspiring young English-born artist should have taken the unprecedented decision of coming to train in Scotland, but it could have had something to do with the fact that Wright's father was a Scot. Presumably, he came into contact with his future master during Jamesone's one and only trip south of the Border in 1633.

Wright's apprenticeship to Jamesone lasted five years and this was followed by several spent in Rome and elsewhere on the Continent. Upon his return he based himself in London and, following the Restoration of the monarchy in 1660, became the Dutch portraitist Sir Peter Lely's chief rival at the court of Charles II. In his early London years Wright cleverly made use of the Scottish patrons he had met through Jamesone.

The pattern of John Michael Wright's career was followed by all the most prominent Scottish portrait painters over the next two centuries: training in Scotland, a prolonged stay in Italy and then success in England achieved with the support of the Scottish nobility resident in London.

6 JOHN MICHAEL WRIGHT

Sir William Bruce *c.* 1664   Oil on canvas 72.4 × 61 National Galleries of Scotland

Wright was clearly a portrait painter of considerable merit, and his portrait of Charles II's Surveyor and Master of Works is an inspired creation; the relaxed way in which he has managed to convey the engaging presence of the subject makes it unique among his work. Wright's wide experience of art on the Continent is clearly shown in the polished manner of the picture's execution. It is tempting to regard the sense of atmosphere in this portrait as a legacy of Wright's master, George Jamesone.

Unfortunately there is no picture that can definitely be assigned to Wright's Scottish period and this makes it difficult to assess Jamesone's influence upon him. Even so, his portraits show a directness, a disinclination to flatter, which can be sensed in Jamesone and which was later to become one of the most impressive qualities in the best Scottish portraiture.

While in Rome Wright was elected a member of the prestigious Accademia di San Luca, an honour he shared with the very greatest of his continental contemporaries, Claude, Poussin and Velasquez. No other seventeenth-century British artist is to be found among such elevated company. Not surprisingly there is nothing in the least provincial about his style.

7 JOHN MICHAEL WRIGHT
Sir Mungo Murray   *c.* 1683
Oil on canvas 224.8 × 154.3
National Galleries of Scotland
Apart from being an invaluable document from the point of view of costume, this painting is the first instance in the history of Scottish art of an artist using tartan to create dramatic visual impact. Unusually for a portrait of this date, the believability of the landscape background suggests that it was based upon an actual location.

Wright's portraiture is invariably more naturalistic and relaxed than that of his better known rival Lely, and nowhere is this more apparent than in his superb portrait of Sir William Bruce (Plate 6).

In 1671 Bruce was appointed Surveyor and Master of Works by Charles II, and in this capacity he became responsible for the extension and refurbishment of the king's premier Scottish residence, the Palace of Holyroodhouse; his political importance, therefore, certainly merited a reverential treatment from the painter. But whereas Lely would have undoubtedly made an anonymous, pompous grandee out of his subject, Wright emphasizes the professional side of Bruce's character. The portrait is charmingly relaxed and contrasts starkly with the haughty aristocratic stereotypes which are the norm in portraiture of this period.

A memorable full-length portrait by Wright (Plate 7), though an altogether less intimate conception, earns a place in this book as the first of many tartan extravaganzas in the history of Scottish art. The subject has only recently been identified as Sir Mungo Murray, the fifth son of the Marquis of Atholl. Wright shows him dressed for hunting rather than battle, and in doing so has left us one of the earliest records of full Highland rig.

Wright's Catholicism seemed set to secure him further royal patronage from Charles II's successor, his brother James II. As Duke of York, James had been responsible for something of an artistic renaissance in Edinburgh where he had been sent to manage the King's Scottish affairs. Upon James's accession in 1685, Wright was despatched to Rome with Lord Castlemaine to stage-manage an embassy James hoped would secure papal approval for the reconversion of his new kingdom. Unfortunately for John Michael Wright the Glorious Revolution which brought William and Mary to the throne in 1688 cut short his career as decisively as it terminated the reign of his royal patron.

John de Medina AND Protestant patronage

It might be thought that the Stuarts' Scottish roots would have guaranteed James II support in his northern kingdom; and, indeed, over the course of the next century there were to be three impassioned Jacobite attempts to reinstate Scotland's hereditary monarchy. But the thoroughness of the Reformation in Scotland had ensured that anti-Catholic sentiment was stronger north of the Border than anywhere else in Britain. Several of William and Mary's most prominent supporters were in fact Scots and, after the success of the coup which brought them to power, these were rewarded with lands and more prestigious titles.

One such was the 3rd Earl of Leven who, in luring the artist

8 JOHN DE MEDINA
David Melville, 3rd Earl of Leven, 2nd Earl of Melville 1691
Oil on canvas 127 × 101.7
National Galleries of Scotland
This imposing portrait of John de Medina's patron, the 3rd Earl of Leven, is a fine example of the style which the artist employed when painting grand sitters. Before the 1690s portraits of such sophistication were unknown in Scotland. Not surprisingly, Medina's decision to emigrate north from London led to his cornering the Scottish portraiture market.

David E. of Leven
d. 1728

Painted by
Sir J.B. Medina

John de Medina (*c.* 1659–1710) north from London, was indirectly responsible for infusing Scottish portraiture with a fresh continental sophistication. Medina became the most influential portrait painter working in Scotland in the early years of the eighteenth century. Interestingly, he was the last foreigner to be naturalized a Scot and the last Scot to be knighted before the Act of Union.

Medina's background was thoroughly cosmopolitan. Born in Brussels of Spanish descent, he had moved to London in 1686 to try and take advantage of the upsurge in commissions which occurred after the Restoration. At first dismayed to find the portrait business more or less monopolized by the Dutch-trained court painter Sir Godfrey Kneller, Medina had nevertheless succeeded in forging a reasonably successful career for himself. Only persistent persuasion (including guarantees of commissions!) on the part of the Earl of Leven induced him to take the risk of moving to Scotland in 1694. Once there, however, he found he had the field to himself and stayed on to build up a thriving business.

Medina took a rather craftsmanlike attitude towards his profession,

10 WILLIAM AIKMAN
Self-portrait 1715
Oil on canvas 74.9 × 62.2
National Galleries of Scotland
By catering for the needs of the
Scottish nobility resident in
London in the wake of the Act of
Union, and by producing for them
precisely the sober kind of portraits
they desired, the gentleman-artist
William Aikman carved out a
successful niche for himself. Rarely,
however, did he surpass the
disarming intimacy of this cool and
delicately realized self-portrait.

typical of a gentleman-artist of the period. When preparing to leave
for Scotland, for example, he had no qualms about pre-painting the
bodies, draperies and backgrounds of his portraits to allow for the
completing of the faces from the life after his arrival!

There is nothing particularly Scottish about Medina's portraits of
his grand Leven patrons (Plate 8). His early style – really an exuberant
development of the formal manner originally introduced to England
by Van Dyck – is very close to that of Kneller. But Medina's later
portraits are freer and far more spontaneous, and it was the less
conventional approach evident in works such as the probable portrait
of his son (Plate 9) which had repercussions for Scottish portraiture.
The well-born young Scot who eventually inherited Medina's mantle
as premier painter to Scotland's nobility was fully aware of it.

William Aikman AND THE ORIGINS OF THE *Grand Tour*

The first Scottish painter to achieve real success in London in the
eighteenth century, and the first to study on the Continent for an
extended period, was William Aikman (1682–1731; Plate 10). One of

the benefits of the Act of Union was that it increased the number of professional opportunities for Scots south of the Border. Aikman was exceedingly well connected, so he was in an ideal position to take advantage of them.

Aikman's cousin was Sir John Clerk of Penicuik, the first of a succession of cultivated and generous Lord Clerks who were to support and encourage every important Scottish artist in the eighteenth century. It was through the Clerks that Aikman was introduced to Medina. By 1704 he had moved to London and was already writing of the possibility of painting Queen Anne and her consort. In the same year as the Union, however, Aikman sold his Scottish estate in order to finance a prolonged Grand Tour of the Continent.

Aikman was a trailblazer in this respect. Not only was his Grand Tour one of the earliest undertaken by a Scottish artist, but it was also more wide-ranging than many embarked upon later in the century when such journeys were less unusual. Other cousins of Aikman ran a trading business at Livorno (then the major port of entry into Italy for the British) and these in turn were in touch with similar trading colonies in Turkey. This network enabled Aikman to travel throughout the Mediterranean and into the Levant.

In Rome Aikman studied under Carlo Maratta and met the young English architect William Kent. The two became friends and visited Naples together. Back in England, Kent was to prove extremely useful in introducing new clients to Aikman. In 1711 Aikman returned to Edinburgh where he was quick to take over the niche occupied by Sir John de Medina, who had died the previous year. The commission for a series of commemorative portraits of the city's surgeons (an unusual group still hanging in Edinburgh's Surgeons' Hall) was transferred to Aikman.

As in the case of his predecessor, Aikman was soon enjoying the patronage of a leading pro-Union Scot. The Duke of Argyll, head of the large and powerful Clan Campbell and a hero of the Duke of Marlborough's campaigns on the Continent, put his military expertise to loyal use once again in 1715 by crushing the Old Pretender's first Jacobite rebellion. As far as the ambitious Aikman was concerned, he was the perfect patron. Apart from commissioning numerous portraits of himself, he introduced the artist to other wealthy clients. It was the Duke of Argyll who encouraged Aikman's final move to London in 1721.

Argyll's advice was sound. Godfrey Kneller's career was waning, and just as Aikman had been able to step into Medina's shoes in Edinburgh, he easily slipped into those of Kneller in London; from the 1720s until his premature death a decade later he was London's leading society portraitist, friend of the satirist Alexander Pope and

11 WILLIAM AIKMAN
Allan Ramsay 1722
Oil on canvas 75.7 × 64
National Galleries of Scotland
This portrait of the poet who
penned the popular tale of Scottish
rural life, *The Gentle Shepherd*, was
owned by the artist's cousin and
patron, the connoisseur Sir John
Clerk of Penicuik. Pasted on to the
rear of the canvas is a verse by
Clerk in the style of the poet:
Here painted on this canvas clout
By Aikman's hand is Ramsay's
　snout
The picture's value none might
　doubt
For ten to one I'll venture
The greatest criticks could not tell
Which of the two does most excell
Or in his way should bear the bell
The Poet or the Painter.

of all the leading intellects in London society. The Prime Minister, Robert Walpole, sat for him and Aikman's final work was a group portrait of George I and his family, the first royal conversation piece in British art.

During Aikman's Edinburgh days the poet Allan Ramsay was one of the colourful mainstays of the city's cultural life. Originally a wigmaker, Ramsay graduated to book dealing and writing poetry. He is nowadays best remembered for his delightful pastoral verse drama *The Gentle Shepherd*, an elegiac story of Scottish rural life which anticipates Robert Burns. The fact that the poet was also the father of the artist of the same name tends to be a source of confusion.

Aikman knew the elder Ramsay well and his portrait of his friend (Plate 11) is the kind of sensitive, intimate character study which contrasts tellingly with the bland, mask-like appearance of many of Medina's portraits. The mass-produced look of the typical early eighteenth-century society portrait only rarely crops up in Aikman's mature work.

Not all portrait painters were as socially fortunate as Aikman, and few experienced such untroubled and apparently effortless careers. Many others were blown off course by the aesthetic philosophy first promulgated in Britain by the Earl of Shaftesbury. As early as 1720 Shaftesbury had codified a rigid Classical hierarchy of subjects, according to which historical subjects represented the very noblest kind of painting while portraiture was very definitely an inferior variety – only a notch or two above still-life or genre painting. The conviction that this was indeed the case took root among several generations of Scottish artists; many who would have liked to become portrait painters and were naturally talented in that direction made for Rome, the fountainhead of Classicism, to acquire the training to practise what they had been persuaded was the highest form of art.

Upon their return nearly all of these were devastated by the discovery that there was no market whatsoever for history painting in Scotland, and they were consequently obliged to look further afield for opportunities to practise what became known as High Art. Even for those who were content to paint portraits there was relatively little work in Scotland; only at the end of the eighteenth century did Henry Raeburn prove an exception to the rule that to survive as a portrait painter in Scotland one had also to keep a studio in London.

Among those of Aikman's generation who did stay in Scotland, Richard Waitt (active 1708–32) is an interesting case. Waitt's work, although it has something of the appeal of primitive art, is not of particularly high quality, but he is an unique example of an artist employed by a clan chief to record, in a precocious essay in democratic benevolence, his entire clan. The sitters ranged from the chief's immediate family to his piper and tenants.

The clan system, whereby a chieftain was linked partly by blood, but predominantly by name and tradition, to a vast extended family of tenants was a survival of the medieval feudal system. After the defeat of the 1745 Jacobite Rebellion, the London government took active measures to suppress the clans and these were to a great extent successful. The Presbyterian Clan Grant from the town that later became Grantown-on-Spey had, like their wealthier, more worldly fellow patrons to the west, the Argylls, supported the Protestant succession and William of Orange.

Very little is known about Richard Waitt apart from the Clan Grant commission, but his simplified drawing and raw colouring are consistent with the tradition that he had been a pupil of John Scougal, a member of the prolific but inferior dynasty of Scots portrait painters. Waitt's 1726 portrait of *The Henwife of Grant* (Plate 12) is an extremely rare example of a non-aristocratic portrait in eighteenth-century Scotland. The artist was paid 25 shillings for the picture.

Waitt was an oddity – an artist with no horizons further than the lands of his clan patron. An artist such as the great, cosmopolitan Allan Ramsay (1713–84) would scarcely have been able to conceive of his provincial existence.

Allan Ramsay: ARTIST OF THE ENLIGHTENMENT

Without doubt, Allan Ramsay is the equal of Thomas Gainsborough and Joshua Reynolds, the two great English portrait painters with whom he is frequently compared. For a variety of reasons, however, Ramsay's reputation, which exceeded theirs for most of his lifetime, went in the years before his death into a sharp decline from which it has only recently recovered. In the last years of his life Ramsay painted almost nothing himself (partly because of an accident to his painting arm), while his London studio churned out royal portraits in fulfilment of his brief as Painter in Ordinary to King George III.

Dr Johnson said: 'I love Ramsay. You will not find a man in whose conversation there is more instruction, more information, and more elegance.' This description of the painter as a social creature is the key to understanding him as a man. Ramsay was the flawless embodiment of the Scottish Enlightenment and played a major role in its formation (see Chapter Two). He was multilingual by his early twenties, engaged in all the great debates of his day, and held strong

12 RICHARD WAITT
The Henwife of Grant   c. 1726
Oil on canvas 76.2 × 63.5
Private Collection, Scotland
Not all of Scotland's great families made use of the skills of artists of the calibre of William Aikman. The Clan Grant from Speyside employed Richard Waitt and, in doing so, bequeathed to us a rare record of a Scottish clan. Unlike Aikman, Waitt would have been virtually unknown outside the area in which he worked.

opinions on everything from Gothic architecture to the American Revolution. The idea of being confined by his chosen métier would have struck him as peculiar.

It is in the light of this wide-ranging, Renaissance view of his own role that Ramsay's brilliant achievement as a portraitist can best be appreciated. He really was the most extraordinary personality, growing up in the intensely art-conscious milieu of his father Allan Ramsay the poet's intellectual circle. This included artists such as William Aikman and the Norie family of decorative landscape painters (see Chapter Four). But the most important factor in forming the tastes of the young Allan Ramsay was his association with the Clerks of Penicuik.

It was in the Clerks' house that Ramsay, like Aikman before him, received his earliest artistic education. Sir John Clerk owned works by Holbein, Rubens, Van Dyck and even Rembrandt; not to mention portraits by Lely, Kneller, Medina and, of course, Aikman. The young Ramsay must also have seen the pictures by the contemporary Roman painter Imperiali which Clerk had collected on his Grand Tour. Sir John's dilettante son, James, had in fact spent some time in the studio of Imperiali, and Ramsay was to follow in his footsteps.

Ramsay was a precocious talent and his father did everything he could to encourage him. At sixteen, the young painter's name was already entered on the list of founding members of the Academy of St Luke, a premature Edinburgh attempt to establish a Scottish academy along the lines of the famous Roman one of the same name. Six years later the poet petitioned the Edinburgh Lord Provost to help raise money to send his son to Italy.

In 1736, at the age of twenty-three, Allan Ramsay left for the Continent accompanied by an amusing doctor friend, Alexander Dick Cunyngham. The trip to Rome was to be only the first of four extended sojourns which punctuate his long and productive career and which qualified Ramsay to be the first Scottish artist to strut the European stage with confidence.

Travelling to Italy in the early eighteenth century was a potentially dangerous adventure, and Cunyngham's diary records all kinds of mishaps from theft to a near-fatal shipwreck. Once there, however, the presence of the exiled Jacobite court provided all Scots tourists with a glamorous, ready-made and intriguing society. Cunyngham's family had strong Jacobite sympathies, and during this stay he and Ramsay enjoyed a rumbustious round of Jacobite parties and suppers.

Ramsay had three masters during his first stay in Italy. First he attached himself to Imperiali, as recommended by the Clerks. Both he and Cunyngham struck up good relations with the Italian artist, who seems to have acted as their guide, as was the Roman custom.

Ramsay also benefited from an introduction to the director of the French Academy in Rome, the artist Vleughels, a friend of the great French Rococo artist Watteau. It was, however, in Naples that he encountered the artist who was to have the most profound effect on his early style, the distinguished Italian Baroque master Solimena.

In spite of the fact that most of Ramsay's better known mature portraits, especially those of women, are close in spirit to French painting and, in particular, to the work of Rococo artists such as Nattier and Perronneau, it was the Italian tradition which had the greater impact on him at first. Both Imperiali and Solimena were part of a continuous painting tradition which could be traced back to the Renaissance. They taught sound, sculptural figure drawing and Ramsay, already a skilled draughtsman before leaving Scotland, took to it with ease.

Ramsay's expertise can be judged from the glamorously confident

13 ALLAN RAMSAY
Self-portrait 1740
Oil on canvas 59.7 × 45.7
National Portrait Gallery, London
Allan Ramsay's early self-portrait is the brilliant result of his first period of intensive study in Italy. No British artist of Ramsay's generation was capable of producing a portrait of such panache at this date. It is not hard to understand the impact that Ramsay's arrival had on the London art scene in the 1730s.

self-portrait (Plate 13) that he painted soon after his return. No other artist in Britain at this time was able to describe form with this degree of expertise, and it is difficult to avoid the conclusion that Ramsay was showing off the flashy new continental manner he had acquired in Italy. The combination of a forceful, individual presence described with a slick technique is impressive.

There is nothing in British portraiture of the late 1730s which compares with Ramsay in terms of realism, and although his manner was to change radically over the next two decades the fearless way in which he deliberately emphasizes specific personality at the expense of social type remains the crux of his art. Soon after setting up his first studio in London, Ramsay was able to write, referring to the foreign artists who held sway there: 'I have put all your Vanloos, Soldis and Roscos to flight and now play the first fiddle myself.'

According to the engraver and author of *Notes on Painters*, George Vertue Ramsay was 'much cried up by the Scotch gentry', very much as Aikman had been in his day. And, again like his father's old friend, Ramsay soon benefited from the patronage of the increasingly powerful Campbell family. In the late 1740s he painted John, Duke of Argyll, and then slightly later his younger brother and successor. Engravings of both these full-length portraits did much to establish his reputation. Twenty years later it was through the Campbells' relations, the Butes, that Ramsay gained an introduction to the most important client it was possible for any portrait-painter to have, the future George III.

An exceptional Scottish commission which demonstrates the bravura qualities of Ramsay's early Roman manner, even more dazzlingly than his self-portrait, is the double portrait of the children of Lord Binning. *The Hon. Rachel Hamilton and the Hon. Charles Hamilton* (Plate 14) is a stylish solution to the perennially difficult problem of how to portray the innocence of children without making them look ridiculous. In spite of conventional whimsical activity and the rather contrived scheme, Ramsay's sense of design and the perfectly realized portrait head of the young girl ensure that there is nothing condescending in the picture. In the little girl's dress can be seen the skilled hand of Joseph Van Aken, the drapery painter commonly employed by London portraitists. Ramsay would have shuddered at the thought of 'filling in' faces as Medina had done, but he was not averse to following a professionally acceptable practice.

Later in the century, British art was to be dominated by the forceful presence of Sir Joshua Reynolds. But at this stage Reynolds, ten years Ramsay's junior, was still a West Country provincial yet to visit Italy. Hogarth, under whom it is likely that the young Ramsay studied life drawing during an early stay in London, was the only

14 ALLAN RAMSAY
The Hon. Rachel Hamilton and the Hon. Charles Hamilton 1740
Oil on canvas 157.5 × 139.7
Private Collection
During the 1740s Allan Ramsay made a number of double portraits in which the artist's deliberate intention of impressing his client by means of his compositional skill is clearly discernible. In this, one of the most beautiful, the charming impression that the children's play has been interrupted is as captivating as the innocence of their expressions.

serious competition and Hogarth was never primarily a portrait painter.

Ramsay was prolific in the seventeen years which separate his first and second (1754) visits to Italy. He was painting over forty portraits a year, dividing his time between his London studio and the one his father had set up for him in the oddly shaped house the poet had

15 ALLAN RAMSAY
Dr Richard Mead 1747
Oil on canvas 236.2 × 144.8
Thomas Coram Foundation for
    Children, London
Dr Richard Mead, the celebrated physician and connoisseur, was of great assistance in promoting Ramsay's career after his return from Italy in 1738. He could not have wished for a finer reward than this portrait, painted by Ramsay for Thomas Coram's Foundling Hospital. The painting was a conscious response to Hogarth's much-admired portrait of Coram himself, and Ramsay used the occasion as an opportunity for an essay in what was known as the Italian Grand Manner. Both intellectual prowess and humanity are conveyed by Mead's imposing presence.

built in the shadow of Edinburgh Castle. But even more impressive than the sheer number of portraits Ramsay completed is his range: from the standard oval to the grand three-quarter and full-lengths. It was in the latter format that Ramsay made one of his most original contributions to eighteenth-century British portraiture: the naturalistic treatment of a sitter in the formal portrait.

Ramsay's first great essay in this respect is the portrait of his friend and promoter, the famous doctor and connoisseur, Richard Mead (Plate 15). In this formidable picture Ramsay was responding to the highly original and much praised portrait of Captain Coram by Hogarth. Ramsay's Mead is just as naturalistic as, if rather less jolly than Hogarth's Coram but there is a sense of authority in Ramsay's characterization of Mead which is absent from Hogarth's earlier portrait.

But it is his great early masterpiece, the portrait of Lord Drummore

16 ALLAN RAMSAY

Hew Dalrymple, Lord Drummore 1754
Oil on canvas 127 × 102.2
National Galleries of Scotland
By the time Ramsay came to paint the convivial Lord Drummore (a contemporary referred to his 'keen relish of social enjoyments') the artist had exhausted the possibilities of the Baroque portrait tradition. In Drummore no trace of pomposity is allowed to interfere with the naturalistic effect for which Ramsay was striving. The absence of harsh lighting and the sitter's friendly gaze make this one of the most personable examples of British portraiture.

(Plate 16), that is the most dramatic instance of Ramsay introducing this fresh, new concept of portraiture into British art. It is hard to think of a more sympathetic portrait. Lord Drummore exudes intelligence and humanity; one can almost sense the rational mind working behind the honest gaze. In place of the brittle manner of his earlier full-length portraits, Ramsay painted Drummore in an altogether gentler way, allowing a subtle light to play across his robust form. The atmosphere surrounding the sitter is almost tangible.

As the leading portraitist in London during the 1740s, Ramsay was the foremost British – as opposed to merely Scottish – artist of the day. But the artist's regular visits to Edinburgh meant that he never completely lost touch with Scottish intellectual life.

Although the 1745 Jacobite Rebellion divided loyalties at all levels of Scottish society, it did not impede the burgeoning of creative and often radical thought which was to transform Scotland later in the century into the spiritual heart of the Age of Reason. Ramsay was in the thick of it, and not only because of the 'enlightened' nature of his own art.

Ramsay's roots predisposed him towards literary pursuits and it is no coincidence that in the 1750s David Hume, the philosopher and most important theorist of the Scottish Enlightenment, became a close friend. That Hume held Allan Ramsay in high regard is evidenced by the fact that he asked the artist for an opinion on his *History of England*, and Ramsay's own three publications of the early 1750s – *A Dialogue on Taste*, *On Ridicule* and *A Letter to Earl ——— on the Affair of Elizabeth Canning* – constitute an impressive achievement in themselves.

Drummore had been painted during an extended visit to Edinburgh between 1753 and 1754, and it was during this stay that Ramsay was instrumental in founding the Select Society. In an era bristling with debating clubs and associations, some more serious than others, the Select Society was the most influential. Along with Hume and Ramsay, the Select Society included all the key figures in the early years of the Scottish Enlightenment – Adam Smith, Adam Ferguson, James Burnet, Lord Kames – and several intellectually inclined members of the nobility. All sorts of topics were debated and prizes awarded. Unfortunately, Ramsay's society foundered in the next decade mainly because it ceased to be as 'select' as Ramsay had intended it. For a short time, however, Ramsay was a mainstay of the most advanced intellectual discussion group in Europe.

By the time Ramsay arrived in Rome on his second visit in 1754 he was an established artist with a new and well-connected wife. Margaret Lindsay, although also a Scot, was the niece of the English Chancellor. Her snobbish parents had not thought a painter – even a successful one like Ramsay – a good enough match for their daughter and so the couple had been obliged to elope. In Rome the newly-weds saw much of the young architect Robert Adam and his wife, but carefully avoided contact with the now twice-defeated Jacobites – almost certainly for fear of damaging Ramsay's prospects after his return to Hanoverian England.

During this visit Ramsay paid much more attention to earlier Italian painting than he had on his first visit; he looked at the work of Domenichino, for example, copying one of the artist's frescos in

17 ALLAN RAMSAY
Margaret Lindsay, the Artist's Wife
c. 1758–60 Oil on canvas 76.2 × 63.5
National Galleries of Scotland
The influence of French portraiture on Ramsay in the 1750s cannot be overestimated, and nowhere is it more apparent than in this ravishing portrait of his second wife. In both the softness of Ramsay's technique and in the muted palette, the picture is highly reminiscent of female portraits by artists such as Nattier and Perronneau. Ramsay's draughtsmanship and natural sense of restraint rescue the picture from artificiality.

the church of San Luigi dei Francesi. On his way home he even stopped off in Venice; however, none of the sensuality of Venetian painting that had so impressed Reynolds, and with the inspiration of which the younger artist was busy making his name back in England, rubbed off on Ramsay. On the contrary, in the portraits he produced in the late 1750s – and they are among his finest – the rhetorical elegance Reynolds espoused is entirely absent.

Ramsay's painting of his wife, *Margaret Lindsay* (Plate 17) is the most intimate and sympathetic female portrait in eighteenth-century British art. It was possibly painted while the pair were still in Italy, and it shows how Ramsay successfully combined the delicacy of the French portraiture he came across there with his instinctively direct Scottish approach. In *A Dialogue on Taste* Ramsay refers to Quentin de la Tour, and it is quite possible that he was thinking of the French pastel artist in modifying his style in this way. The colouring is indeed pastel-like and the drawing extremely sensitive; but in spite of the prettiness of the lace fichu and the flowers there is nothing fussy about the picture. Compared with Ramsay's overwhelmingly naturalistic rendering of feminine beauty, the portraits produced by Medina and Aikman only fifty years earlier look stiff and artificial.

Margaret Lindsay is, of course, an informal portrait of a sitter whom Ramsay knew intimately. Nevertheless he was to continue to imbue his subjects, both male and female, with a similarly sensitive quality. The increasingly elevated personages whom he later painted come across as real people rather than as symbols of political and social power because of the breakthrough he made in this remarkable portrait. Horace Walpole's observation still rings true: 'Mr Reynolds … is bold and has a kind of tempestuous colouring, yet with dignity and grace; the latter [Ramsay] is all delicacy. Mr Reynolds seldom succeeds in women, Mr Ramsay is formed to paint them.'

It was in 1757, shortly after returning from his second visit to Italy, that Ramsay received a commission which propelled him into the highest court circles. The dashing Earl of Bute, the nephew of Ramsay's enthusiastic patron, the Duke of Argyll, was the closest personal friend and political ally of the Prince of Wales. Bute recommended Ramsay to the Prince and the royal portrait was duly executed; it was a great success, and subsequently became extremely well known through engravings.

Although Ramsay was not officially appointed Principal Painter to the King until 1767, he held that position in all but name from the time of the Prince's accession as George III in 1760. In the following years British art was increasingly dominated by Sir Joshua Reynolds, in direct relation to the expanding influence of the Royal Academy of which Reynolds was first President. Nevertheless, Ramsay remained secure in royal favour. Indeed, when Lord Eglinton suggested to the King that he should, perhaps, sit for Reynolds, George III made no bones about his preference: 'Mr Ramsay is my painter, my Lord' came the retort.

Ramsay's portrait of Bute (Plate 18), a reciprocal commission from

18 ALLAN RAMSAY
John Stuart, 3rd Earl of Bute 1758
Oil on canvas 236.2 × 147.3
National Trust for Scotland
The relish with which Ramsay has painted Bute's glorious ermined robes is immensely enjoyable, but that alone could not have made this work the great portrait it undoubtedly is. The nonchalant pose (a great favourite among the aristocracy in eighteenth-century England) is perfectly captured and this, together with the finely perceived head, tells all one needs to know about Bute's character.

JOHN third EARL of BUTE
Knight of the Thistle and of the Garter
appointed
First Lord of the Treasury
1762
when he concluded the Treaty at Paris called
Peace of Paris
the original Picture, painted by order of
The Prince of Wales, afterwards George
the Third, was given by His Majesty in
1822 to John Lord Mountstuart.

the Prince, is if anything an even more virtuosic performance than
the royal picture. Bute, who was to become Prime Minister in 1762
and, incidentally, one of the most unpopular of all time because of
his blatant promotion of fellow Scots, was a gift to Ramsay. Bute
wears court robes and sports the Order of the Thistle; he is observed

making the charmingly vain gesture of lifting the hem of his cape to display the fine calf of which he was reputedly inordinately proud. It is an appropriately theatrical picture of an elegant, self-confident statesman.

Ramsay went on to paint all the members of the royal family, both individually and in groups, many times over. By the 1770s his chief assistant, Philip Reinagle, was organizing the production of hundreds of official portraits each year. Most of these are in the standard Van Dyck tradition, but occasionally Ramsay would stray from the accepted convention of the royal portrait and come up with something radically different.

A case in point is the intriguing profile portrait of Queen Charlotte in which Ramsay has transformed the most unprepossessing royal consort in British history into a bewitching work of art (Plate 19). Reynolds's biographer, James Northcote, made the most perspicacious criticism of this unusual portrait:

> I have seen a picture of his of the Queen, soon after she was married – a profile, and a fan in her hand: Lord! how she held that fan! It was weak in execution and ordinary in features – all I can say of it is, that it was the farthest possible removed from anything like vulgarity.

Ramsay's subjects during his later productive period, however, were not exclusively royal. One who solicited a particularly satisfying response from the artist was his old friend David Hume, who in his capacity as secretary to an official military legation on the Continent had acquired the fine military outfit in which the artist chose to paint him.

Hume's portrait (Plate 20) was intended as a pair to a brilliant though rather unusual one of the French-Swiss philosopher Jean-Jacques Rousseau (Plate 21). Hume had befriended the radical thinker (at this time something of an international celebrity) while he was fleeing persecution by the French authorities, and had helped to find him sanctuary in England. Ramsay painted Rousseau as a present to Hume and the result was a tormented, precociously Romantic image of the philosopher wearing the Armenian costume he affected while in London.

By contrast, the portrait of the Scottish philosopher radiates good humour and reason. Hume's looks apparently were no match for his intellect, and so Ramsay made clever use of dramatic shadows to make his subject more visually interesting. The relaxed simplicity of the pose and the absence of clutter anticipates Sir Henry Raeburn's portraits of his own intellectual contemporaries.

Ramsay died at Dover in 1784, returning from his fourth stay in Rome, the centre of civilization which had meant so much to him.

19 ALLAN RAMSAY
Queen Charlotte with a Fan 1763
Oil on canvas 76.2 × 63.5
The Rt Hon. The Earl of Seafield
It is a measure of Ramsay's genius that he could manage to make a beautiful portrait of such an unpromising subject. With supreme artistic cunning he realized that the Queen's features required some kind of foil to distract the viewer's attention. His solution was the exquisite device of the closed fan dangling from a half-closed hand. Only Goya exceeded Ramsay's skill at painting black lace.

His final years had been spent in a search for Horace's villa in the
Sabine Hills, a retirement activity entirely in keeping with the
proclivities of a man whose intellectual background attached great
importance to the verification of facts. It is ironic that in the same
year the young Henry Raeburn (1756–1823) visited Rome for the
first and only time, and that his experience of the city, unlike
Ramsay's, was to have no significant effect upon his art.

Left 20 ALLAN RAMSAY
David Hume 1766
Oil on canvas 76.2 × 63.5
National Galleries of Scotland
Ramsay probably chose to paint
his friend, the great philosopher
David Hume, in fancy garb to
complement the Armenian costume
worn by the Scotsman's continental
colleague, Jean-Jacques Rousseau,
for his portrait. Having specially
asked to see the picture, King
George III remarked that he
considered the dress 'too fine'. 'I
wished posterity should see that one
philosopher during your Majesty's
reign had a good coat on his back,'
the painter wittily replied.

Right 21 ALLAN RAMSAY
Jean-Jacques Rousseau 1766
Oil on canvas 75 × 64.8
National Galleries of Scotland
This portrait of the radical French-
Swiss philosopher, painted as a gift
for his friend David Hume, became
the focus of an altercation between
the two great thinkers. Rousseau
accused Hume of having
deliberately arranged to make him
look like a 'Cyclops', presumably
because he thought the picture
insufficiently flattering. Hume
politely denied Rousseau's
paranoid theory, his admiration for
the continental genius remaining
unbounded. Whatever the truth of
the matter, Ramsay painted a
masterpiece. The dramatic use of
light in the portrait owes much to
Rembrandt.

Henry Raeburn: THE QUINTESSENTIAL *Scottish genius*

If any artist has a claim to be the quintessential genius of Scottish art, it is Henry Raeburn. No Scottish portraitist of the age could ignore Ramsay's example – and he certainly influenced Raeburn – but Raeburn's personality, lifestyle and development are all fundamentally different from those of Scotland's great courtier painter.

By the time Raeburn was painting the great pictures of his maturity around the turn of the eighteenth century, the horrors of the French Revolution had undermined the watertight faith of the intelligentsia in progress and the beneficial effects of rational analysis; in spite of

the astonishing scientific discoveries being made by many of the men whom Raeburn painted, it was clear that solutions to problems (even those arrived at by painters) could in no way be definitive, and Raeburn's mature work reflects the uncertainty of the Romantic era. As Raeburn was immortalizing the major protagonists of this new age, his slightly younger contemporary, Walter Scott, had already started to romanticize Scotland's history to such widespread acclaim that even today Scotland remains synonymous with Romanticism in the public's mind.

Raeburn's beginnings were inauspicious. His father, an Edinburgh mill-owner, died before he was nine years old and the young Henry was then looked after by his elder brother. He attended Edinburgh's well-known George Heriot's school for orphans. Raeburn's fortunes improved dramatically, however, when in his twenties he married a wealthy widow twelve years his senior. The countess, as she was known locally, owned an imposing house in Stockbridge, then a village just outside the Scottish capital.

In later life Raeburn briefly went bankrupt and was reduced to making copies of other artists' pictures as well as being obliged to sell the grand house and studio he had built for himself. In general, however, he remained as solidly bourgeois as the majority of his sitters. In the final year of his life he was knighted by George IV and made King's Limner in Scotland, although he died before making anything of the role.

At sixteen Raeburn was apprenticed to an Edinburgh goldsmith called James Gilliland, but he soon demonstrated his bent for making portraits by painting miniatures in watercolour. Although it is unknown whether or not he actually met Ramsay while in Rome, Raeburn certainly met the artist who had been his great predecessor's principal Scottish assistant, David Martin (1737–97).

Martin is a rare example of a Scottish artist who, having made a success in London, decided to return to Scotland. He was strongly influenced by Reynolds and, naturally enough, by Ramsay. But although he was the best of the portraitists working in Scotland during the time that Raeburn was developing there is nothing particularly inspiring about his work. It does appear, however, that he gave the young Raeburn pictures of his to copy; and, in 1791, he won a commission from the Royal Company of Archers to paint their President of Council at the expense of the younger man. Nevertheless, in spite of this help from Martin, Raeburn cannot be said to have had any formal training, and it is perhaps because of this that drawing never played any part in his method. Astonishingly, there are in fact no drawings by Raeburn in existence.

Raeburn himself certainly met Reynolds, and perhaps even spent some time in his studio before leaving for Rome. Unfortunately, however, there are no portraits by Raeburn which pre-date his return. A portrait of the pioneer geologist *James Hutton* is an immature work which could conceivably have been painted before he set out; but the composition (the three-quarter length figure seated at an angle which Raeburn was to make his own) is derived from Raphael's portrait of Pope Julius II, then on view in Rome. Whatever it was

22 HENRY RAEBURN
Sir John and Lady Clerk of Penicuik
1792 Oil on canvas 145 × 206
National Gallery of Ireland, Dublin
This superb early double portrait
set a standard in naturalism which
Raeburn was to continue to pursue
in his more formal, studio
portraiture. The artist has truthfully
recorded the transitory effect of
evening light on both his sitters and
on the landscape. In doing so he
has enhanced the feeling of
intimacy between man and wife
and suggested their close
involvement with their estates.

that Raeburn learned from Reynolds, though, it was certainly not
the Grand Manner. The style that Raeburn evolved in the 1790s is
idiosyncratic – the antithesis of everything Sir Joshua had advocated.

The double portrait of *Sir John and Lady Clerk of Penicuik* (Plate 22)
is a milestone in Raeburn's development, in which he solves the
difficult problem of convincingly combining a portrait and a landscape setting. The convention of pretending that a portrait had been
painted out of doors, by including a few cursory brushstrokes to
indicate foliage, sky and garden ornament, had grown increasingly
hackneyed in the course of the eighteenth century. In the portraiture
of Gainsborough and Reynolds it becomes a tired cliché; but even
Ramsay had on occasion resorted to it. In Rome, the Scottish
antiquarian James Byres had told Raeburn 'never to copy any object
from memory, but from the principal figure to the minutest accessory
to have it placed before him', and in the Clerk portrait, where as
much respect is paid to the Pentland Hills as it is to the features of
Sir John and Lady Clerk, the artist is clearly following this advice.

In earlier works, such as *Mrs Ferguson of Raith with her Children* and
two full-length portraits of uniformed gentlemen, *John Sinclair of
Ulbster* and *Dr Nathaniel Spens*, the landscape settings are too detailed

and detract from the subjects. In the Clerk portrait, however, both elements are in perfect harmony and the whole is unified by superb manipulation of light. Just as a photographer 'brings up' the lights in subjects shot with the light source directly behind them, Raeburn skilfully organizes his half-tones to convey a naturalistic *contre-jour* effect. Technically, Raeburn's picture is a ravishing *tour de force*.

The Clerk portrait was the first that Raeburn sent to London, where the level of press comment indicates that it was immediately recognized as an important picture. In common with most Scottish artists of this period, Raeburn always aspired to London success; in a letter to the genre painter David Wilkie, written late in life, he says he feels as if Edinburgh is the Cape of Good Hope. He was particularly aggrieved that he was nearly sixty before he was made a Royal Academician. In 1810 he actually moved to London, perhaps hoping to take over the late John Hoppner's clientele, but there he found Sir Thomas Lawrence's monopoly unbreakable. In Edinburgh at least he was unchallenged.

From 1798 he also had the advantage of a specially designed and equipped studio in the house he had built for himself in the city's Georgian New Town. The house still exists (sadly, now poorly converted into a nondescript suite of offices) and it is still possible to make out the large room with the huge window looking north over the Firth of Forth where Raeburn worked his well-ordered nine-to-five day. At one time there were adjustable shutters at the windows which allowed Raeburn to vary the amount of light that entered.

The use of light for dramatic effect had been a feature of Ramsay's later work. Nevertheless, the earlier artist's method of painting a portrait remained conventional throughout his career: preparatory drawings were made, the design transferred on to the canvas, and then the image was built up in tone and colour with the artist's knowledge of anatomical structure and texture informing his brush-strokes.

By contrast, Raeburn's method – in the absence of any formal training – was one he more or less had to invent himself. No drawings were made, paint was applied directly to the canvas and the features of the sitter swiftly laid in, the silhouette was indicated, and then the more precise image summoned up in coloured light and shade. Anatomical structure was of very little concern. This method of painting a portrait was extraordinarily advanced for the early nine-teenth century; the nearest precedent for it is to be found in the work of the seventeenth-century Dutch master Frans Hals.

In much of his work Raeburn lays on his pigment very thinly and his range of colours is limited. He uses a square-ended brush and allows the individual strokes to overlap, giving a remarkably

23 HENRY RAEBURN
Lord Newton 1806
Oil on canvas 127 × 101.6
The Earl of Rosebery
In the massive person of Lord
Newton, Raeburn was presented
with a subject who lent himself to
the broad treatment at which, by
the 1800s, the artist had become
adept. In the painting of the head,
in particular, Raeburn's use of the
square-ended brush conveys a vivid
impression of monumentality.

'impressionistic' look to many passages of painting. In focusing on
the head he often leaves the less important parts of the picture
unresolved and sketchy-looking.

At the time this aspect of his work gave rise to objections. In 1819,
for example, the Duke of Buccleuch wrote to Walter Scott about a
proposed portrait of the writer that he had commissioned Raeburn
to paint: 'Raeburn should be warned that I will not take a half-
finished picture off his hands. Many of his works are shamefully
finished. The face is studied but everything else is neglected.'

If the economy of Raeburn's mature style occasionally made his
natural clientele yearn for something flashier, however (and many
members of the Scottish nobility did turn to Sir Thomas Lawrence),
then it was perfectly suited to the taste of the lawyers, academics
and general 'literati' who constituted Edinburgh's professional class.
The historian William Robertson, the philosophers Thomas Reid
and Adam Ferguson, the cleric and literary critic Hugh Blair, and,
not least, his friend, the lawyer and collector, John Clerk of Eldin of

whom Raeburn made an especially fine job, all sat for him. Usually they are depicted in their everyday clothes against a draped curtain, their books or other professional accoutrements placed beside them.

His portrait of *Lord Newton* (Plate 23), although exceptional even for Raeburn because of the freedom with which the paint has been handled, is a masterpiece; a vivid, concise visual description of the bibulous Lord of Sessions' formidable presence. Nothing is included which might detract from the stout physicality of the sitter. Broad shadows are used throughout to describe the form and, unusually for Raeburn, Newton's right hand gestures as if explaining some point. It is impossible to look at the panache with which the drapery has been painted without recalling Hals, although Ramsay's Lord Drummore is the most obvious specific prototype.

Two of Raeburn's most memorable pictures are full-blooded, romantic full-lengths depicting Highland chiefs. When Raeburn painted the finer of them, *Col. Alastair Macdonnell of Glengarry* (Plate 24), in 1812, the Jacobite cause had long since ceased to represent any real threat to the political establishment (in 1819 a monument to the Stuarts was erected in St Peter's in Rome at George III's expense!). The proscription of Highland dress, one of several spiteful, retributory measures taken by the London government after the failure of the '45, had been suspended in 1782, and tartan-clad Scottish regiments had been raised ever since the Seven Years' War of 1756–63.

In Rome Raeburn would definitely have been aware of the theatrical treatment that the Roman portraitist Pompeo Batoni had accorded his Grand Tour compatriots (Plate 35) and of the flamboyant, picturesque use he had made of tartan. Ramsay himself had once rather awkwardly managed to wed the plaid to a Classical allusion in his vaguely comical portrait of the MacLeod of MacLeod, a picture in which a periwigged Highland chief alights on the seashore of his native Skye in the attitude of the revered Roman statue, the Apollo Belvedere (Dunvegan Castle, Skye).

In Raeburn's Macdonnell, however, Ramsay's Neo-Classical pretensions have been replaced by down-to-earth if slightly sentimental description. Macdonnell is portrayed heroically, even though the subject's military bearing and air of independent authority were in fact at odds with the reality of his position: the Macdonnell was the leader of a powerless clan, many of whose members were at this time being removed from their traditional lands in the infamous Highland Clearances. Walter Scott based the character of Fergus MacIvor, the doomed Highland chief of his first successful novel, *Waverley*, on Macdonnell and it has been suggested that Raeburn's portrait inspired him in his characterization.

24 HENRY RAEBURN
Col. Alastair Macdonnell of Glengarry
c. 1812 Oil on canvas 241 × 150
National Galleries of Scotland
This is, arguably, Raeburn's finest full-length portrait. Inclined merely to indicate details which he considered irrelevant to characterization, the artist took a far more thorough approach when he made this heroic image of the Highland chief. In terms of painting, however, the portrait is a model of economy: not a brushstroke is wasted.

In the Macdonnell the sense of poignancy is heightened by the feeling that the figure is bathed in atmosphere. Raeburn has observed and described the play of light across the figure from its high source so accurately that we do not question the complex arrangement of shadows and half-shadows. Neither the elaborate nature of the costume nor the ancestral bric-à-brac in the background are allowed to detract from the psychological depth conveyed in the subject's face. It is highly likely that Raeburn painted Macdonnell at home in Invergarry. The sense of place certainly suggests it.

Raeburn's romantic series of Highland chiefs has always been highly praised. Sir Thomas Lawrence described his portrait of the *MacNab*, painted a full decade earlier than Macdonnell, as 'the finest representation of a human being [he had] ever seen'. And the series reached a climax in the Byronic *John, 2nd Marquess of Bute*, a picture in which Raeburn's conscious adoption of Rembrandt's device of using deep shadow to suggest psychological intensity is particularly striking.

It might be assumed that Raeburn's robust, muscular approach to portraiture would not have been suited to female sitters. Yet, fascinatingly, the contrary is true. Raeburn was a painter who could not have flattered if he had tried, although with both sexes he turned in his best performances when he was interested by the sitter.

Probably his finest female portrait is the picture of *Mrs James Campbell* (Private Collection). Only Rembrandt ever managed to convey the depth of experience and philosophical resignation to old age as well as Raeburn in this justly famous portrait. Nevertheless, Raeburn's portraits of Scottish matriarchs are the exceptions rather than the rule, and when it came to painting pretty young women the results were frequently ravishing.

There is no better proof of this than the splendidly unadorned beauty of *Mrs Scott Moncrieff* (Plate 25). This, the simplest of all Raeburns, is as uncompromisingly honest a portrait as his stoutest, flabby-jowled judge. The nondescript, idealized 'beauty' which both Gainsborough and Reynolds frequently impose upon their female sitters is alien to Raeburn. Mrs Scott Moncrieff is beautiful in Raeburn's portrait because she was beautiful in life.

Raeburn was made King's Limner in Scotland (the official royal artist) and then knighted by George IV at Hopetoun House during the king's famous Scottish 'jaunt' of 1822. A portrait of the king was commissioned, but the painter died before he could begin it. Had the portrait of George IV in the Stuart tartan he wore for his Edinburgh visit come to fruition, it is safe to assume, on the evidence of the *MacNab* and the *Macdonnell*, that it would have been a masterpiece of royal portraiture.

David Octavius Hill AND *Robert Adamson*: PORTRAIT PHOTOGRAPHY AS ART

Portrait painting in Scotland did not cease upon the death of her pre-eminent artist in this field. A range of Scottish artists from Sir

25 HENRY RAEBURN
Mrs Scott Moncrieff c. 1814
Oil on canvas 75 × 62.3
National Galleries of Scotland
Raeburn had very strict ideas about what his sitters should wear, and in general he preferred to avoid the idiosyncrasies of fashion. When he came to paint half-length portraits of youthful beauties such as Mrs Scott Moncrieff, for example, he would suggest that the bodice of the lady's garment should be drawn apart so that no busy detail in the lower portion of the picture would divert the viewer's attention from the face.

David Wilkie and Sir John Watson Gordon, Raeburn's successors to the official court position in Scotland, to the prolific Sir Daniel Macnee produced throughout the Victorian period 'commodity' portraits which are all indebted in varying degrees to Raeburn. None, however, was anything like his equal.

There is, none the less, one area in which Scottish artists have left us many minor masterpieces of the portrait-maker's art. Had Raeburn lived to a ripe old age he would doubtless have experimented with

26 DAVID OCTAVIUS HILL AND
   ROBERT ADAMSON
Newhaven Fishwives (unknown
   woman and perhaps Mrs Hall)
c. 1845 calotype 29.9 × 22.8
National Galleries of Scotland
The calotype process which Hill and Adamson employed for their Newhaven fisherfolk project in the 1840s allowed for some very 'artistic' effects. A consciousness of the Dutch genre tradition informs all the Newhaven photographs.

photography; Edinburgh was at the forefront of the new 'science' from the time of its invention in the 1830s. During the 1840s two pioneers, David Hill and his partner Robert Adamson, succeeded in producing numerous portrait photographs which nowadays only extreme purists would deny are art. (The debate as to whether or not photography really constitutes an 'art', incidentally, was already raging during the brief period of Hill and Adamson's collaboration.)

David Octavius Hill (1802–70) was an artist himself and an industrious secretary to the Royal Scottish Academy. With Robert Adamson, his technician, he rapidly brought the calotype technique (the first photographic process to employ a negative) invented by

William Henry Fox Talbot to a level of sophistication which enabled very beautiful images to be produced. Although Hill and Adamson made calotype portraits of virtually every person of importance in the Edinburgh of the 1840s, some of their most beguiling work was done in the pretty fishing village of Newhaven on the Firth of Forth (Plates 26 and 27).

In many of Hill and Adamson's calotypes there is a conscious effort to mimic artistic effects, but in the true tradition of Scottish

27 DAVID OCTAVIUS HILL AND
   ROBERT ADAMSON
*Willie Liston, Redding [preparing] the
   Line* c. 1845
calotype 20.8 × 15.7
National Galleries of Scotland
Scottish portrait painters' interest
in character as opposed to
generalized ideas of beauty, which
reached its zenith in the work of
Henry Raeburn, is clearly
discernible in the work of Hill and
Adamson. Photography, of course,
naturally lent itself to this priority.

portraiture best exemplified by the work of Ramsay and Raeburn they are dedicated to exploring the individual personalities of their subjects. Many of their portraits consciously emulate Raeburn. There was very little doubt about their success and their status as artists amongst their contemporary supporters. Elizabeth Rigby, the future wife of Sir Charles Eastlake, President of the Royal Academy, wrote: '... the beautiful and wonderful Calotype drawings – so precious in every real artist's sight, not only for their own matchless truth to Nature, but as the triumphant proof of all to be most revered as truth in art. Every painter, high or low, to whom Nature has ever revealed herself, here finds his justification.'

28 DAVID WILKIE

King George IV Entering the Palace of
 Holyroodhouse 1828
Oil on panel 55.6 × 91.4
National Galleries of Scotland
Although Raeburn had been
knighted by George IV in 1822 and
was appointed the king's official

artist in Scotland the following
year, his death within a few days of
receiving the honour meant that
the task of making a record of the
King's momentous visit to Scotland
fell to his successor in the post,
David Wilkie. In this vivid little

picture, Wilkie was inspired by
Rubens's treatment of similar
occasions in the life of Marie de'
Medici. Wilkie had visited the
Louvre, where the famous series of
canvases celebrating the queen's
life is still housed, in 1814.

CHAPTER TWO

Enlightened TASTE

The history of Scotland is rich in colourful events, yet there are few quite so bizarre as the grandiose national pageant that Sir Walter Scott stage-managed in honour of George IV's visit to Edinburgh in 1822. Following the tradition established by Scotland's ancient monarchs, Scott had arranged for the former Prince Regent to arrive by ship at Leith, Edinburgh's port. From there the new king made a royal progress to the centre of the city where the massed ranks of the Scottish nobility were waiting to greet him (Plate 28).

From a theatrical point of view the author of the Waverley novels excelled himself. The king, who by all accounts had never enjoyed himself more in his life, sported pink tights beneath his Royal Stuart tartan kilt, and even Lowland families, to whom the tradition of the plaid was entirely alien, were kitted out in Highland outfits specially designed for the occasion.

There was more than a little irony in George IV wearing Stuart costume. His forebears were only very distantly related to Scotland's native royal dynasty, and, in the view of the few remaining Jacobites at least, had usurped the British throne from its rightful incumbents, the Stuarts.

There was, however, a more general cultural irony in the setting and timing of the event. The first twenty years of the nineteenth century had seen the culmination of nearly a century of astonishing Scottish intellectual achievement, the period now known as the Scottish Enlightenment; and the rational essence of 'enlightened' Scottish thought was out of sympathy with the Romantic tenor of Scott's nationalistic piece of pomp.

Very few of the main protagonists of the Scottish Enlightenment, however, would have condemned the political impulse behind George

IV's visit. He was the first British monarch to visit Scotland since Charles II's surreptitious Scottish coronation in the Cromwellian era, and this Hanoverian 'triumph' was intended to stamp the royal seal on Scotland as an integrated part of the Great British state. One hundred and fifteen years had passed since the Act of Union, and, notwithstanding two major Jacobite rebellions over that period this was to a great extent what it had become.

The INTELLECTUAL *power-house of Europe*

The achievements of the two greatest Scottish artists of the eighteenth and early nineteenth centuries, Allan Ramsay and Henry Raeburn, together with those of numerous lesser artists, can only be fully appreciated in the context of the Scottish Enlightenment. It was an extraordinary and unexpected phenomenon: the cultural trans-formation of one of the most poverty-stricken, backward countries in western Europe into the intellectual power-house of the whole continent. During the course of a single century Scotland produced the most progressive philosophers, the most imaginative authors, the most inventive scientists and a substantial handful of first-rank artists.

A roll-call of some of the best-known figures of the Scottish Enlightenment will give an idea of their world-wide influence on virtually every field of human thought and activity: the philosophers David Hume, Thomas Reid and Dugald Stewart; Adam Smith, economist and author of *The Wealth of Nations*; the historian William Robertson; Adam Ferguson, the father of modern sociology; the chemist Joseph Black, discoverer of carbon dioxide; James Hutton, the virtual founder of the science of geology; the architects Robert and James Adam; and, of course, the two artists Allan Ramsay and Henry Raeburn (see Chapter One). Although he was referring specifically to literature, David Hume might have been making a point about the whole range of creative pursuits when he wrote:

> Is it not strange that, at a time when we have lost our Princes,
> our Parliaments, our independent Government, even the presence
> of our chief Nobility, are unhappy, in our accent and
> Pronunciation, speak a very corrupt Dialect of Tongue which we
> make use of; is it not strange, I say, that, in these Circumstances,
> we shou'd really be the People most distinguish'd for Literature
> in Europe?

The Act of Union AND ITS *political implications*

The reasons for this intellectual flowering in Scotland are immensely complex and the subject of intense controversy, and the extent to which the Act of Union of 1707 contributed to it is still hotly debated.

29 Anon.

*The Duke of Queensberry, on behalf of
Scotland, presenting the Treaty of
Union to Queen Anne* 1707

Engraving 15.3 × 10.8

British Museum, London

The primary motivation behind
those in the English Parliament
who pushed through the Act of
Union of 1707 was the sense of
national insecurity which had
prevailed since the Glorious
Revolution of 1688. With a Jacobite
court in exile it was feared that a
Franco-Scottish alliance to restore
the Stuarts might threaten England
through her 'back door' – Scotland.
Many years were to pass before the
economic benefits of the Union
permeated all levels of society, but
the increase in wealth among the
Scottish aristocracy meant that
artists in Scotland were very soon
enjoying more enthusiastic
patronage.

It does, however, seem certain that without the economic stability
created by the legal binding together of Scotland and England,
Scotland's relative prosperity in the later eighteenth century and the
nineteenth would have been delayed and the progress of the arts
accordingly less marked.

The ostensible purpose of the Act of Union was to ensure the
Protestant succession. Queen Anne had succeeded her brother-in-
law, William III, who had ruled jointly with Anne's sister Mary until
Mary's death in 1694. In the year of Anne's accession, 1701, a so-
called Act of Settlement was passed by the English Parliament
designed to make it impossible for Anne's Catholic half-brother, the
Old Pretender, to succeed. Upon Anne's death the crown was to
pass to the Electress Sophia of Hanover, a granddaughter through
the female line of James I. All of Anne's seventeen children died in
infancy; and so, as the years passed, it became increasingly important
to make sure that the Scottish Parliament did not, upon her death,
unilaterally choose to ignore the Act of Settlement and restore her
Stuart half-brother to an independent Scottish throne – hence the
Act of Union.

This further absorption of Scotland into a unified British state
dominated politically and economically by England was in fact just
a further step in a process which had been going on since the Middle
Ages. The previous milestone in this political amalgamation had
been the Union of the Crowns of 1603, when Mary Queen of Scots'
son, James VI of Scotland, had inherited the English throne from
his distant Tudor cousin, the childless Elizabeth I.

Since the Act of Union was, to all intents and purposes, being
foisted upon Scotland by a Whig majority in the English House of
Commons, united opposition to it both in the Scottish Parliament
and across Scotland might have been expected. This, however, was
far from the case, for Scotland was something of a ragbag of political
allegiances (Plate 29).

Jacobite sentiment, for example, which had grown up since James
II had fled into exile after the Glorious Revolution of 1688, and
which was to give the government in London two severe jolts over
the next half-century, was more or less confined to the Highlands.
In the Lowlands the strength of Presbyterianism meant that the
inhabitants were, if not downright hostile, then at least unsympathetic
to the Catholic Stuarts. In addition, the increased prosperity and
relative security that the land-owning Lowland gentry had already
been enjoying gave them much in common with their Whig-sup-
porting neighbours south of the Border.

Furthermore, the Scottish Parliament which, because of the country's turbulent medieval history, had never developed into anything

approaching a practical democratic assembly, had been an impotent governing body for most of the seventeenth century. Since James VI and his court had migrated to London in 1603, Scotland had been ruled by the Lords of the Articles, an institution invented by the king to manage his Scottish affairs. The immediate impact of the Union with England was slight. After the Scottish Parliament abolished itself in compliance with the Act of Union, a succession of powerful aristocratic political 'managers' merely assumed the powers which had previously been exercised by the Lords of the Articles. The greater part of Scottish society experienced very little real change.

A newly PROSPEROUS society

The major benefit that Scotland received in exchange for binding itself to the Protestant succession and signing away its independent Parliament was 'full freedom and intercourse of trade and navigation'. This meant that ultimately Scotland was able to partake of the fruits of England's imperial expansion.

But the economic benefits of the Union were far from immediately apparent. The general feeling of depression in Scotland, which had been exacerbated in the 1690s by famine and financial catastrophe after the Scottish Parliament had virtually bankrupted the country by speculating on a doomed, foolhardy scheme to found an independent Scottish colony in Central America, persisted for many years. Only after the middle of the eighteenth century did ordinary people's lives begin to improve as a result of increased trade and the beginnings of industrialization.

The removal of border tariffs and other restrictions previously imposed by the English had given Scottish traders a chance to compete. In the latter part of the eighteenth century, Scotland's principal exports, of linen and cattle, increased dramatically, as did its share of the lucrative tobacco trade with America. An extensive road-building programme under the direction of General Wade, instituted with the objective of military subjugation after the abortive 1719 Jacobite Rebellion, also brought internal economic benefits to the country.

This was the general economic context in which the Scottish Enlightenment blossomed. More directly pertinent to the major factor which influenced the growth of the arts, patronage, was the increase in the wealth of individuals, and this is best reflected in the growth of modern banking. In this area Scotland was a pioneer. The Bank of Scotland was founded as early as 1695 and the Royal Bank of Scotland in 1727; the assets of both rose enormously in the second half of the eighteenth century. Hopetoun House, Mellerstain,

Inverary, Culzean (Plate 30) – virtually all Scotland's great country houses – were either built or extended during the eighteenth century. By 1800 many wealthy, noble patrons of the arts were keeping houses in both Edinburgh and London.

CULTURAL LEADERS: *Lawyers* AND *academics*

There was a further provision of the Act of Union which was to have a far-reaching effect on Scottish cultural life and, in particular, on the intellectual heart of the Scottish Enlightenment – Edinburgh. Scotland was to retain its own legal system.

The Scottish Enlightenment was essentially an urban phenomenon, and after the Union law became the cultural linchpin of the city at its centre, Edinburgh. Lawyers, a cosmopolitan group many of whom had attended continental universities to round off their Scottish educations, were the leaders of society and in the vanguard of intellectual thought. Consequently, because of the role it played in the life of what was now Britain's subordinate capital, the law became closely bound up with the national sense of identity.

Even before the Union, practical Scottish law had had a prestigious history, having first been properly codified as early as 1689 in Viscount Stair's *Institutions of the Law of Scotland*. Following the Union, however, its scope broadened and Scottish legal academics consciously developed the connections between their subject and the other main areas of abstract thought: politics, history and philosophy. The far-ranging debate which resulted became central to the Enlightenment.

If law then played a major role in the development of the Scottish Enlightenment, the position of education was only slightly less important. The University of Edinburgh in particular was a magnet which attracted and developed the greatest minds of the day. In the latter part of the eighteenth century nearly all the leading Enlightenment figures held official positions there, and the university's medical school, founded in 1726, replaced that of Leyden as Europe's most advanced. The Scottish higher education system throughout benefited from dedicated teaching, partly because professors were paid from students' fees and received no fixed salaries; the more students they attracted, the greater their incomes. The high standing of Scottish education in the public mind today is largely a result of the reputation it achieved in the eighteenth century.

Enlightenment THOUGHT AND *David Hume*

The main concerns and patterns of thought which developed during the Scottish Enlightenment were of a distinct and special cast. What all the leading figures of the movement had in common – and most of them knew one another well and argued out their theories in the many debating societies which are a feature of the period – was an insatiable desire to understand every aspect of existence and, having understood, to improve things if possible. The *Encyclopedia Britannica* was an Edinburgh product typical of the age.

The aim to 'improve' gripped the Enlightenment mind and manifested itself in numerous practical developments. These ranged from the development of steam power by James Watt, through attempts at agricultural betterment like those of the philosopher and legal theoretician Lord Kames, to the building of that great physical monument to the Enlightenment, the Edinburgh New Town itself (Plate 31), an ambitious Neo-Classical effort to improve upon the insanitary, crowded, medieval Old Town.

The portraiture of Allan Ramsay and Henry Raeburn is the most important artistic result of this progressive attitude. By painting their sitters in a straightforward, naturalistic way Ramsay and Raeburn were striving to improve upon the flattering conventions they had inherited. The difference between a portrait by either Ramsay or Raeburn and, say, one by John de Medina or William Aikman, is analogous to the difference between a well-proportioned apartment in Edinburgh's New Town and a medieval tenement in its Old.

The most profound expression of Scottish Enlightenment thought

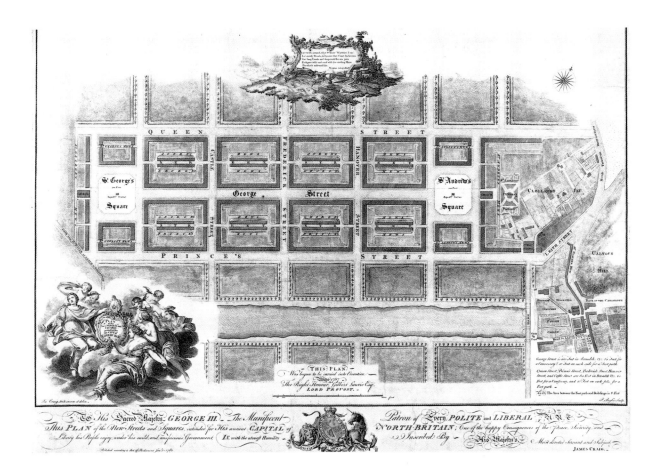

31 JAMES CRAIG
Plan of the Edinburgh New Town
1767 Coloured engraving
40.64 × 65.41
Central Library, Edinburgh
The New Town of Edinburgh is
the most striking manifestation of
the Scottish Enlightenment's
obsessive urge to 'improve'.
Although many individual
buildings have been destroyed or
desecrated by post-war planners
and architects, James Craig's
admirably lucid ground plan
remains intact.

is to be found in the work of David Hume. As a moral philosopher,
he is still generally considered the greatest writer in the English
language, and a little understanding of the basics of his philosophy
is a great help in the appreciation of the art of Scotland's most
intense period of creative change.

Hume's personality comes across vividly in the portrait painted of
him by his friend, Allan Ramsay (Plate 20): he was broad-minded,
sceptical, intensely social, argumentative. Born soon after the Act of
Union, he became, like the majority of his colleagues, a convinced
anglophile, regarding himself as a North Briton first and a Scot
second. He died, it was said, regretting the 'Scotticisms' in his speech
which, in common with his entire class, he had tried desperately to
iron out. Hume was widely travelled, living for periods in France
(during the 1760s he worked as secretary to the British chargé
d'affaires in Paris) and knew or corresponded with the greatest
foreign minds of the age; men such as Jean-Jacques Rousseau,
Voltaire and Benjamin Franklin.

The core of Hume's philosophy is to be found in his *Treatise of
Human Nature*, published first in London in 1739 and then revised
and supplemented ten years later by the *Enquiry concerning Human
Understanding* and the *Enquiry concerning the Principles of Morals*. In these

works he examines the nature of knowledge – how and why things change; Hume insists that, before events can be comprehended properly, we must understand man himself – how much, and in what way, man is able to understand things.

In considering these matters Hume comes to a very worrying conclusion: that reason (the very touchstone of his time), although beneficial and an interesting exercise in itself, has no power to motivate mankind. Man, says Hume, is only ever motivated by his passions: 'Reason is, and ought only to be, the slave of the passions.' It is typical of Hume that by employing reason with ruthless vigour he should have ended up encapsulating a thought which underminded the entire 'reasonable' basis of his society. Though disputed at the time by continental thinkers, Hume's view was vindicated in dramatic fashion by the French Revolution. Hume did not live to witness the event which shattered the Enlightenment's rational view of the world. Had he done so, he would doubtless have argued that the horrors which resulted did not occur because reason had 'gone to sleep', but rather that reason in itself could not have done anything to curb events fired by such passions.

Hume considered all types of human activity, and in view of the milieu he frequented it would have been surprising had art not been one of them. In 1757 he published an essay entitled *Of the Standard of Taste*, and the ideas he expresses in it constitute one of the earliest ventures into what is now called 'aesthetics'.

Naturally enough, Hume takes a common-sense view, maintaining that beauty is a 'power' in objects which gives rise to pleasure; in other words an abstract quality. He does, however, stress that, although abstract, this 'power' is real enough, and not just a matter of subjective opinion. Rational people, he contends, given the right circumstances, should always arrive at the same aesthetic conclusions (Plate 32).

In *The Treatise of Human Nature* Hume states that 'everything in nature is individual', a belief very much in tune with Allan Ramsay's approach to portraiture – the very tenet, in fact, which sets Ramsay apart from contemporaries such as Sir Joshua Reynolds. And Ramsay – like Hume – penned a precocious essay dealing with aesthetic matters. In 1755 the painter published a *Dialogue on Taste* in which he contends that the 'agreeable' (a characteristic eighteenth-century epithet encompassing the meanings 'graceful' and 'elegant') and the 'exact' (meaning precise and accurate drawing) are not mutually exclusive.

Included in Ramsay's *Dialogue* is an extensive section dealing with the respective merits of Classical and Gothic architecture. Coupled with the fact that he was eventually to give up painting altogether

32 DAVID ALLAN
The Connoisseurs   After 1780
Oil on canvas 86.4 × 97.8
National Galleries of Scotland
Allan's picture of three gentlemen contemplating a print epitomizes the late eighteenth-century attitude to appreciating fine art. The connoisseurs, whom the artist identified by means of an unfortunately now hidden key on the reverse of the canvas, are clearly discussing the merit of the work in question. The great philosopher of the Scottish Enlightenment, David Hume, contended that – provided they each took a 'reasonable' approach to their task – they would all arrive at the same conclusion.

and to end his days searching for the whereabouts of Horace's villa outside Rome, it is a solid indication of the artist's interest in history for its own sake, an interest which amounted to something of an obsession with the leading figures of the Scottish Enlightenment. 'This is the historical age and we are the historical people,' declared David Hume.

The LURE OF *Italy*

The Scottish Enlightenment's passionate interest in history was largely the result of the tumultuous events which had moulded Scotland's history in the eighteenth century, from the Act of Union to the Jacobite Rebellions. The leading figures of the Enlightenment found themselves in an entirely new historical situation – Scotland as part of a legally united kingdom – and much of their thinking was geared towards trying to make sense of this new circumstance. Scottish history was their priority, but it was far from being their only interest.

Paramount in the first age since the Renaissance to venerate the classical heritage of Greece and Rome was an interest in ancient history. Most educated Scots received a classical education, and both the Scottish social elite and the artists who served it aspired to drink at the fountainhead of classical culture, Rome.

The Scottish attitude towards Rome, however, was ambivalent for two reasons. The residency of the Pope guaranteed the city a status in the minds of religious Presbyterian Scots analogous to that which Moscow occupied in the minds of right-wing Americans during the Cold War; in one of his letters Allan Ramsay's father refers to Rome as 'the Seat of the Beast'. In addition, the exiled Jacobite community in Rome presented a great deal of social embarrassment to supporters of the Union and the Hanoverian cause – not to mention, during the early eighteenth century when the Jacobite threat was a reality, an element of danger.

Nevertheless, the lively Scottish community in Rome which persisted until Napoleon's conquest of the city in the 1790s is an exciting historical phenomenon which had numerous and significant cultural repercussions for art in Scotland. The influences of contemporary Roman artists, of artists from other continental countries working in Rome and of the visual evidence of Antiquity conspired to ensure that Scottish art, which in view of the country's geographical position on the edge of Europe could so easily have become backward, remained in the European mainstream.

The SCOTTISH *artistic community in Rome*

In the later eighteenth century the Scottish community in Rome was a thriving social mix of artists, dilettantes and aristocratic patrons. Similar types of visitors were also flocking to Rome from other parts of Europe during this period, and there were sizeable artistic communities of Germans and Scandinavians. But by any standards the Scottish artistic presence was formidable and it is not too fanciful to think of Rome at this time as a second centre of Scottish art.

Their imaginations fired by such works as Joseph Addison's *Remarks on Several Parts of Italy*, published in 1705, and Jonathan Richardson's *Accounts of the Statues and Bas-Reliefs, Drawings and Pictures in Italy* of 1722, English visitors to Rome were some of the earliest. And, later in the eighteenth century, Sir Joshua Reynolds's experience of Italian art, transmitted through his famous Royal Academy 'Discourses', had far-reaching implications for English art. Generally speaking, however, the Scots in eighteenth-century Rome constituted a higher-powered and more influential group.

33 AGOSTINO MASUCCI
*The Marriage of Prince James Francis
Edward Stewart to Princess Maria
Clementina Sobieska on 1st September
1719* c. 1735
Oil on canvas 243.5 × 342
National Galleries of Scotland
The marriage of the Old Pretender
to a wealthy Polish princess in 1719
did much to restore the waning
spirits of the Jacobite court in
Rome, and the cause was further
encouraged by the birth of Prince
Charles Edward (Bonnie Prince
Charlie) the following year. The
presence of the Jacobites
contributed a thrilling social frisson
to the experience of the many
Scottish artists who studied in
Rome in the eighteenth century.

Moreover the experience enjoyed by the Scots tended to be more
colourful because of the presence of the exiled Jacobite court. The
Old Pretender, Prince James Edward Stuart, had been invited to
take up residence by Pope Clement XI after the failure of the 1715
Jacobite Rebellion. About fifty prominent Jacobites accompanied
him, and after his marriage to the Polish Princess Maria Clementina
Sobieska in 1719 (Plate 33) the court became a permanent fixture in
the Palazzo Muti, near what is today the Piazza Venezia. The
birth of Prince Charles Edward in 1720 encouraged an increasingly
optimistic mood about the likelihood of a Stuart restoration.

For any Scot visiting Rome, therefore, the Jacobite court was a
source of intense curiosity. It was virtually impossible to avoid contact
with Jacobites; and in any case, they could be extremely helpful.
Before issuing a visa to a Scots artist wishing to visit Naples, for
example, the papal authority demanded the approval of a senior
Jacobite. There were of course no formal diplomatic relations between
Georgian England and the Vatican precisely because of its support
for the Jacobites.

From the point of view of visiting artists and Grand Tourists, by
far the most useful group of permanent residents in Rome were the

antiquaries – a fascinating group of multilingual, antique-dealing, cultural guides. The most famous was in fact an Englishman, Thomas Jenkins. But Jenkins was the exception. After the middle of the century his business was monopolized by Scots, and many of these were Jacobite by inclination, if not openly so.

James Byres (1734–1817; Plate 34) was a typical example. From a family of Aberdeenshire Jacobites, Byres had come to Rome with the intention of studying architecture. In this he had not been unsuccessful, but since life in Rome was expensive he used the contacts he had made to set up as an antiquary. Acting as 'cicerone', or guide, it was Byres who helped the very greatest British visitors to explore the Eternal City; the historian Edward Gibbon, the collector Charles Townley and any number of dukes and earls were among his clients.

But for Byres, guiding was merely a sideline to the more important and remunerative business of the antiquary: discovering and exporting works of art. It was from Byres that Sir William Hamilton acquired the famous Portland Vase and the Duke of Rutland bought the seventeenth-century French artist Poussin's first set of *Seven Sacraments*. Byres also collected contemporary pictures – David Allan's *Origin of Painting* was in his collection – and helped young painters to secure commissions. In the 1780s Byres arranged for Henry Raeburn to paint a miniature of Lord Spencer.

The Jacobite sympathies of Andrew Lumisden (1720–1801) were far more obvious than those of Byres. Lumisden served as Bonnie Prince Charlie's secretary during the 1745 Rebellion and, after the young Prince's crushing defeat at Culloden, returned to Rome as under-secretary to his master's ageing father. As 'cicerone' he was as adept as Byres, but he was even more learned; Lumisden's *Remarks on the Antiquities of Rome and its Environs*, published after his ultimate return to Scotland in 1768, ran to two editions.

What is more, Lumisden seems to have taken a purposeful interest in his compatriot artist-visitors; a whole range of Scottish artists including Cosmo Alexander, George Willison and David Allan were in his debt in one way or another. He was also acquainted with the greatest of them all, Allan Ramsay; although, when he arrived to pay his respects to the successful portrait painter on Ramsay's second visit to Rome in the 1750s, Lumisden was apparently received with a certain coolness which contrasted with their friendly relations of twenty years earlier. Mr Ramsay, it seems, was not keen to associate openly with Jacobites now that his success in Hanoverian England had been established.

Gavin Hamilton, David Allan AND THE *Runcimans*

Most Grand Touring Scottish artists made Rome the focus of their continental travels, usually staying for three or four years, and the majority of them never went further east than Italy; William Aikman's unusually extensive Grand Tour early in the century (see Chapter One) was an exception, as was the visit in the late 1750s of the architect Robert Adam to the Dalmatian coast.

Gavin Hamilton (1723–98) is unique among eighteenth-century Scottish artists since he spent most of his extremely influential career in Rome, becoming the artistic focus for all Scottish visitors, artists and aristocrats alike. Hamilton is the epitome of the Scots artist in Rome, and his activities and range of interests are typical. But he is something more than just a good example of the species: Hamilton was the most important European exponent of the early phase of Neo-Classical history painting, and served as a model not only to Scottish artists who aspired to success in what was then considered the highest genre of painting, but to all other nationalities. Even the greatest Neo-Classical painter of all, the artist in whose work the ideals of revolutionary France found their fullest expression, Jacques-Louis David, owed a debt to Hamilton.

Hamilton graduated in humanities at Glasgow University when he was fifteen and at the age of twenty-one was already in Rome. He studied under the Italian master Agostino Masucci (Plate 33) who, like the more popular Pompeo Batoni (Plate 35), specialized in painting the portraits of visiting Grand Tourists.

Although most of his career was spent in Rome, Hamilton returned to London in the early 1750s and spent six years trying to establish himself as a portrait painter. A portrait of *Elizabeth Gunning, Duchess of Hamilton* (Plate 36) suggests that he might have been able to compete with Ramsay had he not decided to return to Italy. Hamilton has painted the Duchess (one of a pair of ravishing Irish beauties known about London as the 'Hibernian Maids') in an icily elegant

Left 35 POMPEO BATONI
Colonel William Gordon of Fyvie
1766 Oil on canvas 258.2 × 186
National Trust for Scotland
Batoni was the leading portraitist
in Rome for much of the
eighteenth century, specializing in
flattering mementoes of the many
wealthy Grand Tourists who visited
the city. Apart from being one of
his finest works, this magnificent
portrait of Colonel Gordon is an
especially flamboyant conception.
No Scottish artist ever managed to
make tartan appear quite as exotic
as Batoni does here.

Right 36 GAVIN HAMILTON
Elizabeth Gunning, Duchess of Hamilton
c. 1752–5 Oil on canvas
    238.7 × 147.3
The Duke of Hamilton,
    Lennoxlove
In this portrait of the renowned
beauty Elizabeth Gunning, the icy
spirit of the Neo-Classicism which
Hamilton was to espouse in his
more dramatic depictions of
Homeric subjects seems already
apparent. Hamilton's attempt to set
up a portrait practice in London
was short-lived, and he soon
returned to Rome where he spent
the rest of his life.

manner with the glossy technique he had acquired from his Italian
master.

Back in Rome, having embarked upon a subsidiary career as an
antiquary, Hamilton began painting a ground-breaking series of
extremely large Neo-Classical history pictures illustrating scenes from
Homer. Over the years he was to make a considerable success of
these works, securing commissions from the English grandees he
came across in his role of antiquary and for whom he acquired
important Roman and Renaissance works of art.

It is ironic that a Scot should have played such an important role in forging the Neo-Classical style in painting given that the exuberantly decorative French Rococo style, against which the cool and restrained Neo-Classicism was a self-conscious reaction, had had virtually no effect on the arts in Scotland. Nevertheless, the thoroughness of Hamilton's Scottish education must have made him an easy convert to Neo-Classical values. Moreover, Neo-Classicism developed hand-in-glove with the Enlightenment and Hamilton, of course, hailed from the most 'enlightened' country in Europe.

The Rome in which Gavin Hamilton found himself in the mid-1750s was convulsed by what was in effect a Neo-Classical revolution. He was surrounded by zealous advocates of the return to what they called 'the true style', the chief advocate of which was the German Johann Joachim Winckelmann. The ideas expounded by Winck-elmann in his two major works – the *Gedanken über die Nachahmung der Griechischen Werke* (Thoughts on the Imitation of Greek Works), published in 1755, and the *Geschichte der Kunst des Altertums* (History of the Art of Antiquity), published in 1764 – were those which must have gripped and convinced Hamilton.

In the controversy which raged during this period over the respective merits of Greek and Roman art, Hamilton sided firmly with Winckelmann in his admiration for all things Greek. It was in Greek art that he perceived 'noble simplicity and calm grandeur', to use Winckelmann's phrase, and in looking to Homer for subject matter he sought to emulate these values. It was for this reason that he had chosen to illustrate Homer's *Iliad*. In his choice of subject matter he was ahead of his time; for most of the eighteenth century Homer's reputation was no greater than that of ancient Roman writers like Virgil.

Nevertheless, the idea of turning to Homer for subjects had been in the air for a long time. In his *Treatise on Ancient Painting*, published in 1740, the Scottish writer George Turnbull maintained that Homer had been the source of all classical Greek art; while the Earl of Shaftesbury, one of the earliest British statesmen to view Ancient Greece as a political model, suggested the naturalism of Homer's portrayal of emotions as suitable for painters. In France, the influential connoisseur, the Comte de Caylus, also detailed a Homeric pro-gramme for artists in his *Tableaux Tirés de l'Iliade ... de Homère*.

The six pictures by Gavin Hamilton depicting episodes drawn from Homer's *Iliad* were painted over a fifteen-year period beginning in 1760. They were all commissioned by British patrons, probably on the suggestion of Hamilton himself while he was sharing with them his antiquarian expertise. (Hamilton, incidentally, was a dealer of consequence; it is thanks to him that Raphael's *Ansidei Madonna*,

37 GAVIN HAMILTON
Achilles Lamenting the Death of Patroclus
1760–3 Oil on canvas 227.3 × 391.2
National Galleries of Scotland
The orderly composition and
rhetorical gestures in this, one of
six scenes from Homer's *Iliad* which
Hamilton painted in the 1760s,
suggest that the Scottish artist's
most vital source of inspiration was
the seventeenth-century French
Classicist, Poussin. In both scale
and concept, however, Hamilton's
revival of the Classical spirit is more
grandiose than that of the earlier
artist.

among other great Renaissance masterpieces, now hangs in the
National Gallery in London.)

There are few better examples of a Neo-Classical artist striving to
realize an ennobling theme than Hamilton's *Achilles Lamenting the
Death of Patroclus* (Plate 37). The theme of the entire series is the anger
of Achilles, and this canvas is pivotal to the story. The picture was
commissioned by James Grant of Grant, and Hamilton was paid
what was at the time the considerable sum of £350. In 1763, when
the completed painting arrived in London, a number of Scots begged
Sir James Grant to allow it to be shown at the Society of Arts before
it was sent on to Scotland.

Hamilton's orderly 'stage-set' composition is organized so as to
allow the meaning of the action to be easily understood. The
elaborate rhythms of interlaced figures which tend to cloud the issue
in Baroque painting – that of Rubens for example – are carefully
avoided. Hamilton's composition is static; and the emotions of his
protagonists are expressed by rhetorical gestures alone. The point of
the picture is to set a moral example; the object of the exercise is to
'improve' the spectator.

The influence of Hamilton's Neo-Classical history pictures
extended beyond his immediate circle through the engravings of
them which he commissioned from Domenico Cunego. Not-

anding their influence on a range of illustrious continental
(of whom David is by far the most famous), their most far-
reaching effect was upon the sensibilities of Scottish artists visiting
Rome. Hamilton's engravings confirmed many of them in their latent
ambition to succeed as painters of history. Unlike Hamilton, however,
the majority of eighteenth-century Scottish artists returned home to
try to fulfil the ambitions fired in them by the experience of Antiquity,
the Renaissance and the new Neo-Classical artistic creed. The
consequences of Hamilton's influence for art back in Scotland were,
therefore, very great indeed.

Before looking at the most important of those who, initially at
least, attempted to fulfil Hamilton's Neo-Classical ideals after their
return to Scotland, it is worth mentioning one or two lesser talents
who were content to pursue the less esteemed though more lucrative
genre of portraiture. For these the stay in Rome tended to be used
as an opportunity to internationalize their provincial style. Allan
Ramsay (see Chapter One), who took on board the polish and
refinement of the Roman masters under whom he studied as well as
the delicacy and elegance of the French portrait painters he
encountered, is, of course, the pre-eminent example. But there were
others.

William Mosman (1700–71), for example, an artist patronized by
the Jacobites and who worked alongside Ramsay in Imperiali's studio
in the 1730s, shows a less inspired but more extreme assimilation of
the Roman manner. His portrait of Sir Thomas Kennedy of Culzean
is an Italianiate *tour de force*. The baronet stands in the pose of a well-
known classical statue and the precious treatment of his garments,
not to mention the sweet colouring, are thoroughly Roman and
recall the manner of Antonio David. John Alexander (1686–1766)
and his son Cosmo (1724–72) – like Mosman, Jacobites from the
north-east of Scotland – also developed thoroughly Italianized styles.
The elder artist's decorations for the Duke of Gordon's castle (Plate
38), carried out as early as the 1720s, are evidence that even Scottish
painters working early in the century cherished the ambition to
recreate the grand Italian decorative manner back home in Scotland.
In general, however, the Alexanders were content to put their
sophisticated, continental techniques at the service of clients who
merely wanted their portraits painted.

For most of the Scottish artists who visited Rome after the middle
of the century, however, the experience turned out to be a very
mixed blessing indeed. Having fallen victim to the dogma of High
Art, they became convinced of the superiority of history painting
above all other varieties; but on returning home, they suffered the
bitter disappointment of finding out that their services in this field

38 JOHN ALEXANDER
The Rape of Proserpine 1720
Oil on canvas 71.1 × 80.7
National Galleries of Scotland
John Alexander's study for a large
canvas which once decorated the
staircase of the Duke of Gordon's
castle in Morayshire gives a good
idea of the quality of painting in
north-east Scotland early in the
eighteenth century. Pluto, in the
process of abducting Proserpine in
his chariot, is preceded by a figure
representing Love holding
Cerberus on a leash.

were simply not required. Gavin Hamilton was unique in being a
portrait painter who turned to history painting and found patrons
willing to commission him. He was clever enough to realize that his
role as a practitioner of High Art obliged him to reside in the cradle
of the Classical revival.

All the tensions and contradictions which resulted from a prolonged
stay by a young Scottish artist in Rome can be traced in the schizoid
career of David Allan (1744–96). Allan arrived in Rome in 1767 and
spent the next decade there, for much of the time the foremost of
Gavin Hamilton's several protégés. Born in Alloa, at the tender age
of eleven Allan had left for Glasgow to study art at the Foulis
Academy.

For a young boy with an ambition to be an artist in mid-eighteenth
century Scotland, there was no better place. Founded by Robert

Foulis and his brother Andrew, this early Glasgow art school was an extraordinary, precocious attempt to found an academy along continental lines. It had been preceded by the short-lived Academy of St Luke, founded by Allan Ramsay the poet and his associates in the 1720s, but the Edinburgh school was a small-scale, half-hearted affair by comparison, and it is the Foulis Academy which can

39 DAVID ALLAN
View of the Foulis Academy   *c.* 1762
Oil on canvas 33 × 40.6
Hunterian Art Gallery, University of Glasgow
Allan's picture of the art school he attended before departing for Italy indicates that the Foulis Academy was as professional in its approach as the continental prototypes upon which it was modelled. The studying of Old Masters and Antique casts was standard procedure in art schools throughout the eighteenth century, and remained so for much of the nineteenth.

justifiably lay claim to being Britain's first continental-style art academy.

At the Foulis brothers' school students had the benefit of a remarkable collection of three hundred works of art (Plate 39) – everything from original pictures by Rubens to copies after Raphael and Antique busts – and it was the contemplating and copying of these works which formed the basis of their art education. Rather surprisingly, print-making also played a part in the academy's curriculum; the Foulis Press printed some of the highest-quality books of the period. Presbyterian propriety, however, prohibited the conducting of life classes.

For a student like David Allan, however, it was the progressive philosophy to which he was introduced there which was to have the most significant impact on his career. The Foulis brothers were firm believers in the hierarchy of genres as delineated by the Earl of Shaftesbury in his essay *The Judgement of Hercules*. 'The merely natural must pay homage to the historical or moral,' Shaftesbury had written; and David Allan who, paradoxically, was ultimately to contribute most to the formation of a Scottish School by his choice of 'natural'

40 DAVID ALLAN

Hector's Farewell to Andromache 1773
Oil on canvas 74 × 100
Accademia Nazionale di San Luca,
 Rome

Sir William Hamilton, the British ambassador in Naples, was well acquainted with the artist David Allan, whom he described as 'one of the greatest geniuses I ever met with – he is indefatigable'. In 1773 the indefatigable Mr Allan won a gold medal at Rome's Accademia di San Luca with this accomplished essay in Neo-Classical painting. Later, however, he was to forsake his vocation as a painter of history subjects in order to concentrate on genre.

subjects from everyday Scottish life, was never to shake off this conviction.

Remarkably, the Foulis Academy actually paid for students to travel to Rome; but, even if it helped Allan with his initial costs, it certainly could not have subsidized his entire ten-year stay there. Allan, like most of his fellow Scottish artists in Rome, was sponsored by the gentry from his home town.

Once in Rome Allan was imbued through his mentor, Gavin Hamilton, with an enthusiasm for Homer, and in 1773 he won the Concorso Balestra, a prestigious prize awarded by the Accademia di San Luca. The subject of his successful picture was *Hector's Farewell to Andromache* (Plate 40), and its composition was based on a design by Hamilton. Allan was the only British artist to win the Concorso in the eighteenth century.

Unlike his master, however, he was never to accept the Earl of Shaftesbury's recommendation that history pictures should be painted on the gigantic scale it was imagined the ancients had employed. But two other pictures from his Roman period are evidence that Allan was, during his Roman stay, doing his best to fulfil all the

other philosophical tenets of Neo-Classicism. Neither in *The Continence of Scipio* (Plate 41), the favourite Roman subject of Neo-Classical artists, nor in *The Origin of Painting* (NGS) is there any indication that Allan would later abandon the heroics of Antique history in favour of lassies and laddies cavorting in rural Scottish settings. There is no sign that he was destined to be the progenitor of the nineteenth-century school of British genre painting.

In 1777 Allan returned to Britain for good and, after spending two years trying to establish himself as a portrait painter in London (his ambition to be a painter of history had clearly already waned to some extent), he moved back to Scotland where his career proceeded to develop in the very different direction of genre painting (see Chapter Three).

He was never, however, to dissent from the artistic philosophy which, in a way, had waylaid his progress; in the dedication he made to his old Roman master Gavin Hamilton, in the work for which, ironically, he became best known – his illustrations to Allan Ramsay's

42 JOHN RUNCIMAN
Self-portrait 1767–8
Oil on canvas 68.7 × 55.6
National Galleries of Scotland
Within a year of painting this fine
self-portrait John Runciman died,
probably by his own land, which
makes his inclusion of a figure from
Michelangelo's Medici funeral
chapel in Florence seem ominous.
The apparently more gifted of the
Runciman brothers, he might well
have gone on to achieve even
greater things than his elder
brother.

The Gentle Shepherd (Plate 52) – he wrote: 'It must be the source of just regret to every lover of the art of painting, to remark how much its progress is retarded in Great Britain by the little demand there is for public and great works in the historical line.'

The effect of Rome on the other major Scottish artist to emerge in the late eighteenth century, Alexander Runciman (1736–85), was very different. Seeds of ambition to follow the highest artistic calling were sown in both Alexander and his short-lived, younger brother John Runciman (1744–68) immediately they arrived there. Alexander Runciman was to become the most persistent and imaginative Scottish history painter of the century.

But the narrow dogmas of Neo-Classical taste did not guide the Runcimans as exclusively as they did Gavin Hamilton and David Allan. In addition to Antique art the Runciman brothers took High Renaissance and Baroque artists such as Michelangelo and Rubens as their guides, an idea that would have appalled the strict theoretician of the movement, Winckelmann.

John Runciman was thought to be extremely promising while he was in Rome. The Swiss-born English artist Henry Fuseli, a friend and inspiration to the brothers, commented that he thought John had 'livelier expectations' than Alexander, and a pensive self-portrait by John painted at this time certainly suggests sensitivity and a competent hand (Plate 42). Behind the artist, Michelangelo's funerary sculpture *Day*, from the Medici Chapel, is indicative of his broad interests. Unfortunately, John was to die in mysterious circumstances shortly after painting this picture and, sadly, many of the paintings which he did while he was in Rome seem to have been deliberately destroyed.

Nevertheless, John Runciman's most interesting work from a long-term historical perspective was executed before leaving Scotland. It is a small picture, *King Lear in the Storm* (Plate 43), a precursor of the romanticized interpretations of literary subjects which were to become two-a-penny in the next century. Not only has John Runciman transferred Lear from stormy heath to stormy shore to make the incident more melodramatic, but he has used free brushwork borrowed from Rubens to evoke the turbulence of the elements. This is

43 JOHN RUNCIMAN
King Lear in the Storm   1767
Oil on panel 44.4 × 61
National Galleries of Scotland
The fact that this remarkable tiny picture was painted before John Runciman had set out on his search for a Neo-Classical education in Rome only serves to emphasize the fact that – as with so many Scottish artists of the period – his natural, painterly inclination was directly opposed to the controlled Classicism to which he aspired.

44 ALEXANDER RUNCIMAN
*Agrippina Landing at Brundisium with
the Ashes of Germanicus*
1780 Oil on canvas 100.2 × 133.2
National Galleries of Scotland
The most striking aspects of this
picture – its 'stage-set' composition
and sombre colour range, the
Classical poses and rhetorical
gestures of the figures – are the
hallmarks of the serious, late
eighteenth-century history painter.
The subject had previously been
tackled by Runciman's compatriot
and mentor in Rome, Gavin
Hamilton.

a startlingly precocious essay in Romantic painting, by an artist who
unfortunately did not live to fulfil his promise.

John's more important elder brother, Alexander, was apprenticed
to the Norie firm of decorative house painters (see Chapter Four) at
about the same time that David Allan was studying at the Foulis
Academy. His early career is, however, irrelevant to his ultimate
development, except that a number of drawings of contemporary
events that he made in Scotland suggest an interest in his country's
history typical of the Scottish Enlightenment and this must have
prepared him well for the Neo-Classical historicism he was to find
in Rome.

It was not long after his arrival there that he wrote to a friend, 'I
find since I came here I have been on a wrong plan of study for
painting all my life but I have begun an entire new system of which
I hope to show something if I come home.' Clearly, Runciman had
been bitten by the High Art bug, and within two years he was
painting a gigantic picture of a Homeric subject, *Ulysses Surprising
Nausicaa.* Unfortunately the work is now lost but it is likely to have
been executed in the manner of Gavin Hamilton. Most of the other

subjects he tackled over the next couple of years, either as drawings or as full-scale paintings, were also Neo-Classical favourites. They included *The Origin of Painting*, a story from Pliny which appealed to the Enlightenment mind because of its theme of primitive discovery, and *Agrippina Landing at Brundisium with the Ashes of Germanicus*, a subject from the historian Tacitus that exemplified stoic Roman virtue (Plate 44).

The influence of Henry Fuseli, however, not to mention his admiration for the muscular drawing of Michelangelo and the colouring of Venetian art, combined to divert the painter's style in a clearly Romantic direction and Runciman's new cast of mind is reflected in his subsequent choice of subjects. Refusing to restrict himself to the orthodox, Neo-Classically approved canon from Greek and Roman history, he began to tackle mythological stories. A drawing showing *Orestes Pursued by the Furies* (Plate 45) is a characteristically ebullient and freely expressed attempt to realize an imaginary scene.

Runciman's taste for mythological and literary subjects sets him apart from Gavin Hamilton and his ilk. Hamilton would have nothing to do with the unobservable (no representations of Greek gods interfere with the sober supposed reality of his Homeric series, for example), and in this he was in tune with other great minds of the Scottish Enlightenment. In general they disapproved of the imaginary; Ramsay, for example, disliked passages in Shakespeare such as the ghost scenes in *Hamlet* and *Macbeth*, while Hume took a sceptical view of Christian miracles.

Sponsorship of the Runciman brothers' sojourn in Rome had been provided by Sir James Clerk of Penicuik on condition that the two artists should decorate his new house upon their return. Because of John's death this duty fell solely to Alexander, who began work on the scheme as soon as he got back to Scotland in 1771.

Runciman's work at Penicuik House turned out to be the greatest large-scale painted decoration in eighteenth-century Scotland (Plate 46); the only comparable enterprise south of the Border was that accomplished by Runciman's friend, James Barry, for the Society of Arts in London later in the same decade. Tragically, however, this single epic manifestation of eighteenth-century Scottish artists' obsession with High Art was destroyed by fire at the end of the nineteenth century. Etchings, photographs and a written account remain, however, and these give a reasonable idea of how the Penicuik House scheme looked.

Correspondence between the artist and Sir James Clerk shows that Runciman considered several themes for his subject matter and

46 *Photograph of The Fire at Penicuik House* June 1899
Sir John Clerk of Penicuik
The destruction of Alexander Runciman's great Ossianic decorative scheme at Penicuik House in 1899 robbed Scotland of a series of paintings unique in their theme, scale and ambition. As various records made of the decoration attest, however, the effect of Runciman's pictures must have been dazzling.

at one time a Homeric one, the life of Achilles, was projected. Eventually, however, a far more 'national' subject was chosen.

In 1762 the poet James Macpherson had published *Fragments of Ancient Poetry, collected in the Highlands of Scotland, and translated from the Gaelic or Erse Language*. In spite of a preface by the highly respected Professor of Rhetoric and Belles Lettres at Edinburgh University, Hugh Blair, this and the poems, supposedly by the ancient Gaelic bard Ossian, which followed, turned out to be fraudulent. But that was not before the whole of literary Europe had been captivated by what it thought to be an authentic, primitive, Caledonian muse.

Alexander Runciman had no doubts; for his Penicuik House decorations he enthusiastically embraced an Ossianic theme.

Entering 'Ossian's Hall', as it came to be known, must have been
an extraordinary experience – rather like coming across the Sistine
Chapel in the heart of the Scottish Lowlands. In the central roundel
of the ceiling the ancient bard himself was depicted playing his harp
(Plate 47); while in the coving Runciman painted twelve separate
scenes illustrating episodes described in Ossian's song. In the four
spandrels surrounding the central oval reclined four river gods,
personifications of Scotland's four major rivers.

Apart from 'Ossian's Hall' – actually Penicuik House's main
drawing room – Runciman decorated the ceiling of one of the
house's oval staircases. Here he took his theme from real history,
depicting a series of scenes from the life of St Margaret (Plate 48).

The fact that Runciman saw fit to extend his Ossianic scheme
with scenes from the life of a real historical figure proves beyond
doubt that he intended the Penicuik House decorations to be a large-

47 ALEXANDER RUNCIMAN
The Blind Ossian Singing and
Accompanying Himself on the Harp
1772 Pen and ink wash, with oil
46.1 × 59.8
National Galleries of Scotland
This was a preparatory study for
the central oval of the ceiling of
'Ossian's Hall' at Penicuik House,
in which Alexander Runciman
depicted the ancient bard
performing songs which told of
Scotland's mythical past. The
ghosts of the heroes of whom
Ossian tells appear in the clouds.

scale essay in history painting. Various elements in the compositions, however, not least the ghosts of Ossian's heroes and St Margaret rising to heaven from Edinburgh Castle, show Runciman aspiring to the spirit of Baroque art and reneging on strict Neo-Classical convention.

In contrast to David Allan, Runciman's output of history paintings

48 ALEXANDER RUNCIMAN
The Landing of St Margaret c. 1772
Etching 22.3 × 18.1
National Galleries of Scotland
Alexander Runciman's pictures depicting scenes from the life of Scotland's medieval queen, St Margaret, decorated one of the two oval staircases at Penicuik House. In common with the Ossian pictures (though in stark contrast with the staid easel pictures which the artist later produced for the annual exhibitions at the Royal Academy) these were full of movement and energy. Welcomed from Norway by King Malcolm, the fair-haired Margaret approaches a group of waiting monks. According to a description, the painting was intensely coloured.

did not drastically decline after his return from Italy and he continued to send pictures such as *Agrippina Landing at Brundisium* (Plate 44) of 1784 to the Royal Academy in London. He was widely regarded as Scotland's leading painter of serious subjects. Yet these late efforts to perpetuate the Neo-Classical history painting in its pure form lack the excitement, ambition and imaginativeness – in short the proto-Romantic spirit – which characterizes many of Runciman's drawings and which make him such an interesting artist.

The owner of *Agrippina Landing at Brundisium* wrote that the picture 'must be interesting as a principal work of an artist who was the father of the Scottish School of Painting which we have every reason to hope will one day assume a place in the history of art'. To call Runciman the father of the Scottish School is overstating the case perhaps. Nevertheless, he certainly set an example of grand ambition which inspired a number of Scottish artists in the next century, the morose and tragic David Scott (1806–49) most notable among them.

CHAPTER THREE

Victorian

VALUES

49 EDWIN LANDSEER
The Monarch of the Glen 1851
Oil on canvas 63.8 × 68.9
United Distillers PLC
The picture which has come to
epitomize Victorian infatuation
with the Highlands was originally
intended to hang above the dado
in the Refreshment Room of the
House of Lords; the artist wanted
the work to be seen from a low
viewpoint. In his poem 'The Lady
of the Lake' Walter Scott refers to
the stag as 'The antler'd monarch
of the waste'.

It is ironic that the best known painting of a Scottish subject was
painted by an Englishman. Edwin Landseer's *Monarch of the Glen*
(Plate 49) is without doubt one of the most famous images in
British art. It has been endlessly reproduced on everything from tea
towels to whisky labels; there was a time when no respectable,
middle-class parlour in the country was thought complete without
an engraving of Sir Edwin's noble stag.

Queen Victoria and 'BALMORALITY'

Edwin Landseer (1802–73) had begun painting in the Scottish Highlands as early as 1824. Consequently, by the time Queen Victoria
ascended the throne in 1837 he had already completed a number of
pictures of Highland subjects. It was the combined effect of these
and the writings of Walter Scott that initially fired the young Victoria's
imagination and prompted her desire to explore the northern part
of her kingdom.

In 1842 the young queen and her husband of two years, Prince
Albert, made the first of what was to become a lifetime of annual
visits. She made the journey by sea, having taken heed of warnings
that a royal progress through the north of England might be
spoilt by political agitation from the Chartists, and disembarked at
Edinburgh's nearest port, Leith. Like most first-time visitors, Victoria
was immediately captivated by the romantic situation of the Scottish
capital.

But it was Victoria's first experience of the Highlands which really
initiated her love affair with Scotland. In honour of the visit of the
royal couple to their wonderfully located Perthshire castle, Taymouth,
the Earl and Countess of Breadalbane had had the ancient building
specially enlarged and remodelled after the 'baronial' fashion of

Walter Scott's Borders home, Abbotsford. Avenues of lantern-carrying, kilted retainers laid on to welcome them drew an ecstatic reaction from the queen, and Albert was soon taking advantage of the opportunity to indulge his Germanic passion for hunting. After his excursions, apparently, Victoria would read aloud to him from the works of Walter Scott.

A cruise off the west coast of Scotland in 1847 confirmed the couple in their adoration of the Highlands and it was after this trip that the industrious Albert immediately set to work on plans for a new royal residence north of the Border. Weather, it seems, was a prime consideration. To avoid the squally horrors of the west, an east coast site was decided upon.

As luck would have it, the picturesque old castle on the Deeside estate of Balmoral was vacant and, having first leased it, Albert eventually had the building demolished and replaced with a new 'baronial' pile. Not only was the new residence equipped with all the latest conveniences such as sophisticated plumbing, but it was decked out lavishly with thistle-strewn wallpapers and tartan carpets. The concept now known as 'Balmorality' had been born.

Although Queen Victoria's dedication to the Highlands did much to popularize Scotland in the public mind, her enthusiasm was really only part of a larger trend that had begun approximately eighty years earlier. Over that period Scotland had been steadily transformed into a favourite tourist destination as visitors hungry for dramatic scenery, like the poet William Wordsworth and his sister Dorothy for example, came in ever increasing numbers. Not surprisingly, this trend is best reflected in the boom in Scottish landscape painting (see Chapter Four), but it also lay behind the type of painting which was to become the most popular of the Victorian age, 'genre' painting.

While some painters concentrated on Scotland's natural beauty – initially in the Lowlands but ultimately almost exclusively in the Highlands – others, from towards the end of the eighteenth century, took to recording everyday scenes in Scotland's towns and villages. Even before 1800, when the Industrial Revolution was still in its infancy, the customs of rural Scotland came to be seen as quaint and were valued as such by a number of artists. A taste for the pictures they produced developed rapidly amongst important collectors.

David Allan AND ROBERT BURNS

When the artist David Allan (1744–96) returned from his ten-year stay in Rome in 1777 (see Chapter Two) he was, like many other artists of his generation, unable to find commissions for the history subjects his Neo-Classical training had qualified and encouraged him to wish to paint. Having first tried his luck with portraiture, he eventually opted to concentrate almost exclusively on the painting of genre subjects.

Allan's conversation pieces (usually small-scale family groups) contain the seeds of much later nineteenth-century genre painting. The *4th Duke of Atholl and Family* (Plate 50), painted in 1780, is a fine example and the most natural and pleasing of these group portraits. Allan shows the young duke in full Highland dress with his wife,

50 DAVID ALLAN
The 4th Duke of Atholl and Family
1780 Oil on canvas 91.5 × 101.5
The Duke of Atholl, Blair Castle
As was frequently the case with eighteenth-century Scottish artists, David Allan's studies in Italy had been sponsored by local gentry, in his case the Cathcarts of Schawfield. After his return to Scotland Allan continued to benefit from their patronage; the Duchess of Atholl shown here was Lord Cathcart's eldest daughter. This delightful picture, painted with Allan's characteristic freshness, is interesting for two reasons: it is an example of a Scottish artist treating landscape naturalistically at an early date, and a prototype of Allan's later painting of genre subjects in which less elevated personages are shown engaged in similarly relaxed activities.

children and gamekeeper, surrounded by the trophies of the hunt. The setting is Glen Tilt, later to become a favourite haunt of Queen Victoria, with Blair Castle in the background. Fifty years later Landseer painted the very same duke in old age, posed in a similar manner in the same glen.

It was during his stay at Blair Atholl that Allan also painted a picture of an al fresco Highland dance. Intended as a pair to a similar one of a Neapolitan dance he had sketched during his stay in Italy, it is a charming, naturalistically observed oil, which stands at the head of a succession of Scottish country dances painted by Scots artists during the course of the next century. Later Allan himself was to adapt the composition he had invented for his own important watercolour *The Penny Wedding* (Plate 51), and this subject (a 'penny wedding' was a rural marriage celebration at which the guests

51 DAVID ALLAN
The Penny Wedding 1795
Pen and watercolour 33.6 × 45.7
National Galleries of Scotland
The tradition of painting rural
wedding celebrations can be traced
back to the sixteenth-century
Netherlandish master, Breughel.
Within the Scottish context,
however, it was David Allan who
imbued the subject with artistic
authority. His skilful rendering of
comic incidents was to have a
profound influence upon his most
distinguished successor in the field
of genre painting, David Wilkie.

contributed to the cost and the happy couple reaped any profit)
was subsequently taken up by the most influential Scottish genre
painter, David Wilkie, in one of his most popular pictures
(Plate 56).

Allan's own greatest contribution to the formation of the nineteenth-century British genre tradition, however, were his illustrations
to Allan Ramsay's pastoral verse-drama *The Gentle Shepherd* (Plate 52).
The dedication Allan felt it necessary to include in the work is to his
former master during his Roman sojourn, the artist Gavin Hamilton
(see Chapter Two) and it provides a revealing insight into the mind
of a Scottish artist of Allan's generation. In it Allan justifies – almost
apologetically – his choice of lowly subject matter by claiming that
it was faithfully derived from nature following the example of the
poet. Using a literary excuse to legitimize a work of art was to
become a constant refrain among later genre painters.

The contemporary writer whose work naturally lent itself to David
Allan's talent was clearly the 'ploughman poet' himself, Robert
Burns, and Allan did in fact eventually illustrate Burns. Although,
unfortunately, the two never met, the poet admired the artist
immensely, considering him his only equal in the evocation of pastoral
life. There can have been few more complementary collaborations
between a writer and an artist; Burns's ennobling of peasant themes
was wholly in tune with Allan's attitude.

George Thomson, the publisher of Burns's Scots songs, sent the
poet a gift of Allan's painting based on his most celebrated poem
'The Cotter's Saturday Night'. Tragically, the painting has since
been lost, yet the poem eloquently encapsulates the philosophy which

52 DAVID ALLAN
*Glaud and Peggy (from The Gentle
Shepherd)* 1789
Etching with watercolour
23.1 × 18.2
National Galleries of Scotland
David Allan was not the first artist
to illustrate Allan Ramsay's popular
verse-drama *The Gentle Shepherd* but
Allan's version provides the perfect
artistic accompaniment to the text.

53 DAVID WILKIE
The Cotter's Saturday Night 1837
Oil on panel 83.8 × 108
Glasgow Museums and Art
  Galleries
By the time David Wilkie came to
paint this intimate evocation of
Robert Burns's famous poem of the
same name, his artistic priorities
had changed. The artist's early
preoccupation with the description
of precise detail has here been
replaced with an overwhelming
desire to create a unified
composition by the careful
manipulation of light effects to
convey the sense of simple,
domestic piety articulated by Burns.

lay behind the predilection of artists like Allan for painting genre
subjects:

> From scenes like these old Scotia's grandeur springs.
>   That makes her loved at home, revered abroad:
> Princes and lords are but the breath of kings,
>   'An honest man's the noblest work of God:'
> And certes, in fair virtue's heavenly road,
>   The cottage leaves the palace far behind.

A later treatment of the poem by Allan's greatest successor in the
field of genre painting, David Wilkie (1785–1841), does however
survive (Plate 53). It is in fact one of his masterpieces, a late work
produced at a time when the artist was employing the dramatic
lighting effects he had observed in the work of the great Dutch
master, Rembrandt. It was by depicting simple, rustic scenes like this
with scrupulous regard for accuracy that Wilkie had made his original
reputation, and the way in which he developed the kind of Scottish

picture Allan had originally conceived, eventually resulted in genre painting achieving an unprecedented status.

David Wilkie AND genre painting

David Wilkie studied at the Trustees' Academy in Edinburgh, Scotland's first permanent art school, where David Allan had been master until his death a few years before Wilkie's arrival. Upon graduating from the Trustees' at the age of nineteen, Wilkie returned home to the family manse in Cults, a small village in the county of

Fife on the other side of the Forth estuary, and it was here that he set about painting what turned out to be a very remarkable picture indeed: his aim was to create a portrait of an entire village.

Wilkie chose as a subject for his first major picture an authentic rural gathering, the annual cattle fair in nearby Pitlessie. He was not the first Scottish artist to paint such an event; Alexander Carse, a lesser follower of David Allan, had depicted a similar scene some years earlier. But, although the figures in Carse's picture of Old-hamstock Fair are grouped in a comparable way to those of Wilkie in *Pitlessie Fair* (Plate 54), the less sophisticated painter had drawn them in the generalized manner he had learnt from Allan. Wilkie's figures, in stark contrast, are described with a regard for detail which proclaims their individual identities. These are real people – members of Wilkie's own family, their neighbours and servants – several of whom the artist had surreptitiously sketched in the fly-leaf of his Bible during Sunday service in his father's kirk.

54 DAVID WILKIE
Pitlessie Fair 1804
Oil on canvas 58.5 × 106.7
National Galleries of Scotland
The small scale and crowded nature of David Wilkie's earliest masterpiece make the nineteen-year-old artist's observation and skill all the more impressive. Particularly convincing is his grouping of the various figures engaged in the myriad incidents described in the picture.

Nevertheless, in spite of the originality of Wilkie's *Pitlessie Fair* in the context of Scottish art, the picture owes much to Dutch seventeenth-century genre painting. The Dutch school, which had always been popular amongst British collectors, served as a model for all nineteenth-century genre artists. At this stage in his own career, however, Wilkie was doing little more than including in his pictures bawdy incidents (the urinating 'peasant' and the squabbling children in Pitlessie) typical of Dutch genre painting; later, after first-hand experience in London of the works he had known only from prints in Scotland, he would consciously work to achieve a Dutch Old Masterish look to his paintings.

With the £25 that the local laird paid him for *Pitlessie Fair*, together with the income from a number of portrait commissions the picture earned for him, Wilkie set off for London where he enrolled in the Royal Academy schools. Success followed rapidly. Within a year a painting of disputatious drinkers in a Scottish country inn called *The Village Politicians* (The Earl of Mansfield) had received a tumultuous reception at the Royal Academy exhibition and its author acclaimed a genius in the London press. It was not long before eminent connoisseurs such as Sir George Beaumont and even the Prince of Wales himself were competing for the privilege of acquiring the pictures Wilkie painstakingly produced.

Much of the success of *The Village Politicians* had been due to the convincing psychological truth Wilkie had managed to achieve in the facial expressions of his subjects (at this time there was a general interest in the correlation between expression and emotion and Wilkie had attended lectures delivered by his friend, the surgeon Charles Bell, on precisely this topic) and the same is true of his next important picture *The Letter of Introduction* (Plate 55). If anything he achieves a convincing psychological exchange here by even subtler means than in the earlier work: the suspicious expression of the old man, the diffident body language of the youngster – these qualities imbue this meeting of country cousin and rich relation with a profound emotional tension. The incident is almost certainly autobiographical.

The praise of influential critics for pictures such as *The Letter of Introduction*, however – many thought Wilkie superior to his Dutch precursors and the nickname equating him with the great Dutch genre painter, 'The Scottish Teniers', soon stuck – was insufficient to remove the nagging doubt at the back of the artist's mind that he ought to be tackling more ambitious subjects, doing something more significant; a trip in 1814 to Paris, where he was awed by the power and scale of the Old Masters he experienced in the Louvre, only accentuated this latent anxiety. But Wilkie was not ready to forsake

55 DAVID WILKIE
The Letter of Introduction 1813
Oil on wood 61 × 50.2
National Galleries of Scotland
Especially striking in this picture is Wilkie's intention that the spectator should glean as much information about the encounter from decor and attire as from facial expression. While the bust and Oriental vase in the old man's study mark him as a man of intellectual and artistic tastes, the crumpled morning coat, gloves and top hat of the youngster suggest the newcomer to the big city.

the territory he had made his own and, following a commission from the Prince of Wales to paint a Scottish subject as a pendant to a picture already owned by the Prince called *Blind Man's Buff* (HM The Queen), Wilkie returned to Scotland in search of inspiration.

In its general conception the composition of the picture which resulted from the commission, *The Penny Wedding* (Plate 56), pays homage to David Allan's watercolour of the same subject (Plate 51), but a closer analysis of the work betrays a more interesting twist in the artist's treatment of Scottish genre subjects. To the left of the picture can be seen the legendary Scottish fiddler Neil Gow in a pose lifted directly from his portrait by Henry Raeburn; Gow had already been dead some twelve years when Wilkie painted this picture in 1818. Taken with the fact that the tradition of the 'penny wedding' itself was virtually extinct by this date, it is clear that here Wilkie was nostalgically recreating a scene from the earlier rural life of his homeland rather than painting a contemporary one.

This means that, in contrast to a work such as *The Letter of Introduction*, Wilkie in *The Penny Wedding* was engaging in an act of historical reconstruction. He himself spoke of Scotland as being a 'volume of history' and this attitude colours all his subsequent renderings of Scottish themes. Yet a picture like *The Penny Wedding* cannot have satisfied his yearning to paint historical subjects of greater

56 DAVID WILKIE
The Penny Wedding 1818
Oil on panel 64.4 × 95.6
Royal Collection
Wilkie's enchanting picture of an old-fashioned Scottish country wedding celebration is imbued with an intense nostalgia for a tradition which was already extinct by the time he chose to depict it. The deep shadows and rich brown colouring of the picture are, in themselves, nostalgic in an artistic sense for the Dutch Old Master tradition of which the artist was an ardent admirer.

significance. During this same period, however, an opportunity arose which allowed him to do just that.

Not long after the event itself, the Duke of Wellington hit upon the idea of commissioning Wilkie to paint a picture commemorating his famous victory at Waterloo. The result – although the picture was not in fact unveiled until 1822 – was *The Chelsea Pensioners Receiving the Waterloo Despatch* (Plate 57). The picture, in effect a modern history subject, depicts the moment when the news of the British victory was brought to veterans of earlier campaigns seated in the street outside the Royal Hospital in Chelsea. The Duke paid Wilkie what

57 DAVID WILKIE
The Chelsea Pensioners Receiving the Waterloo Despatch 1822
Oil on panel 97 × 158
Apsley House, London
Although some of his later pictures are both larger in scale and grander in conception, Wilkie's imagined scene of Napoleonic War veterans receiving news of Wellington's victory at Waterloo remains his most complex and ambitious work.

at that time was the extraordinary sum of 1200 guineas for the picture, a record price for a contemporary British work. When exhibited at the Royal Academy Wilkie's most ambitious essay to date proved so popular that for the first time in the institution's history, crush barriers were needed to protect an exhibit.

The Chelsea Pensioners is an extremely complex piece of theatre, painted with a bravura reminiscent of seventeenth-century Baroque art and, in particular, of the series of pictures glorifying the life of Marie de' Medici by the greatest northern Baroque master, Rubens; Wilkie had paid close attention to Rubens's famous pictures during his visit to the Louvre in 1814. Yet the picture is still painted on the small scale of a genre work and, even if the technique employed is a far cry from the fastidiousness of *Pitlessie Fair*, the impact of the work as a whole still depends on accuracy and detail.

In his later work, however, Wilkie strove to expand his style still further with frequently uncertain results. In 1823 he was called upon to paint a commemorative picture of his old patron, now George IV, making his triumphant entry into the Palace of Holyroodhouse (Plate 28) during his visit to Edinburgh of the same year. Wilkie's failure to convey the pomp and swagger of the occasion in the Rubenesque way to which he aspired is only too plain; it is hardly surprising that the failure of nerve which accompanied the production of this picture led to the artist suffering a complete mental breakdown.

Along with almost his entire generation, David Wilkie was utterly seduced by the works of Walter Scott and waited with bated breath for the appearance of each new Waverley novel. The admiration in this case was mutual; Wilkie's descriptive, narrative painting was precisely to the author's taste even if he expressed greater enthusiasm for what he considered the masterly animal paintings of Edwin Landseer. Scott disliked what he saw as a 'lack of finish' in the portraits of Henry Raeburn.

The cordial relations between Scott and Wilkie are perfectly reflected in a charming watercolour of the author and his family outside their home, Abbotsford, which Wilkie made during a sketching trip to Scotland in 1817. The artist's association with the writer was, however, predominantly professional; Wilkie – along with dozens of other Scottish and English artists – was engaged by the Edinburgh publisher, Cadell, to provide illustrations for his edition of the Waverley novels.

The other major Scottish artist involved in the work and whom Scott considered on a par with Wilkie was William Allan.

Walter Scott AND HISTORY PAINTING: *William Allan* AND THE LATER *Wilkie*

William Allan (1782–1850) had been a fellow student of Wilkie's at the Trustees' Academy, but rather than making the time-honoured journey south like his colleague after graduating, Allan had taken the more exotic course of embarking upon a ten-year tour of Russia. There he was much favoured by members of the imperial family, among whom he found a ready market for his Byronic costume pieces of Tartar horsemen and Circassian slave girls. *Slave Market, Constantinople* (Plate 58) is an excellent example of the luxurious subject matter in which Allan specialized and of the zestful panache with which he painted it.

In 1814 Allan returned to Edinburgh, where he installed himself

58 WILLIAM ALLAN
Slave Market, Constantinople 1838
Oil on panel 129 × 198
National Galleries of Scotland
No nineteenth-century Scottish artist enjoyed depicting exotic costume as much as Sir William Allan. Painted a year after his election to the presidency of the Royal Scottish Academy, his *Slave Market, Constantinople* is a vividly coloured picture which contrasts with the sober treatment the artist accorded to subjects drawn from Scottish history. The craze for the Orient which began during this period inspired Scottish artists in much the same way that it did continental masters such as Delacroix.

in a fantastically bizarre studio decorated with all manner of memorabilia gleaned on his travels; walls were hung with weird armour and colourful tapestries while the artist – the very model of the Orient-infatuated nineteenth-century British traveller – wore a Circassian jacket when he painted. In this role Allan is the first representative of a prestigious band of nineteenth-century Scottish artists who drew their inspiration primarily from foreign lands; David Roberts, the artist whose watercolours of Ancient Egyptian sites are still much reproduced, is the most famous of those who followed in Allan's footsteps.

Allan himself, however, did not paint exclusively foreign subjects. Under the personal direction of his friend, Walter Scott, he turned to interpreting episodes from his native history and, in particular, from the melodramatic career of Mary Queen of Scots. Not surprisingly, the eventful life of Scotland's martyr queen was the subject most favoured by nineteenth-century Scottish artists, even though the rich store of dramas it encompassed had already been raided by earlier artists; John Alexander, Gavin Hamilton and David Allan all produced Mary Queen of Scots pictures. Allan, however, embarked upon a series intended to illustrate all the crucial incidents in Mary's life.

Of these, the most inspired – not to say the most gory – depicts the murder of Mary's Italian secretary and reputed lover, Rizzio, at the hands of her jealous husband, Lord Darnley and his henchmen. *The Murder of Rizzio* (Plate 59) is a *tour de force* of historical reconstruction largely thanks to the influence of Walter Scott who encouraged Allan to get the details of the setting and costumes historically accurate; in the company of Wilkie the artist visited the apartment in Holyroodhouse where the event had actually occurred. Wilkie himself

was at this time trying to be equally faithful to historical fact in the history pictures he had begun to paint, and the influence of Wilkie's freer late style is apparent in the dramatic lighting and loose handling of paint in Allan's picture.

Scott's influence on a range of Scottish painters of history, however, went a good deal further than advice on historical accuracy. As the author explored and brought to life for his public new areas of Scotland's history in each new novel published, artists tended to turn for new subjects to the territory Scott had mapped out. Scott's novel *Old Mortality*, for example, presented artists with a source of subjects which several found lent themselves especially well to visual interpretation. The book deals with the Covenanting Wars, Scotland's seventeenth-century civil war which had been sparked by the determination of Charles II to impose an Anglican system of bishops and worship on Presbyterian Scotland; the Covenanters were those who had sworn an oath to defend Presbyterianism. Allan, as always close on Scott's heels, chose to paint the murder of Archbishop Sharpe, the turncoat Presbyterian minister whom Charles II had appointed Archbishop of St Andrews. Yet it was George Harvey (1806–76) opting for the more subdued subject of *The Covenanters' Preaching* (Plate 60) who produced the finest picture inspired by *Old Mortality*. Harvey's picture shows a Covenanting minister, having refused to bow to the political edict banning him from preaching,

59 WILLIAM ALLAN
The Murder of Rizzio   1833
Oil on panel 102.9 × 163
National Galleries of Scotland
In spite of William Allan's dedication to accuracy (great trouble was taken to ensure the authenticity of costume and setting) the sense of melodrama in his picture of the infamous murder of Mary Queen of Scots' Italian secretary and presumed lover gives it a period flavour. In common with most of his generation of Scottish artists, Allan viewed his country's history through the Romantic eyes of his friend Walter Scott.

conducting a service in the countryside. The picture is a wholly credible reconstruction of such an event and has come to symbolize the stoic resilience of those faithful to Scotland's national religion.

Both George Harvey and his younger contemporary James Drummond (1818–77) studied under William Allan after he became master of the Trustees' Academy in 1826. Drummond is a somewhat less sympathetic artist than Harvey, since his pictures often have an exaggerated air of pantomime about them. Nevertheless, his most famous picture, *The Porteous Mob* (Plate 61), inspired by the opening scene of Scott's novel *The Heart of Midlothian*, is a convincing essay in historical reconstruction. Captain Porteous, the head of the Edinburgh militia who in 1736 had ordered the town guard to fire on an unarmed crowd, is on the verge of being lynched by Edinburgh's notorious mob. Drummond, a keen antiquarian who made a thorough study of Edinburgh's vanishing medieval buildings, has used his knowledge to good effect in this picture. The setting in which he has staged the incident – the eastern end of the Grassmarket in the shadow of Edinburgh Castle – is also historically correct.

Wilkie was never to come as slavishly under the influence of Walter Scott as an artist like Drummond, despite his personal relationship

60 GEORGE HARVEY
The Covenanters' Preaching 1830
Oil on panel 82.6 × 106.7
Glasgow Museums and Art
    Galleries
Harvey, a mainstay of the Royal Scottish Academy in its early years and eventually its President, was one of the few nineteenth-century artists who eschewed the overblown rhetoric which became the norm in the painting of subjects from Scottish history. Although his output was uneven in quality, this, the first of three pictures of Covenanting subjects, is one of the most convincing recreations of an historical event by a nineteenth-century Scottish artist.

with him. With a few exceptions – the most notable being two pictures depicting events in the life of John Knox – he continued to try to develop the modern history picture, his first attempt at which had been *The Chelsea Pensioners Receiving the Waterloo Despatch* (Plate 57).

In an attempt to shift the artistic block which resulted from the mental breakdown he had suffered, Wilkie returned to the Continent in 1825, travelling extensively over a three-year period. But whereas in 1814 it had been the work of Rubens which impressed him most, during this far longer sojourn it was the painting of the sixteenth-century Italian artist Correggio and seventeenth-century Spanish masters such as Velasquez and Murillo which had the greatest impact on his style. Upon his return to England Wilkie painted three canvases depicting incidents from the Peninsular War. They are distinguished from all his earlier work not only by their comparatively vast scale but by the grandeur of their conception, richness of colour and exuberant brushwork.

Nowhere is Wilkie's abandoning of the fastidious, detailed style with which he had established his original reputation as a painter of genre pictures more striking than in *The Defence of Saragossa* (Plate 62). It is a picture which depends for its impact on the Romantic sweep of the composition. The lone central figure inspiring others through her heroism is, in its way, an inspired conception, oddly prefiguring the heroine in Delacroix's great picture *Liberty Leading the People*. And indeed Wilkie may have exerted some influence on the French

61 JAMES DRUMMOND
The Porteous Mob 1855
Oil on canvas 112 × 143
National Galleries of Scotland
Following in the footsteps of Walter Scott, artists such as James Drummond became experts in Scottish history, bolstering their immense knowledge with fine collections of antiquities. Drummond in particular was obsessed by the history of the Scottish capital, as can be deduced from this image of a famous riot in the city's Old Town. The artist himself lived in what is today one of Edinburgh's most popular tourist haunts, John Knox's House.

Romantic artist: on his return home through Paris he apparently showed Delacroix some of his Spanish sketches, and both Delacroix and his compatriot Géricault had admired Wilkie's earlier work during a visit to London.

Delacroix, however, was the first to voice misgivings about the change of direction that Wilkie had taken so late in his career. He was especially well qualified to do so; more than most artists, the Frenchman was aware of the problems of large-scale figurative

62 DAVID WILKIE
The Defence of Saragossa 1828
Oil on canvas 94 × 141
Royal Collection
Confronted by a picture such as Wilkie's *Defence of Saragossa*, it is hard to avoid the conclusion that the artist's later dedication to the painting of heroic subjects from modern history was unfortunate. Almost all the qualities for which Wilkie is still generally admired – faithful observation, fastidious technique, ingenuity of imagination – are absent.

painting and of the necessity of achieving a synthesis between the subject and the sentiment motivating it. But whereas Delacroix had the benefit of the local precedents of Jacques-Louis David's Neo-Classical Republican compositions and Baron Gros' aggrandizing paintings of Napoleonic subjects, there were no such glorious ante-cedents in either Scottish or English art to help Wilkie in his modern history pictures. Wilkie was to all intents and purposes breaking fresh ground. It is perhaps surprising then that Wilkie's new style was generally well received.

Without doubt the most successful work that Wilkie painted in his late bolder manner is *Josephine and the Fortune Teller* (Plate 63). The picture illustrates the story of the future Empress of France being told by a gipsy that she 'will become greater than a queen'. The composition is heavily indebted to Correggio; Josephine is portrayed as a madonna surrounded by retainers and children in place of saints and cherubs. Here at least one feels that the Baroque treatment Wilkie has accorded the subject is at one with its essential spirit.

Considering the long-term fidelity to the Dutch precedents Wilkie had shown over the many years in which he specialized in genre subjects, it is surprising how eclectic his sources of inspiration were

64 DAVID WILKIE
*A Persian Prince, his Slave bringing him
    Sherbet* 1840
Chalk and colour wash 45.7 × 31.5
Aberdeen Art Gallery and
    Museums
Anticipating the English Pre-
Raphaelite artist William Holman
Hunt by over a decade, in 1840
Wilkie embarked upon a journey
to the Holy Land in order to
accumulate precise visual
information for a series of biblical
subjects he intended to paint. This
watercolour, one of the finest results
of the exercise, gives some idea of
the kind of picture the artist might
have produced had not his
untimely death intervened.

Left 63 DAVID WILKIE
Josephine and the Fortune Teller
1837 Oil on canvas 211 × 158
National Galleries of Scotland
Although the 'slackness' which an
early commentator perceived in
Wilkie's late painting is evident
here, there is also charm and a
beguiling sense of intimacy. Both
qualities had gone a long way to
ensuring the early success of the
artist's paintings of genre subjects.

for the later modern history pictures. In an enormous picture based
upon an episode of recent British colonial history, for example,
Rembrandt is the overriding influence. Wilkie began *General Sir
David Baird Discovering the Body of Sultan Tippoo Sahib after Storming
Seringapatam* (NGS) in 1834 and took four years to complete it,
largely because of his desire to be absolutely truthful in his account.
Wilkie employed Indian models, borrowed clothes and armour
which had actually been worn at the scene, and even went as
far as corresponding with the general's widow. The posthumous
likeness of Sir David, however, was copied from his portrait by
Raeburn.

Nevertheless, no matter how imposing some of Wilkie's later
history pictures are, it is not in this area that his finest achievements
are to be found. His greatest works from all periods of his career
were painted on a small scale. In a late work such as *The Cotter's
Saturday Night* (Plate 53) for example, he manages a real marriage of
content and expression which eluded him in his more portentous
subjects. In this case, he was returning to his roots by choosing the
poem by Robert Burns which had first been singled out by David
Allan. The image of natural piety conveyed by the reading aloud of
a family Bible after dinner is touching, the handling of the paint
fluent but perfectly complementing the mood of the subject, and the
colouring subtle and harmonious. In contrast to the Sir David Baird
picture, the influence of Rembrandt has here been successfully
assimilated into Wilkie's own stylistic heritage.

In 1840, encouraged by his friend David Roberts, Wilkie made an
artistic pilgrimage to the Holy Land. Unlike Roberts, however, Wilkie
was not motivated by an interest in archaeology; rather his intention
was to collect ethnographical information which would give authenticity to the biblical compositions he planned to paint; the figure
in a delightful watercolour *A Persian Prince, his Slave bringing him Sherbet*
(Plate 64), for example, was probably intended as a model for
Christ himself in some projected picture. Although some of his
preconceptions were confounded (he was upset, for example, to find
that Orientals did not use chairs much and that Leonardo's *Last
Supper* therefore could not be accurate!) it is clear from the large
number of brightly-coloured sketches he made during the trip that
Wilkie found genuine inspiration in the Near East.

It was especially tragic, therefore, that on the journey home the
artist was taken ill with suspected cholera. He died on 1 June 1841
and was buried at sea off Gibraltar. It is a measure of the esteem in
which Wilkie was held by his contemporaries that Turner, who was
in some respects his rival, painted a poignant tribute to the Scottish
artist; when asked why he had made the sails of the ship in his

picture, *Peace, Burial at Sea* (Tate Galley), so black, Turner replied that he had been unable to paint them black enough.

The Westminster Hall Mural Competition AND ITS EFFECT ON *Scottish Artists*

Wilkie's influence continued after his death with the publication of the sketches he had made on his final trip. But it was not until 1854 that the English Pre-Raphaelite painter, William Holman Hunt, fulfilled Wilkie's aspiration to paint biblical subjects in authentic settings.

It is interesting, however, to speculate on what Wilkie might have done next had he lived longer. There are indications, for instance, that he had already been planning a great cycle of religious paintings for the proposed new Houses of Parliament, the competition for which was rumoured before he sailed. It is even possible that he was considering the change of medium which would have been required for the undertaking, since he visited Munich on his way east in order to look at the fresco technique revived by the fashionable group of German painters called the Nazarenes.

In 1834 the ancient medieval Palace of Westminster had been devastated by fire, an event most memorably recorded by Turner who made one of his most dramatic watercolours of the event. It was immediately recognized that the rebuilding of the seat of government would present a perfect opportunity to make a national cultural statement and the attention of the authorities responsible for the project first turned to the architectural form the new buildings should take. Eventually, the Gothic style was chosen and the result was the elaborate edifice which has since become a symbol of British parliamentary democracy.

Yet there was also the question of the interior decoration of the new palace to contend with, and – as Wilkie had suspected – a competition to provide suitable murals for the new Houses of Parliament was announced. The entries were put on show in Westminster Hall in a number of exhibitions in the 1840s and proposals by several Scottish artists were included. The most hopeful of these was David Scott (1806–49), an artist who was convinced that his experience of fresco technique in Italy made him particularly suitable for the commission.

Scott came from an artistic background; his father was an engraver who had trained under David Allan at the Trustees' Academy and his younger brother, William Bell Scott, also became an artist. After early studies at the Trustees' Academy he worked as an engraver in his father's firm before spending a year in Rome, where he familiarized himself with fresco technique by studying Michelangelo's

65 DAVID SCOTT

The Discoverer of the Passage to India Passing the Cape of Good Hope

1841 Oil on canvas 533.4 × 406.4

Trinity House, Leith

This vast canvas is the most energetic bid by any Scottish artist in the early Victorian period to make a major statement in the realm of High Art. At the exhibition of the picture organized by the artist in the winter of 1841 visitors were bewildered by Scott's mammoth conception. His technique, frankly inadequate to the task, can have done little to encourage the public acclaim he craved.

decorations in the Sistine Chapel and Raphael's equally celebrated scheme in the rooms in the Vatican known as the 'Stanze'. Upon his return to Edinburgh Scott embarked upon a career as a history painter but, though well regarded within his profession, he encountered public apathy and critical hostility.

His most ambitious undertaking – a picture which is a monument of its type – was an immense canvas entitled *The Discoverer of the Passage to India Passing the Cape of Good Hope* (Plate 65). The central subject of this complex picture is the Portuguese explorer Vasco da Gama who is posed defiantly on the deck of a storm-tossed ship surrounded by half-naked, cowering, Michelangelesque sailors. Scott had seen Géricault's *Raft of the Medusa* while in Paris, and although he professed to disdain it, it was clearly this picture which inspired his Vasco da Gama composition; the raw energy of Alexander Runciman's Ossianic cycle (Plate 47) may also have served as a model.

Following the example of Géricault, Scott mounted at his own expense a public exhibition of the picture he intended as his *magnum opus*, perhaps with an eye to attracting the attention of the judges of the Westminster competition. Unfortunately, his ploy did not succeed, since both public and critics ignored the exhibition. Even a pamphlet on fresco painting, published to ingratiate himself further, was in vain: Scott's Westminster Hall competition entries received no recognition whatsoever.

Scott's failure in the Westminster Hall competition certainly blighted his career, and a subsequent failure to be appointed master of the Trustees' Academy hastened his rapid psychological decline;

the artist spent the remaining years of his life in melancholy seclusion. In the year of his death, however, his Vasco da Gama picture was purchased by public subscription and installed appropriately in the newly-built Leith maritime headquarters – the first picture bought in this way for any public building in Scotland. Scott's career marks the end of nearly a century of hopes among Scottish artists of establishing a school of history painting in Scotland.

William Dyce AND *pre-Raphaelitism* IN SCOTLAND

Ironically, the man who was eventually to stamp his personality on the decoration of the new Houses of Parliament was not only a close friend of Scott's but had not even bothered to enter the Westminster Hall competition. William Dyce (1806–64) was the archetypal serious Victorian artist: an improver and theoretician with interests in science and religion as well as in art and design. He designed the certificates for the Great Exhibition of 1851, wrote church music and attempted to revive fresco painting in Britain.

Born in Aberdeen, Dyce first studied medicine and then toyed with the idea of entering the Church before enrolling in the Royal Academy Schools. In the course of several visits to Italy he came into contact with the Nazarenes, a pseudo-monastic group of German painters working in Rome who were inspired by fifteenth-century Italian art. Dyce was impressed by their piety and it confirmed him in his belief that an irreligious man could not possibly be qualified to paint religious subjects. Nevertheless, Dyce objected to the Nazarenes' slavish dependence on earlier artistic models at the expense of nature, although this was precisely the criticism which the eminent critic and supporter of the Pre-Raphaelites, John Ruskin, would later make of Dyce's own work.

After his return from Italy Dyce became involved in the reorganization of art and design education, and it was in his official capacity as director of the London Design School that he was called upon to advise the commission set up under the chairmanship of the Prince Consort which was supervising the decoration of the new Houses of Parliament. The Prince had recently returned from Berlin where he had admired a series of pictures executed in the revived fresco technique by the Nazarene painter Cornelius. Dyce was a strong advocate of fresco as a suitable medium for the Westminster decorations and it was this opinion which persuaded the commission that he was the British artist best suited to the task. In 1847 a trial mural above the throne in the House of Lords, *The Baptism of King Ethelbert*, was enthusiastically received. Dyce was subsequently commissioned to decorate the Queen's Robing Room with a cycle of frescos on an Arthurian theme.

66 WILLIAM DYCE
Pegwell Bay: A Recollection of October 5th, 1858 c. 1858
Oil on canvas 73.7 × 88.9
Tate Gallery, London
William Dyce's meticulous technique, forged under the influence of the group of German painters known as the Nazarenes, is employed to admirable effect in this gem-like picture. Not surprisingly, Dyce earned the adulation of the greatest of Victorian art critics, John Ruskin, who identified 'thoroughness' as one of his chief virtues.

The Prince saw in the Palace of Westminster scheme an opportunity not only to elevate the taste of the nation but also to create a British school of monumental historical painting. Unfortunately, however, the project was beset with political and technical difficulties which, rather than helping to unite British artists in any common artistic cause, led to acrimony and general disappointment.

David Scott was not the only competition entrant for whom rejection was too bitter a pill: the English artist Benjamin Robert Haydon, a close friend of David Wilkie and his travelling companion on his first visit to Paris, could never come to terms with his own failure and eventually committed suicide, and the mental condition of the patricide Richard Dadd was in no small part due to similar disillusionment. Even Dyce came to regret his involvement; he died after collapsing while still engaged in the work, the Queen's Robing Room unfinished and the fresco technique he had championed already having shown itself no match for the damp and grime of London.

From the point of view of Dyce's art the Westminster murals were a time-consuming and emotionally draining diversion. In common with most British artists of the period, he was at his best when he was painting easel pictures and it was on a small, manageable scale that he produced his finest works. Probably the best known and by far the most haunting of his smaller pictures is *Pegwell Bay: A Recollection of October 5th, 1858* (Plate 66). This strange beach scene, which appears at first to be almost photographic and topographically accurate, is in fact subtly distorted to enhance the overall effect of heightened reality. The result is an eerie stillness, which is underlined by the frozen poses of the figures and the mysterious comet in the sky; it seems as if time has stood still at a particular moment. In several other pictures, Dyce superimposed figures on a meticulously observed landscape in a similar manner (see Chapter Four), yet in none of his other pictures does a figure directly engage the spectator as Dyce's young wife does in the right foreground of *Pegwell Bay*.

Dyce was a friend of and an inspiration to the English artists who called themselves the Pre-Raphaelite Brotherhood rather than a member of the group, and it is he who is credited with having first drawn the attention of the man who was to become the virtual high priest of the movement, John Ruskin, to their work. Ruskin, who for the first part of his career had honed his critical faculties by tirelessly promoting Turner in his famous first volume of *Modern Painters*, redirected his powers after the great landscape painter's death in 1851 in favour of the Pre-Raphaelites, and in particular of the young leader of the group, John Everett Millais. In the precision of Millais' painting Ruskin perceived the perfect realization of his own theories about the importance in art of careful observation.

Millais, of course, was no Scot, but like Turner he earns a place in any history of Scottish art because of the example he set to many Scottish painters after the middle of the nineteenth century. Moreover, his connections with the country where he was eventually to live and work began early in his career when, in 1853, he accompanied Ruskin and his young Scottish wife Effie on a holiday in the Highlands. It was on this fateful trip (Effie was eventually to secure the annulment of her marriage to the writer in one of the most scandalous divorces of the age; she subsequently married Millais) that Millais painted his celebrated portrait of Ruskin at Glenfinlas (Private Collection). The picture is a *tour de force* of Pre-Raphaelite detail painting, especially in the bubbling water and lichens of the burn before which Ruskin was posed.

The aesthetic philosophy of Ruskin, however, was never to be as influential north of the Border as it was in England, and Ruskin even managed to make himself personally unpopular in the Scottish capital by making disparaging remarks about the city's architecture. Nevertheless, he did gain some converts to his cause, chief among them Joseph Noel Paton (1821–1901). Paton had studied at the Royal Academy Schools alongside Millais and Richard Dadd to whose painting his own best work bears striking similarities, so as a young man he was already aware of the ideas these progressive English artists were developing.

Paton's finest works are a pair of so-called 'fairy pictures' now in the National Galleries of Scotland, the finer of which is *The Reconciliation of Oberon and Titania* (Plate 67). The picture, which illustrates a scene from Shakespeare's *A Midsummer Night's Dream*, is a frenzied mix of

67 JOSEPH NOEL PATON
The Reconciliation of Oberon and Titania
1847 Oil on canvas 76.2 × 122.6
National Galleries of Scotland
A close friend of the English Pre-Raphaelite artist John Everett Millais, Joseph Noel Paton had as glittering a career as that of any Scottish artist in the Victorian period. The skill and inventiveness of his 'fairy pictures' account for their popularity.

elves and nymphs (some shown in postures sexually provocative
enough to alarm a Freudian analyst!) painted in glowing colours,
every leaf and transparent wing described in minute detail. In Paton's
later work sentimentally conceived religious themes replace the
fantasy of his fairy pictures; in their moralizing tone these often come
uncomfortably close to the evangelical lantern slides so popular
during the Victorian period.

Paton was – at least for a brief period – a Scottish artist who
embraced a thoroughly Pre-Raphaelite approach to painting. Yet if
any artist can lay claim to being Scotland's pre-eminent Pre-Raphaelite, it must be the younger brother of the tragic David Scott, William
Bell Scott (1811–90). Like his brother, William Bell Scott worked as
an engraver in his father's firm and took classes at the Trustees'

Academy before leaving for London. There he mixed in literary society and made a modest reputation for himself as a poet; indeed it was Bell Scott's poem 'Rosabell', about a prostitute he had known in Edinburgh, which initially made him popular with Dante Gabriel Rossetti and the other Pre-Raphaelites.

William Bell Scott, again like his brother, entered the Westminster Hall competition and he too was unsuccessful. But the younger Scott does not seem to have been at all discouraged by the experience and went on to develop his career in various other directions. The post of master of the newly-founded Government School of Art and Design in Newcastle took him to Northumberland, and it was there that he executed what is probably his best-known work, a series of paintings illustrating the history of the county at Wallington Hall.

The artist's best and most wholeheartedly Pre-Raphaelite work, however, is the sadly little-known decorative scheme at Penkill Castle in Ayrshire (Plate 68). It was here that Bell Scott decorated the spiral staircase of the building at the behest of his friend and patron Alice Boyd. For subject matter he turned to *The King's Quair*, a courtly ballad written by James I of Scotland while imprisoned by the English. The murals, now unfortunately badly deteriorated, are imbued with the Romantic spirit of medieval courtly love which the Pre-Raphaelites did so much to popularize.

Despite Ruskin's impact on artists like Paton and Bell Scott, Pre-Raphaelitism cannot be said to have had anything more than a superficial effect on art in Scotland. Academic artists like William Fettes Douglas (1822–91) frequently used a Pre-Raphaelite technique to give a gloss to historical dramas such as *The Recusant's Concealment Discovered* (Plate 69) and in the early work of several younger artists who were to achieve their mature styles later in the century can be traced the influence of individual Pre-Raphaelite pictures: Millais' *The Blind Girl*, for example, was particularly admired by William McTaggart.

Nevertheless, general resistance to Ruskin seems to have been fairly solid in Scotland, causing the great man considerable irritation if a letter he wrote in 1858 to a magazine called *The Witness* is anything to go by: 'If in that mighty wise town of Edinburgh, everybody still likes flourishes of brush better than ferns, and dots of paint better than birch leaves, surely there is nothing for it but to leave them in quietude of devotion, to dot, in faith, and flourish.'

Scottish artists and the SENTIMENTALIZING TRADITION

If, however, Scottish-trained artists in general found themselves out of sympathy with the ideals of Pre-Raphaelitism, many excelled at imparting to Scottish subjects the sentimental, sometimes even

68 WILLIAM BELL SCOTT
The King's Quair (detail) 1865–8
Encustic on plaster
Penkill Castle, Ayrshire
The mural cycle executed by David Scott's more successful younger brother, William Bell Scott, at Penkill Castle, Ayrshire, is probably the greatest cycle of Pre-Raphaelite painting in Britain. Bell Scott was one of the few Scottish artists to practise the detailed realism advocated by Ruskin.

Far right 70 TOM FAED
The Last of the Clan 1865
Oil on canvas 144.8 × 182.9
Glasgow Museums and Art
    Galleries
This brilliantly painted, sad commentary on the infamous Highland Clearances was perfectly expounded in the narrative which accompanied the picture's exhibition at the Royal Academy in 1865: 'When the steamer had slowly backed out, and John MacAlpine had thrown off the hawser, we began to feel that our once powerful clan was now represented by a feeble old man and his grand-daughter; who, together with some outlying kith-and-kin, myself among the number, owned not a single blade of grass in the glen that was once our own.'

maudlin, characteristics which are evident in much later Pre-Raphaelite painting and which came to be accepted as the norm in Victorian art after the mid-century. This approach is typified by the mature work of Thomas Faed (1826–1900), the younger brother of the equally accomplished if somewhat more emotionally reticent John Faed (1820–1902).

The roots of Tom Faed's style lie in the genre tradition established by Wilkie and, like Wilkie, his earliest mature pictures are full of echoes of seventeenth-century Dutch genre painting; Faed's most highly wrought early work *The Visit of the Patron and Patroness to the Village School* (Dundee Art Gallery) is packed with the kind of amusing incident which guaranteed Wilkie his original success and which was clearly still appreciated a decade or so after his death. Yet even in this picture painted as early in his career as 1851, a tendency to dwell in a rather voyeuristic way on the emotions of the mischievous children is an indication of the direction Faed's painting was to take.

In *The Last of the Clan* (Plate 70) Faed can be observed relishing the pathos of his subject: a group of contemporary Highlanders left on the Scottish shore after the departure of their fellows for a new life abroad. Every expression and gesture serves to augment the poignancy of the occasion. With pictures of this nature Faed touched the social conscience which was an increasingly important feature of the bourgeois Victorian character. It is hard to think of a title which encapsulates mawkish Victorian sentiment better than that of perhaps Faed's best-known work, *The Mitherless Bairn* (National Gallery of Victoria, Melbourne).

69 WILLIAM FETTES DOUGLAS
The Recusant's Concealment Discovered: Persecution in Scotland 1859
Oil on canvas 101.2 × 50.5
Glasgow Museums and Art Galleries

An uneven painter, though one of great skill, with this picture Fettes Douglas succeeded in producing one of the few wholly satisfying Pre-Raphaelite essays in Scottish art. For his subject the artist delved into one of the areas of Scottish history most frequently ransacked by native artists – the seventeenth-century Covenanting Wars.

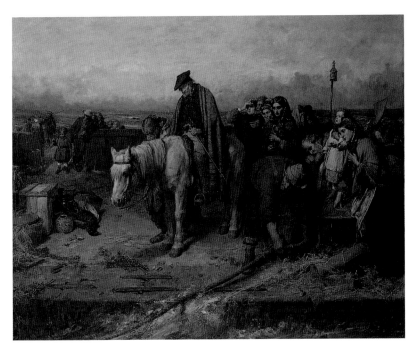

In our more cynical age it has become exceedingly difficult to sympathize with Faed's pictures to the degree the artist intended. Nevertheless, his superb technique – the impeccable rendering of textures of flesh and cloth for example – is still easy to enjoy. If anything, however, Faed was surpassed in this respect by an artist of the same generation who celebrated a wider range of emotions in a manner which made him one of the most popular artists of the nineteenth century.

John Phillip (1817–67), although born in Aberdeen, undertook all his initial artistic training at the Royal Academy Schools in London. Like most of his Scottish peer group, however, Phillip began by painting genre subjects in the Wilkie tradition – pictures such as *A Presbyterian Catechizing* (NGS) – but, in the light of his later development, these works appear a little drab and old-fashioned. In the footsteps of Wilkie, Phillip made several visits to Spain and it is in his paintings of Spanish subjects that he introduced a bright, colourful gaiety to Scottish art which became an increasingly dominant feature in the work of the group of pupils of Robert Scott Lauder who were to make their mark later in the century.

This reaches a kind of ebullient apotheosis in the picture which is generally agreed his masterpiece, *La Gloria – A Spanish Wake* (Plate 71). The convincing realism of the scene, the believability of the

71 JOHN PHILLIP
La Gloria – A Spanish Wake 1864
Oil on canvas 144 × 217
National Galleries of Scotland
Phillip is undoubtedly one of the most enjoyable nineteenth-century Scottish painters. The change in tone of Scottish painting which had occurred over the quarter-century since the death of David Wilkie can be gauged by a comparison between this and the very different pictures which resulted from Wilkie's travels in Spain. Although based outside Scotland for most of his career, Phillip exercised a considerable influence on younger Scottish artists.

forced jollity among the celebrating throng and the contrast between the bright Mediterranean light illuminating the merrymakers and the shadows engulfing the grieving mother and her consoling friends, all contribute to the success of the picture. Yet it is hard to concentrate on the drama while Phillip's virtuoso skill in describing satins, cotton and wool creates such a stunning effect. Not surprisingly, 'Spanish' Phillip as he was dubbed by that other favourite of Queen Victoria, Edwin Landseer, became immensely highly regarded among younger artists in his homeland. His love of colour signals a break with the tradition of emulating the honeyed tones of Old Master painting which had more or less dominated Scottish painting since the days of Wilkie.

National Art Institutions AND THE LATER VICTORIANS

When the artist Robert Scott Lauder (1803–69) returned to Scotland in 1852 to take charge of the school in which he had studied some thirty years earlier under William Allan, the Scottish art scene he found had changed beyond all recognition. The Trustees' Academy was no longer housed in the cramped and dingy tenement he had known but had, since 1826, been installed in a noble, purpose-built suite of galleries on Princes Street, the finest location in the city.

The Trustees' Academy had – as its name implies – been administered since its foundation in 1760 by the Board of Trustees for Improving Fisheries and Manufactures in Scotland, a far-sighted and uniquely Scottish body whose primary aim in setting up the art school had been to promote better standards of design in industry. Originally, many of the students were apprentice tradesmen – coach-painters, goldsmiths and so on – but a sizeable number had always attended the Trustees' classes with the ultimate goal of becoming fine artists.

Alongside the Trustees' had grown up various other professional bodies of artists, the most important of which were the Royal Institution and the Royal Scottish Academy. The Royal Institution had been founded in 1819 as an exhibition-organizing body by a group of gentleman amateurs; in 1826, however, most of the serious artists who had taken part in its exhibitions had broken away from the Institution in order to form their own, more artist-orientated professional organization, and it was this body that, after receiving a Royal Charter in 1838, was recognized as the Royal Scottish Academy.

The building in which Scott Lauder found himself teaching had been designed by the pre-eminent Scottish architect of the day, William Henry Playfair, and completed in 1826. It was modelled on a Greek temple and built in a severe Doric style, although this aspect of the building was softened by the addition of another row of columns around its perimeter and various other prettifying architectural embellishments in 1835. Apart from the Trustees' it also housed the Royal Institution and the Society of Antiquaries. Not until 1835, after several years of acrimony between the Royal Institution and its offspring, was the Academy (which remains in control of the building to this day) allowed to hold its annual exhibition in the fine new premises.

Eventually, the Royal Institution more or less faded away since its function had been usurped by the more dynamic Academy, but it did leave one great legacy: over the years the Institution had increasingly devoted itself to assembling a distinguished collection of Old Masters with the intention of assembling the basis for a national gallery. In 1850 the Prince Consort laid the foundation stone for a second Neo-Classical building designed by Playfair to the rear of his original building. Playfair's new Ionic-style building, the National Gallery of Scotland, was intended primarily to provide a home for the national collection, but from the time of its completion in 1858 until the early years of this century it also housed the Royal Scottish Academy which transferred there from the Royal Institution.

Robert Scott Lauder, as Director of the Trustees' Academy, was, of course, in the midst of these physical changes in the way art was presented in the Scottish capital. But he was also part of and instrumental in bringing about radical changes in the way art was taught within the new buildings. His period of influence at the Trustees' Academy is now accepted as having ushered in something of a golden age of Scottish painting in the late nineteenth century. After the important life-class, to which he attached such store, was taken over by the Academy in 1859, and even more rapidly after he was obliged to retire in the early 1860s, the Trustees' Academy ceased to play a major role in the art life of Scotland and the forging ground for Scotland's most important artists moved to the west.

Never himself considered in the first rank of Scottish artists, Scott Lauder's own painting is of interest chiefly because of the painterly qualities embodied within it; these he transmitted through his teaching and example to an important younger generation of Scottish artists destined to have an important impact on late Victorian art in Britain. Under William Allan at the Trustees' Scott Lauder had become aware of Wilkie's fluid late style; but it was probably the Rev. Thomson of Duddingston (see Chapter Four) – Scott Lauder married his daughter – who gave him the confidence to conceive of a picture from the outset in painterly terms and not simply as a kind of coloured-in drawing. Scott Lauder spent five years in Italy but, unlike

72 ROBERT SCOTT LAUDER
Christ Teacheth Humility 1847
Oil on canvas 234 × 353
National Galleries of Scotland
The virtues of rich colour and the free handling of paint espoused by Scott Lauder can be seen to good advantage in this, his major religious picture. The New Testament passage that the artist has chosen to illustrate comes from St Matthew's Gospel: the disciples are asking Jesus who will be the greatest in the kingdom of heaven. Scott Lauder's wife and children posed for some of the figures.

his near contemporary David Scott, the experience fired no similar, debilitating ambition in him to become solely a painter of historical subjects.

Christ Teacheth Humility (Plate 72), the work for which he is best known and for which he was most celebrated in his lifetime, was Lauder's unsuccessful entry for the 1847 Westminster Hall competition. The colour is rich in the manner of the Venetian sixteenth- and seventeenth-century masters the artist venerated, and the paint itself is remarkably freely handled by the standards of most contemporaneous British painting. The contrast between the way Lauder's picture is painted and Paton's treatment of *The Reconciliation of Oberon and Titania* (Plate 67) could not be greater; that Paton's picture was awarded a premium when exhibited alongside *Christ Teacheth Humility* in Westminster Hall is a significant indication of mid-nineteenth-century taste. *Christ Teacheth Humility*, however, was well received back in Scotland and was, in fact, the first work purchased by the Association for the Promotion of the Fine Arts for the new National Gallery of Scotland.

The qualities apparent in *Christ Teacheth Humility* were precisely those Scott Lauder tried to inculcate into his pupils at the Trustees' Academy. His overriding aim was to ensure that the discipline of drawing, as taught in both the classes where students were presented with the nude model and in those where only casts of antique statues were provided, was seen as a means towards creating fine paintings rather than as an end in itself.

In his designated teaching capacity as Director of the Antique he tried to achieve this end by arranging the plaster casts at his disposal in groups instead of individually as was traditional; the point of the exercise being to make students appreciate the spatial and tonal relationships between what might to all intents and purposes have been elements in a projected composition. Many surviving studies, not to mention later paintings by those schooled by Scott Lauder in this way, bear witness to the success of his method.

73 JOHN PETTIE
The Drumhead Court Martial 1865
Oil on canvas 69.5 × 104
Sheffield City Art Galleries
Typically of the later generation of Victorian painters of historical and literary subjects, the incident portrayed here by the gifted John Pettie was invented by the artist for theatrical effect. The idea that historical subjects might be exploited for fun rather than for their ability to convey a moral message was one that inspired much of the best work of Pettie and his associates.

The most concentrated effect of Scott Lauder's influence is to be found in the work of a group of Scottish painters who migrated to London in the early 1860s and who, during the remainder of the century, virtually dominated the Establishment art world of the metropolis. The leading lights of this group were William Quiller Orchardson (1832–1910) and his friend John Pettie (1839–93), but a number of other artists of the same generation, most notably Tom Graham (1840–1906) and John MacWhirter (1839–1911), were also part of the group. They became known as 'the London Scottish'.

The work of Orchardson and Pettie was almost always historical or literary in content, but whereas previous generations of Scottish artists had done their utmost to imbue such subjects with a sober *gravitas*, these painters specialized in rendering them in a light-hearted, theatrical fashion. Although extremely popular in their time, it is only very recently that such pictures have begun to be appreciated again.

John Pettie, whose enthusiasm for historical costume dramas was initially fired by the older history painter, James Drummond, originally made his name in London with a picture entitled *The Drumhead Court Martial* (Plate 73). The work contains all the elements which were to become hallmarks of Pettie's painting for the rest of his career: a dramatic – though in this case fictitious – historical incident (the trial of a Cavalier by a group of Roundheads at a makeshift battlefield court), a sense of immediacy – of interrupted action, and a telling characterization and delineation of the emotions of the protagonists in the drama. However, the way Pettie has actually painted the scene – high colour, a shimmering paint surface dependent upon lively brushwork – both balances and complements the artist's narrative concerns.

Thirty years later when Pettie painted *Bonnie Prince Charlie entering the Ballroom at Holyrood* (Plate 74), his approach to painting a dramatic incident had scarcely altered: in his treatment of what in this case is a factual historical incident – Prince Charles Edward Stuart's arrival at the ball he hosted in Edinburgh during the 1745 Jacobite Rebellion – precisely the same qualities are evident. Pettie was an artist who would draw inspiration from a whole variety of sources if he thought they would help him make a good picture, and here the greatest of Raeburn's Highland chiefs, the *Macdonnell of Glengarry* (Plate 24), has clearly influenced his conception.

There is less of a feeling of fancy dress about the superficially similar pictures of Pettie's older and more interesting rival, William Quiller Orchardson. Like that of Pettie, Orchardson's initial success in London was due primarily to the clarity and readability of his compositions. English artists of the period tended to overcrowd their pictures in an effort to impress by sheer technical bravura. By contrast, Orchardson and Pettie – perhaps in an unconscious acknowledgement of one of Wilkie's great strengths – understood the power a picture might gain when the subject is allowed room to breathe. Orchardson, however, was also adept at conveying a precise moment of psychological drama in his pictures and it is this that makes him an ultimately more rewarding artist than his younger colleague.

The emotional relationship, or rather the lack of it, between the fashionable, bored young wife and her wealthy, unsuited older husband in the better of the two pictures Orchardson entitled *Le Mariage de Convenance* (Plate 75), is a perfect example of the artist's facility in this respect. The staging and costumes are immaculate, the lighting organized so as to cast a fitting gloom over what is after all a moralistic scene meant to convey intense domestic unhappiness. But even if the sense of melodrama which pervades the picture now appears slightly ludicrous, stemming as it does from the Victorian

75 WILLIAM QUILLER ORCHARDSON
Le Mariage de Convenance 1883
Oil on canvas 104.8 × 154.3
Glasgow Museums and Art
  Galleries
Orchardson excelled at conveying
a subtle message in a painterly
language which is impressively
succinct. The bleak atmosphere
which surrounds these two partners
in an unhappy marriage is as
meaningful as their postures and
expressions.

Left 74 JOHN PETTIE
*Bonnie Prince Charlie entering the
  Ballroom at Holyrood* 1892
Oil on canvas 158.8 × 114.3
Royal Collection
A romantic late-Victorian view of
Scotland's Jacobite past is evident
in this picture of the Young
Pretender.

age's unquestioning acceptance of family values, the beauty of
Orchardson's painting is still worth contemplating.

Technically, Orchardson's *Mariage de Convenance*, together with
much of his other work, owes much to Scott Lauder's influence, and
in particular to the importance he attached to preserving a fresh,
spontaneous look in a finished picture. Ultimately, this very Scottish
painterly concern was descended via William Allan from the exuberant late style of David Wilkie and, interestingly, in a ravishing though
unfinished picture by Orchardson called *The Last Dance* (Private
Collection) he can be observed to have adopted a method of
painting – working outwards from the areas of most interest – very
similar to that known to have been employed by Wilkie.

Orchardson enjoyed greater personal fame and success probably
more than any other Scottish artist before or since; his works sold
for unheard of prices and were appreciated by a range of artists
whose admiration counted for much, from Whistler and Sickert to
the French Impressionist Degas, who was taken by his somewhat
atypical picture depicting his wife and baby son, *Master Baby* (NGS).
Orchardson was, however, especially in his later years, very much a
pillar of the English art establishment.

For art back in Scotland, the innovative approach of the two

further ex-pupils of Robert Scott Lauder who remained north of the Border was to be of far greater moment as far as subsequent twentieth-century developments in Scottish art are concerned. In his most important picture *The Legend* (Plate 76), George Paul Chalmers (1833–78) can be observed describing subtle interior light effects in a fresh, expressive way and with a very daring palette which, in spite of the traditional genre interest of the subject, stakes more of a claim on the spectator's attention than the implicit narrative. Chalmers died tragically young and was therefore unable to experiment further. William McTaggart (1835–1910), on the other hand, outliving him by over thirty years, had a long life in which to courageously extend the painterly lesson he had first learnt from Robert Scott Lauder (see Chapter Four).

76 GEORGE PAUL CHALMERS
The Legend   *c.* 1864–7
Oil on canvas 102.9 × 154.3
National Galleries of Scotland
Although unfinished (the artist agonized over this picture for several years), *The Legend* is Chalmers's most interesting picture. Suggested by an episode in Walter Scott's 'Pirate', a group of children are here depicted spellbound by the tales of an old Scottish 'seer'. Chalmers's effort at narrative, however, was clearly usurped by his desire to evoke the magical atmosphere of the scene by the use of subtle colour effects.

CHAPTER FOUR

Land OF THE *Mountain* AND THE *Flood*

These days it is unthinkable that a country with such a varied, dramatic and universally admired landscape as Scotland should have remained unpainted until the eighteenth century. Yet the tradition of painting the Scottish landscape is even shorter than the history of portrait painting in Scotland. Not surprisingly, precisely the same conditions prevailed against it in the sixteenth and seventeenth centuries: religious and political strife, poverty and a general feeling of cultural inadequacy. When the rare occasion arose that the skills of a landscapist were needed it was invariably a foreign artist who received the commission.

Scotland's climate has, of course, never been suitable for the practical, outdoor activity of landscape painting. But even taking account of the fact that painting the landscape out-of-doors – an activity we regard as conventional nowadays – only became the norm from the middle of the nineteenth century, it is safe to say that an artist such as the seventeenth-century French landscape painter Claude would certainly have been less prolific had he been working in Scotland rather than Italy.

Yet lack of patronage was always a far more dissuasive factor than mere wind and rain. The well-off bourgeoisie of the kind which created the fertile economic conditions in which the seventeenth-century Dutch school of landscape painters flourished scarcely existed in Scotland before the mid-nineteenth century.

Until the latter part of the eighteenth century, however, something more difficult for us to grasp inhibited artists from conceiving of the Scottish landscape as potential subject matter: taste itself militated against it. The same instinct which prompted the cultivated traveller to pull down the carriage blinds as he or she traversed the Alps put the most significant part of Scotland's landscape, the Highlands, out

demand. Artists who specialized in this kind of upmarket interior decoration also tended to be involved in theatrical work, painting backdrops for the stage in Edinburgh and Glasgow, and several of them were more or less men of the theatre.

The most gifted independent artist of this kind working in mid-eighteenth-century Scotland was William Delacour (active 1740–67), a Frenchman who came to Scotland in 1757 and took charge of the Trustees' Academy, the newly established forerunner of the city's art college, in 1760. Delacour painted the most complete surviving decorative scheme for the Marquess of Tweeddale at Yester House, East Lothian (Plate 78). It was an ambitious undertaking: seven large canvases for the Great Saloon of the magnificent house designed by William Adam, father of the more famous Robert. Delacour's decorations are a mixture of real scenes and fictitious arrangements of Roman ruins, very much akin to those popularized on the Continent by Giovanni Panini. They are the best of this kind in Scotland.

Delacour may have been the most sophisticated individual operating in this field, but he certainly did not have it to himself. The decorating business in the Lowlands was in fact dominated by a famous Edinburgh firm, known as the Nories. James Norie (1684–1757) had founded the company in the 1720s, and by the middle of the century his more gifted sons, James Junior (1711–36) and Robert (died 1766), had joined him in the business. The Nories carried out all kinds of humdrum decorating work, but they specialized in producing painted scenes of mountains, waterfalls and classical ruins in a rather cruder manner than that of Delacour.

Although their work almost always had a functional purpose however – and the Nories were first and foremost artisans – it is obvious that they were also regarded by their peers as artists. Both James Norie Senior and Junior, for example, were, like Allan Ramsay the poet and his eponymous son, members of the short-lived Academy of St Luke set up in Edinburgh during the 1720s.

While neither 'Old Norie', as he was nicknamed, nor his elder son could be described as landscape painters in the modern sense, Robert Norie was a different commodity. It is highly likely that it was he, the longest-surviving member of the family business, who was the first to realize that the local Scottish landscape might serve as well as, if not better than, the Italianate conventions he had inherited. In a set of four panels commissioned by the Duke of Hamilton in the 1740s for the Palace of Holyroodhouse, two are still conventional Italianate fictions while the others show scenes which are obviously Scottish in character. In one of them the central feature is probably the much admired Perthshire mountain, Ben Lawers (Plate 79).

78 WILLIAM DELACOUR
Decorative Paintings in the Great Saloon, Yester House, East Lothian 1761
Royal Commission on the Ancient and Historical Monuments of Scotland
Delacour's work for the finest room in the mansion originally designed by Robert Adam's father, William, for the Marquess of Tweeddale, is a splendid example of late eighteenth-century Italianate decorative painting.

Right 79 ROBERT NORIE
Landscape with a View of Ben Lawers
1741 Oil on canvas 175 × 107
The Duke of Hamilton
James Norie sent both his sons to London to study under the landscape artist George Lambert. From the English artist it appears that Robert learned that his native landscape could be exploited. This panel is an early example of a real Scottish location being inserted into a decorative scheme.

An interesting connection between the Scottish decorative land-scape tradition and the High Art of history painting is to be found in the career of Alexander Runciman (1736–85). In spite of his ultimate role as Scotland's most widely respected, 'serious' late eighteenth-century painter, Runciman had been apprenticed to the Norie firm at the early age of fourteen, and had it seems achieved a degree of fame as a decorative landscape painter before leaving for Italy. Some of the earliest pictures he exhibited were landscapes and he continued the practice of drawing landscape in Italy, concentrating

80 ALEXANDER RUNCIMAN
The Tomb of the Horatii on the Appian Way 1767–8
Pen and wash 22 × 31.1
National Galleries of Scotland
Although Runciman's major achievement lies in the area of history painting, he learned a love of landscape at an early age during his time at the Foulis Academy in Glasgow; it seems that – unusually for the period – the Academy encouraged its students to sketch out of doors. It was in the studio of the Nories, however, that Runciman must have absorbed the spirit of Rococo art, and it is this decorative attitude which informs several very beautiful landscape drawings made after the artist's arrival in Rome in 1767.

on classical ruins set in the Roman Campagna (Plate 80). The spirited pen-and-ink manner of Runciman's Italian drawings recalls the work of Piranesi.

It was not, however, only in the Nories' workshop that young artists in mid-eighteenth-century Scotland were being encouraged to think in terms of landscape. As a contemporary print suggests (Plate 39), the major activities of the students of Scotland's first school of art, the Foulis Academy in Glasgow (see Chapter Two), was the copying of the Old Masters and antique casts, but it appears that they were also sent out into the countryside to draw. David Allan (1744–96), ultimately the most successful of the Foulis Academy students, certainly drew landscape while there and, even after his training in Rome as a Neo-Classical painter of history, he continued to treat the landscape elements in his pictures with respect.

Jacob More: THE *British Claude*

While Runciman's experience under the Nories left him interested in rather than dedicated to landscape, that of Jacob More (1740–97) was to have a far more decisive influence on his career. More followed in the footsteps of Runciman and many other ambitious Scottish artists of his generation and went to study in Rome. But whereas Runciman departed after a few years a convinced history painter, More stayed on for twenty to become the pre-eminent Classical landscapist of the age. He is sometimes referred to as the British Claude or, more frequently, More of Rome.

Jacob More was without doubt the most talented British disciple of the greatest of all seventeenth-century Classical landscape painters, the French-born Claude Lorraine, usually referred to as Claude. During his years in Rome the Scottish artist did his best to imitate the master's manner, and the paintings by him which survive from this period are often almost indistinguishable from the idyllic, generalized Classical scenes of the earlier artist. He was, however, already a convinced follower of Claude even before he left Scotland.

Nevertheless, in the early 1770s More painted a number of majestic pictures of specific locations which constitute the first full-blown, authentic treatment of the Scottish landscape. There was nothing particularly original about More's choice of subject: the Falls of Clyde (the upper reaches of the river stretch into Lanarkshire in what is now the centre of the Scottish industrial belt) had become, by the time More chose to paint them, one of the most famous tourist sites in Britain. Not only were they very beautiful and visually dramatic, but they were associated in the minds of the eighteenth-century intelligentsia with the medieval Scottish patriot hero William Wallace. Neither was More the first artist to choose to paint the Falls of Clyde. As early as the 1740s they had been drawn by the English artist Paul Sandby, who, although in Scotland as part of a military surveying operation after the failed 1745 Jacobite Rebellion, often forsook his brief to draw and make watercolours of the Scottish landscape purely for pleasure. Sandby's pictures, however, are slight in comparison with those of More.

The cataract of the Falls of Clyde is divided into three separate waterfalls – Cora Linn, Bonnington Linn and Stonebyres Linn. More painted all three and made two sets of paintings. His picture of Cora Linn (Plate 81), generally agreed to be the most dramatic of the falls, is a radical departure from the unspecific, stylized decorations which he must have been used to painting in the Nories' workshop.

Although More's general inspiration in this picture is Claude, it seems that he was specifically influenced here by a contemporary landscapist, the French artist Claude-Joseph Vernet. A fine picture by Vernet called *Landscape with Waterfall* hung in Dalkeith Palace near Edinburgh, and More must surely have known it. More's picture,

however, asserts itself far more authoritatively than Vernet's as a depiction of a precise location: the flavour might be that of a Classical idyll, but the gnarled tree and the figures in the foreground are credible elements in the landscape rather than pictorial devices. On the other hand, More has still thought it necessary to tame the waterfall somewhat for fear of offending the delicate sensibilities of the prospective connoisseur.

In the second set of Falls of Clyde pictures More painted, the figures are clothed in Antique costume and this imbues each scene with a far stronger Claudian atmosphere. More's decision in this respect is a sign of things to come in his Italian work. If to the modern eye these second versions of More's Falls of Clyde pictures lack the freshness of the first and are generally less appealing, it is worth remembering that it was pictures in this vein which achieved for More his international reputation. Making one's pictures conform to public taste was not at this time considered demeaning.

In spite of More's respect for Classical formulae, however, once in

81 JACOB MORE
The Falls of Clyde – Cora Linn
c. 1771 Oil on canvas 79.4 × 100.4
National Galleries of Scotland
In spite of conventional pictorial devices from the seventeenth-century French Classicist Claude, such as the use of the rocky promontory in the foreground for example, More's original set of Falls of Clyde pictures constitutes the first convincing celebration of an idiosyncratic feature of the Scottish landscape.

Italy he continued to sketch and draw from nature as he and his fellow young landscape enthusiasts had done in Scotland. He also took with him the pseudo-scientific fascination for natural phenomena which was part of the intellectual baggage of the Scottish Enlightenment. *Mount Vesuvius in Eruption: The Last Days of Pompeii* (Plate 82) is a remarkably dramatic picture to have been painted as early as 1780. More, fascinated by the eruption of the volcano which occurred while he was staying in Naples, has used the scene to evoke the destruction of the town in the first century AD. This is a very early

82 JACOB MORE
Mount Vesuvius in Eruption: The Last Days of Pompeii 1780
Oil on canvas 151 × 201
National Galleries of Scotland
Although More gained his international reputation as a painter of tranquil Classical landscapes, he could also be inspired by nature at her most volatile. Mount Vesuvius provided the artist with material for one of his most extraordinary pictures.

example of a Romantic interpretation of landscape which anticipates the depictions of cataclysmic natural phenomena by the English artist John Martin and even those by Turner.

Alexander Nasmyth: FATHER OF *Scottish landscape painting*

In spite of his important early landscapes of Scotland and his high standing abroad, however, More's role in shaping the standard nineteenth-century vision of the Scottish landscape is very slight. Within a generation he was virtually forgotten. Alexander Nasmyth (1758–1840), by contrast, while still representing the last gasp of the picturesque, Claudian spirit of Scotland, also did much to prepare the way for nineteenth-century artists who imposed a wild, Romantic vision on the Scottish landscape.

Nasmyth benefited from a very thorough art education. He attended the Trustees' Academy in Edinburgh during Alexander Runciman's period as master, and spent four years in Allan Ramsay's London studio from 1774 to 1778. Ramsay was, of course, no landscape painter, but he did insist on drawing as a prerequisite to painting and this was an important legacy to Nasmyth, who continued to draw for the rest of his career. The king's official painter, a consummate professional, must also have served as a role model for Nasmyth. Especially during Nasmyth's two years in Italy (Ramsay employed him to record his researches into the whereabouts of Horace's villa), the idea of the artist as a man of general learning and wide interests must have impressed itself on the younger artist.

Indeed, throughout his early years it seems that Nasmyth fully intended to follow in the footsteps of his great master and become a portrait painter. Had he done so he might well have gone on to compete with his friend Henry Raeburn. The two met in Italy and they remained close friends until the latter's death. Raeburn built his own studio opposite Nasmyth's in Edinburgh New Town in the late 1790s. In spite of this contact with the two portrait painters in Italy, however, it seems that it was also in Rome that Nasmyth's enthusiasm for landscape was initially fired. With the resident Jacob More at the height of his powers, it is logical to assume that it was More's example which inspired him.

In 1785 Nasmyth returned to Edinburgh from Rome and for a short time succeeded in making his living as a portrait painter. It was during this period that he made his well-known portrait of his close friend Robert Burns (Plate 83). This picture of Scotland's best loved poet has become a virtual icon of Scottish culture. Ironically, Nasmyth's other friend and neighbour, Henry Raeburn, who painted almost every other notable figure of the period, was never to have the opportunity of this ideal subject.

Nasmyth's practice as a portrait painter was, it seems, cut short by word of his radical political sympathies getting out among his clientele. Consequently, during the 1790s, he concentrated on teaching at the school he set up in his own house, as well as on painting a great number of theatrical backcloths for theatres all over Scotland. It was not until the end of the century that he finally devoted himself to landscape.

Even when Nasmyth was eventually able to turn his full attention to the painting of landscape, however, it was still usually as part of some practical scheme. Many of his pictures were commissioned by patrons wishing to replan their estates. Nasmyth's function was to inform them about how a proposed Neo-Classical temple or bridge, for instance, would look in the completed scheme.

For the Duke of Argyll, for example, whose estate at Inverary on Loch Fyne in the west of Scotland is one of the prettiest spots in the country, Nasmyth painted a view across the loch with the new, planned town (the first in Scotland) set upon the shore of the

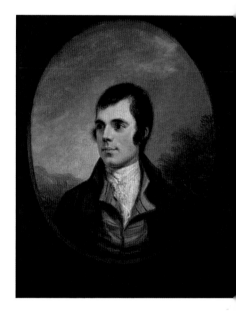

83 ALEXANDER NASMYTH
Robert Burns 1787
Oil on canvas 38.4 × 32.4
National Galleries of Scotland
In the 1780s, during his sojourns
in the city he poetically dubbed
'Scotia's darling seat', Robert
Burns met and befriended all the
leading Edinburgh-based artists of
the day with the exception of
Raeburn. Nasmyth became a close
friend, and it was he who
bequeathed the world this image
of the much loved poet.

loch. It was a commission perfectly suited to the artist's practical,
Enlightenment frame of mind: Nasmyth designed gardens, bridges
and buildings. A charming Neo-Classical well head by Nasmyth is
still one of Edinburgh's most charming architectural features, and at
Inverary itself Nasmyth helped to lay out the grounds.

In the earlier landscapes Nasmyth produced in Scotland the
influence of Claude, which in Jacob More's work overwhelms, is to
some extent also present and it is known that Nasmyth had actually
copied a picture by Claude while in Italy. But close comparisons
with Claude are misleading. Nasmyth tended to select scenes which
in compositional terms were Claude-like. When it came to specifics,
however, such as weather conditions, the effect of light or the
positioning of buildings, he was usually scrupulously accurate. He
never introduced an imaginary building, for example, unless there
were actual plans to build it.

Nasmyth's landscapes are very rarely devoid of signs of human
presence; even where there is no trace of castle, house or proposed
bridge there is usually some suggestion of habitation if not figures
themselves. In this the artist's thinking is typical of the Scottish

85 ALEXANDER NASMYTH
Edinburgh from Calton Hill   1825
Oil on canvas 119.9 × 164.5
City Art Centre, Edinburgh
Nasmyth's technical accomplishment
is strikingly clear in this fine view
of Edinburgh from its most
awe-inspiring vantage point.
Unfortunately, soon after
this picture was painted
the skill and control demonstrated here began to be
considered old-fashioned.

86 ALEXANDER NASMYTH
Edinburgh from Dean Village
Date uncertain Gouache on
    prepared paper 41 × 46.3
Fitzwilliam Museum,
    Cambridge
Nasmyth made many paintings of
the Scottish capital from every
conceivable vantage point. Here he was
viewing the city from the area in which his
friend Henry Raeburn had been born.

Enlightenment which saw humanity as part and parcel of its environment and not detached from it. The balance between the activity of man and that of nature is a salient feature of all Nasmyth's work. Like all his intellectual contemporaries he was passionately keen on 'improving' things, but this did not stretch so far as wishing completely to organize nature as Claude had done.

A further fact which it helps to bear in mind in appreciating Nasmyth's pictures is that he, in common with all the most creative figures of the Enlightenment, was essentially an urban creature. And nowhere is this better illustrated than in a series of cityscapes of Edinburgh he painted in the 1820s when the city's Georgian New Town was expanding to the east and west (Plates 84, 85 and 86). Apart from their intrinsic value as architectural evidence of the city at a crucial stage of its development, Nasmyth's pictures betray a rational, eighteenth-century view of the transformation of what (as Kenneth Clark among others has pointed out) is by virtue of its topography a naturally romantic town.

Nasmyth lived on into the reign of Queen Victoria, so it is little wonder that even in his lifetime his pictures were already beginning to be thought old-fashioned, though on a small scale he could be more spontaneous (Plate 87). When in 1821 he engraved a series of vignettes to illustrate Walter Scott's Waverley novels, Scotland's great Romantic novelist thought them too tame – too polite – and solicited the services of Turner instead.

Nevertheless, through his pupils, Alexander Nasmyth had an extraordinarily pervasive influence on nineteenth-century Scottish landscape painting. These included his children, of whom Patrick Nasmyth (1787–1831) was to win a reputation as great as his father's south of the Border; David Roberts, William Allan, Hugh William Williams and curiously enough John Ruskin's father. David Wilkie, although never a pupil in the proper sense, called Nasmyth the 'father of Scottish landscape painting'.

The BEGINNINGS OF *Romanticism*

The transition from the Picturesque way of looking at the Scottish landscape to its treatment by painters in the full-blown, Romantic fashion which became standard during the Victorian age was gradual. Yet in the 1800s it was spurred on by an alliance (in artistic terms mutually profitable though socially rocky) between two of the greatest figures in the British Romantic movement, Walter Scott and J. M. W. Turner.

It was Scott who, in his immensely widely-read poetry and novels, was the first to voice the quintessential Romantic reaction to Scotland's landscape and nowhere is the author's passionate love of

87 ALEXANDER NASMYTH
Six designs for stage sets with views of Old Edinburgh for The Heart of Midlothian 1820
Pen 16.0 × 11.8
National Galleries of Scotland
In common with most landscape painters of his generation, Nasmyth was also employed in the theatre. These rapidly executed, spirited little sketches, for a dramatization of one of Scott's novels, provide a marked contrast with the polish of his finished oil paintings. They also show that Nasmyth referred directly to nature in his subsidiary capacity of set designer.

it more memorably encapsulated than in some of the most famous lines from his poem *The Lady of the Lake*:

> Breathes there a man with soul so dead,
>   Who never to himself has said,
> This is my own, my native land.
>   Land of brown heath and shaggy wood,
> Land of mountain and the flood,
>   Land of my sires! What mortal hand
> Can e'er untie the filial band
>   That knits me to thy rugged strand!

Scott's romanticization of his homeland relies for its potency on the cultural and historical associations of various locations. Yet in celebrating these links Scott was merely building upon a tradition which had sprung up over the previous half century; the diaries of travellers to Scotland in the later part of the eighteenth century are dense with references to the most famous characters from Scottish history (heroes such as William Wallace and Robert the Bruce) and the spurious Celtic bard Ossian (see Chapter Two) crops up in relation to all sorts of unlikely places.

Once the cult surrounding Scott had become established, however, many other beauty spots such as Loch Katrine, the setting glorified in *The Lady of the Lake*, were added to the accepted canon owing to their often fictitious literary associations. Many wild, windswept locations in the Highlands extended the tourist itineraries and places such as the passes of Glencoe and Killiecrankie – scenes of real historical events – acquired extra glamour thanks to the author's pen.

This romantic reputation that Scotland achieved thanks to Scott and its popularity amongst the landscape painters was aided and abetted by the international political situation. From the 1790s, for some twenty years the Napoleonic Wars prohibited almost all travel to the Continent. This meant that landscapists who in earlier times would have made haste to Italy were obliged to look for an artistic education at home. One of the reasons for the success of Alexander Nasmyth's Edinburgh school was the ready pool of high-born young ladies who found in Scotland a substitute for the Continent.

It was not, of course, only students who were affected by these travel restrictions. Established artists were in exactly the same position, and in one case in particular this state of affairs worked wholly to the benefit of and had far-reaching repercussions for Scottish landscape painting: the greatest English Romantic landscape painter of the age, J. M. W. Turner, discovered Scotland. Turner made a total of six visits to Scotland during his lifetime, his first to the Highlands in

88 JOSEPH MALLORD WILLIAM
  TURNER
Loch Coruisk, Skye c. 1831
Watercolour with scraping on
  paper 8.9 × 14.3
National Galleries of Scotland
Turner's ravishing interpretations
of Scotland's natural glories (this
watercolour of the most dramatic
location on the Isle of Skye was
intended as an illustration to Walter
Scott's description in *The Lord of the
Isles*) inspired Scottish artists to
capitalize on their country's more
sublime assets.

1801. The artist was immediately filled with enthusiasm for the range
of subjects the country presented and Wales, his previous major
source of inspiration in Britain, subsequently took second place in
his affections.

The most significant aspect of Turner's visits to Scotland was his
collaboration with Walter Scott. In 1818 Scott decided to publish a
compendium of Scottish historical material to be called *Provincial
Antiquities and Picturesque Scenery of Scotland*. Turner was involved in the
project both as illustrator and shareholder and it was this speculative
financial venture which turned out to be the most important part of
their collaboration.

Turner's illustrations to Scott depict the various locations as they
were in his own day; the artist consciously attempts not to evoke any
of their historical associations. Nevertheless, Turner's imagination
was fed by Scott's works, and it is known that the author personally
recounted stories to him, particularly during his long stay with the
author at his new baronial mansion, Abbotsford, in the year before
Scott's death.

The superb watercolour of the dramatically situated *Loch Coruisk*,
on the Isle of Skye (Plate 88), is an exceptionally fine example of the
kind of inspired interpretation of the Scottish landscape which Turner
produced to accompany Scott's works. Painted in 1831 and intended
to be engraved as an illustration to *The Lord of the Isles*, it evokes the

awesome, fleeting weather conditions characteristic of the mountainous gulley, while at the same time describing the intricate geological formation which gives rise to them. Typically, although there is no overt reference in the work to its literary justification, its restless, romantic mood is in tune with the spirit of Scott's ballad. Ruskin thought it a model of topographical exactitude.

Turner's association with the national bard – not to mention his passion for Scotland – guaranteed him a high standing north of the Border. But the example he set also meant that his approach to landscape had a decisive influence on the way nineteenth-century Scottish landscape painters perceived their own country.

Minister OF THE KIRK AND *Romantic painter*

During his 1822 visit Turner became friendly with, and actually accompanied on sketching trips, a close friend of Walter Scott, the interesting, self-confessed amateur artist called the Rev. Thomson of Duddingston (1778–1840). Although a minister of the Kirk by vocation, Thomson was Scotland's first indigenous landscape painter who can properly be labelled Romantic. The Rev. Thomson's energetic painting imparted confidence to a range of younger Scottish artists.

Thomson, himself a 'son of the manse', studied divinity at Edinburgh University and proceeded to follow in his father's footsteps. Although he attended Nasmyth's drawing classes, he really had no formal training, a circumstance that probably saved him from the Picturesque conventions which would surely have hindered his original, unfettered approach to landscape. For most of his life Thomson worked from the manse which still stands in the shadow of the geological feature which dominates Edinburgh's skyline, the rocky, volcanic outcrop called Arthur's Seat. Through his friendship with Scott, Thomson's house became something of an intellectual talking-shop.

Whatever his opinion of himself, however, Thomson was an amateur only in a technical sense. In his early years he certainly saw Dutch landscapes by artists like Van de Velde and Ruisdael, knew Claude's works through engravings in that artist's monumental compendium *Liber Veritatis* and, closer to home, was familiar with the freely painted backgrounds which his friend, the portrait painter Henry Raeburn, thought adequate in some of his portraits. Since it was not until the 1820s that the influence of Turner pervaded his work, the logical conclusion must be that Thomson arrived at his unconventional style of rendering the effects of waves breaking on the seashore and similar natural phenomena all by himself.

Fast Castle from Below, St Abb's Head in the Distance (Plate 89) dates

89 THE REV. JOHN THOMSON OF
  DUDDINGSTON
Fast Castle from Below, St Abb's Head
  in the Distance 1824
Oil on canvas 76.2 × 105.4
National Galleries of Scotland
The Rev. Thomson of
Duddingston's several views of the
precipitous Fast Castle constitute
the first thoroughly Romantic
treatment of Scottish scenery. Not
surprisingly, Walter Scott was a
friend and admirer. In 1826
Thomson provided an illustration
of Fast Castle for the author's
Provincial Antiquities and Picturesque
Scenery of Scotland.

from the 1820s and depicts the subject Thomson painted more
frequently than any other. The broad, expressive, generalized treatment of weather and sea effects is undoubtedly what appealed to
Walter Scott and it was thanks to Scott that the castle, perched high
on the Berwickshire coast, already possessed powerful, Romantic
literary associations; the author had been thinking of Fast in his
description of the imaginary Wolf's Crag Castle in *The Bride of*
Lammermoor.

Thomson's picture is less an accurate description of the scene than
a reflection of the artist's feelings about it. And 'feeling' is the key
word. Later he was to write to Scott, *à propos* yet another castle
subject, that he thought it had 'a sufficient allowance of interesting
association, tho' physically it is nothing but a rocky shore and an old
castle gone to its grave. . . . I think I feel this subject and shall at all
events try it.' The Reverend's comment is a clear and unequivocal
expression of a Romantic artist's attitude to his subject.

Thomson's most successful pictures concentrate on Lowland,
usually seaside, locations relatively close to his Edinburgh home.
Later in the century Scottish artists such as David Roberts (1796–
1864) were to extend their range by travelling abroad in search of

more exotic settings, discovering that foreign places with evocative histories could also provide a source of Romantic inspiration.

'Grecian' Williams AND THE *subjective landscape*

Hugh William Williams, better known as 'Grecian' Williams (1773–1829), was, in spite of his Welsh ancestry, an Edinburgh-bred artist of the same generation as Thomson. He made his name and at the same time earned his sobriquet with a group of watercolours made during his travels in Greece, exhibited to much acclaim in Edinburgh in 1822.

In 1820 Williams had published two illustrated volumes based upon his foreign experiences and called *Travels to Italy, Greece and the Ionian Islands*. Significantly, they are dedicated to the Rev. Thomson of Duddingston: in his illustrations Williams had romanticized the classical sites of the eastern Mediterranean in much the same way as Thomson had the medieval ruins of Scotland.

Williams's stylistic development is interesting because it demonstrates more clearly than that of any other British artist of the period the gradual change from the convention-ridden, eighteenth-century Picturesque approach to landscape as practised by More and to a lesser extent by Nasmyth, to the subjective Romantic one which became standard in the nineteenth century.

The work Williams produced before the turn of the century shows a controlled, unadventurous watercolour technique being used to place buildings in parkland in much the same way that Nasmyth encouraged. There is no indication that the artist wants to let go or is even capable of it. Williams's heroes, as his journals reveal, were the respectable Classical exemplars: Claude, Gaspard Poussin and Salvator Rosa. Williams's mature work, by contrast, represents a radical change to an expressive, free use of watercolour to paint land and seascapes in which individual elements are diminished for dramatic effect and weather conditions exaggerated to convey the artist's personal response to the scene. In contrast to the Rev. Thomson of Duddingston who arrived at his personal Romantic style independently, Grecian Williams relied to a large extent on the inspiration provided by Turner.

In *The Temple of Poseidon, Cape Sunion* (Plate 90) the choppy sea and stormy sky are strongly reminiscent of Turner, as is the diminutive scale of the silhouetted Doric peristyle set against the sky. The Picturesque concern for calm topography has been usurped by Williams's desire to express his feeling of awe and sense of melancholy. This is a Byronic view of Antiquity, diametrically opposed to that of Jacob More. The monument itself is no longer the focus of some pastoral, antique idyll; nor is it thought worthy of the Neo-Classical

90 HUGH WILLIAMS
The Temple of Poseidon, Cape Sunion
1828 Pen and Watercolour
    62.3 × 71.8
National Galleries of Scotland
In the light of subsequent
developments, the impact that the
modest-looking pictures of
'Grecian' Williams had on Scottish
artists in the 1820s is hard to
understand. A comparison with
Alexander Nasmyth's attitude
towards scenery, however,
highlights the innovatory subjective
approach of the younger artist.

historicist treatment that Alexander Runciman might have afforded it. It is an integral part of a larger, emotion-suffused entity.

While it is true that Turner had travelled to the western Highlands and painted on the Isle of Skye as early as the 1830s, it was not until rather later that this area became the chief source of landscape subjects for Scottish artists. By the time that the best of these began to tackle the more dramatic aspects of Scotland's scenery, the way it was thought appropriate to paint a landscape had radically altered. Whereas Turner always generalized in his treatments of sublime subjects, Scottish artists in the Victorian period tended to particularize.

The Highlands, Horatio McCulloch AND THE *High Victorian* VISION

Probably the major reason why the Highlands became so extraordinarily popular among tourists and artists alike in the nineteenth century was their greatly increased accessibility. The expansion of the Lowlands' transport system to encompass the Highlands had actually begun with General Wade's military road-building programme in 1724. By the 1820s, however, once the railways and Thomas Telford's engineering skills had made it feasible to connect previously isolated valleys, mountains and lochs with the Lowland cities, the aim was mainly touristic; already in the 1840s the man now venerated as Scotland's first conservationist, Lord Cockburn, was expressing relief that he had been able to enjoy the luxury of the Scottish countryside before the onslaught of the iron horse.

Nevertheless, the main attraction of the Highlands for those from urban centres was the opportunity they presented for isolation and solitary contemplation. Queen Victoria herself first became enamoured of the Highlands precisely because of their 'away-from-

it-all' appeal; in her famous journals the Queen constantly refers to the pleasure of being alone amongst the marvellous scenery. Unfortunately, however, ultimate solitary indulgence was only available to the Prince Consort; deerstalking – pursuing the prey into isolated glens – was an exclusively male preserve.

This idealized, romantic view of the Highlands which eventually became synonymous with the world's image of Scotland as a whole, finds its purest artistic expression in the paintings of Scotland's pre-eminent Victorian landscape painter, Horatio McCulloch (1805–67). The patriotic pride expressed in the writings of Burns and Scott, which some historians have explained as a late-flowering cultural compensation for the political castration of Scotland by the Act of Union, originally found a painterly outlet in the work of the first artists identified by Victorian commentators as members of the Scottish School: in Raeburn's portraiture and in Wilkie's Scottish genre subjects. But it is in the paintings of Horatio McCulloch that it reaches its zenith.

McCulloch came to be admired as the national painter *par excellence*, and it is his vision of the Highlands that, even a century after his death, still epitomizes Scotland in the public mind. McCulloch painted scenery unspoilt by man, with no indication of human habitation or intrusion, emphasizing in his pictures all the features which differentiate Highland scenery from that of other mountainous

91 HORATIO McCULLOCH
Glencoe 1864
Oil on canvas 110.5 × 182.9
Glasgow Museums and Art
 Galleries
Associations of the awesome pass of Glencoe with the treacherous massacre of the MacDonald clan by the Campbells in 1692 are unavoidable. For McCulloch this was a bonus: the scene and its historical connotations dovetailed perfectly with the artist's unfettered Romantic view of the Highlands.

countries: the dappling effect of sunlight breaking through clouds on the colour of the heather, the damp swirling mists, mountains which appear far greater than their actual heights. McCulloch's Scotland and Nasmyth's Scotland could quite easily be different countries.

Even now that McCulloch's immense popularity is almost forgotten it is not hard to appreciate the reasons for the success of a picture like his *Glencoe* (Plate 91). There is undoubtedly something sentimental about it, a quality which is underlined by a comparison with Turner's atmospheric interpretation of the same subject. Even allowing for a barely perceptible narrowing of the pass, however, the fidelity to nature of McCulloch's superb picture is undeniable. If the glowing light behind the mountains, the extraordinary variety of shades in the heather and the alert deer in the foreground appear theatrical, then it is the theatricality of nature. McCulloch did not invent it. The Highlands are intensely theatrical.

McCulloch was born in Glasgow in the year of Trafalgar and, as so often in the history of Scottish landscape painting, he began his career apprenticed to a house painter. From these humble beginnings he moved on to study easel painting under the Glasgow artist John Knox (1778–1845). Knox, who made his reputation painting vast city panoramas, had been a pupil of Alexander Nasmyth and it was through him that McCulloch inherited the Picturesque manner which is evident in his earliest known work.

At the age of twenty, however, McCulloch moved to Edinburgh, where he experienced the watercolours of 'Grecian' Williams and was befriended by the Rev. Thomson of Duddingston. Without doubt the older artists imparted to him the importance of having a 'feeling' for a chosen landscape subject. Yet, while taking account of their emotional commitment, McCulloch's mature work is characterized by a more focused analysis of the individual elements within the landscape. In this he sometimes comes closer to Turner, but he rarely departs from minutely detailed observation of nature and the 'tinted steam' effects so enjoyable in Turner play no part in his work.

McCulloch's picture of *Loch Katrine* (Plate 92), painted two years later than *Glencoe*, is an even more heartstring-tugging performance than the earlier work. Half a century after the publication of Scott's *The Lady of the Lake* (near the start of the poem a king, in pursuit of a stag, chances upon Loch Katrine), this lake had achieved almost mythical significance for Romantic artists. Turner had of course painted it for the engraving to accompany the poem in Scott's collected *Poetical Works*, and McCulloch probably drew some inspiration from Turner. McCulloch, however, capitalized on Scott's description of the location as an isolated Shangri-la to a far greater

extent; the crisp, clear air is almost tangible and no human presence intrudes to break the spell. In the painting of the slopes which tumble from the summit of the mountain named Benvenue into the loch McCulloch has described the variegated rocky surface with the precision of a geologist.

In Victorian Scotland, McCulloch's interpretation of the Highlands became so widely accepted as artistically true that any painter choosing to emphasize a different aspect of the terrain or who treated it in a different manner would have been thought perverse. McCulloch had pioneered the acceptance of the wild, the bleak, the uninhabited and the awesome, and made it his own. Artists could either choose to try to extend his repertoire by selecting more spectacular locations and more dramatic weather effects, or they could ignore it altogether.

The Pre-Raphaelite APPROACH AND McCulloch's legacy

There was, however, one further option open to Scottish landscape painters after the mid-nineteenth century; they could take on board the principles of Pre-Raphaelite painting as espoused by the formidable English critic and connoisseur John Ruskin. This involved zooming in on a selected part of a particular scene and transcribing it in terms of form and colour with the most painstaking attention to detail possible.

92 HORATIO McCULLOCH
Loch Katrine 1866
Oil on canvas 104 × 183
Perth City Art Gallery and Museum
The mass popularity of McCulloch's pictures during the later Victorian period has tended to persuade modern critics to emphasize their defects at the expense of their merits. Here the artist had succeeded in painting the definitive view of the setting of Walter Scott's poem 'The Lady of the Lake'.

Unfortunately, from the point of view of Scottish artists there was a major problem in following this method. Artists who trained at the Trustees' Academy in Edinburgh, for example, had continued to absorb influences in a desultory way from Old Masters, the work of other contemporary artists and even house decoration much as their eighteenth-century predecessors had done; in common with them too

93 WILLIAM DYCE
Christ as the Man of Sorrows 1860
Oil on millboard 34.9 × 48.4
National Galleries of Scotland
The idea of using a characteristically Scottish setting as a backdrop to a biblical scene was perhaps an odd one. Nevertheless, the startlingly meticulous way in which Dyce has represented the vegetation imparts an appropriately sacred atmosphere to this picture.

they believed that to be over-emphatic in the details of a picture was unartistic and, ultimately, detrimental to the finished work. In their minds Raeburn's great example confirmed this to be true; to go along with Ruskin was to renounce Scotland's unique artistic achievement.

William Dyce, however, was anything but hamstrung by the artistic traditions of his homeland (see Chapter Three); yet even his work presents problems to those who would wish to class him along with the English Pre-Raphaelites. In his overtly religious, jewel-like picture *Christ as the Man of Sorrows* (Plate 93), for example, where the artist has imagined a doleful Christ against Scottish moorland, the basic Pre-Raphaelite rule that the setting of a story or incident should be correct has been contravened. While authenticity obliged Holman Hunt to go to the Holy Land to paint *The Scapegoat*, Dyce felt it acceptable merely to look outside his back door.

The advocates of Pre-Raphaelitism maintained that, when applied to landscape, it had overthrown 'the tyranny of the recognizable view'. In the long-term development of the nineteenth-century Scottish School of landscape painters, however, it was those artists who were content to live under that tyranny who were most significant.

Peter Graham (1836–1921), for example, was typical of the school during what might be termed its decadent phase. Graham was an Edinburgh-born, Trustees' Academy student who set out to outdo McCulloch. Not content with the traditional romantic Highland views, he went further afield than the acknowledged master of the genre in a search for ever more desolate subjects. Nothing was too wild or bleak for Graham, and when there was no legitimate literary association with a romantic location he fancied, Graham would ransack the poetry books or, failing that, invent one himself. *A Spate in the Highlands* (Plate 94) is Graham at his action-packed best. An enraged burn has demolished one span of the bridge and the heavens are on the verge of letting loose another downpour. Graham migrated south to enjoy the fortune that this kind of subject brought him; apparently the painter could not supply Agnew's with enough pictures of this kind!

To escape from the kind of post-McCulloch Romantic mannerism

94 PETER GRAHAM
A Spate in the Highlands 1866
Oil on canvas 120 × 176.8
City Art Gallery, Manchester
Graham was just one of a number of Victorian artists who flourished as a result of concentrating on the wilder aspects of Highland scenery. The unspecific title of the picture immediately suggests that the artist's real subject is the mood conjured up by the natural event rather than the river's precise location.

represented by artists like Graham, not to mention a host of facile lesser artists who followed in McCulloch's footsteps, a single-minded genius of originality was required. Fortunately, nineteenth-century Scotland produced one.

The GENIUS OF *William McTaggart*

Only recently, in the wake of the first full-scale retrospective of his work since his death, has anything like true recognition been accorded William McTaggart (1835–1910). He has always been denied critical esteem primarily because of the superficial similarities between his work and that of the French Impressionists. In a way this historical oversight is forgivable since, especially in his later years, McTaggart painted pictures with the detached brushwork and heightened palette which are hallmarks of French Impressionism. Yet this Scottish artist arrived at his sparse, late style by a circuitous route which was more a development of his Pre-Raphaelite origins rather than a reaction against anything of which he particularly disapproved.

McTaggart was born on the Mull of Kintyre, and his childhood, spent by the sea, was to influence his choice of subject matter for the rest of his life. Indeed, it would be more correct to call him a 'seascapist' than a landscapist. Unlike McCulloch, McTaggart hardly ever ventured into the Highlands: he is a painter of the sea and shore, a fact which in itself sets him apart from his Romantic precursors.

After training at the Trustees' Academy, McTaggart briefly painted in a Pre-Raphaelite manner. But even in these early days his application of paint was altogether looser than that of Millais and his followers; McTaggart's natural talent never really lent itself to finicky obsession with detail. Nevertheless, his closeness to mainstream English Victorian painting early in his career can be seen in the somewhat cloying anecdotalism of his first pictures.

Spring (Plate 95), painted in 1864, coincidentally in the same year that McCulloch painted his great *Glencoe*, gives a good idea of the stylistic origins of McTaggart. It shows him to have been a painter as firmly rooted in the sentimental, Victorian tradition as a W. P. Frith or a Luke Fildes. On the other hand it contains all the qualities – a light touch, a fresh approach to colour, a feeling for the outdoors – which are the seeds of the artist's highly individualistic mature style.

In the 1870s, however, McTaggart abandoned the respectable Victorianism of pictures like *Spring* and began to use rougher canvas. His brushwork gradually became much more spirited and he lightened his palette to such an extent that almost every colour seems to have been mixed with quantities of white. In a magnificent series of atmospheric seascapes painted in the 1880s and 1890s, the outline

drawing at which his student studies show him to have been adept plays no part whatsoever.

To move from *Spring* to *Running for Shelter* (Plate 96), painted more than twenty years later, is like leaving a stuffy studio and feeling the wind about one's ears. It is an extraordinarily courageous work to have been painted as early as 1887. The summary treatment of the sails of the cowering yawls in the distance, not to mention the figure painting, would have appalled Ruskin; 'finish' plays no part in McTaggart's painting from this date.

In *Running for Shelter* something of the acute difficulty the artist experienced in integrating his figures into their environment can be perceived. According to McTaggart's dealer McOmish Dott, he would spend weeks trying to achieve a homogeneous effect in the whole; the balance between detail and suggestion was difficult for him. More and more as the years progressed, McTaggart tended to indicate figures with passionate flicks of the brush, often leaving the picture with the appearance of a very mysterious ghostly presence rather than one of real, flesh and blood figures.

By the 1870s, when McTaggart's style was reaching maturity, the

95 WILLIAM McTAGGART
Spring 1864
Oil on canvas 45.1 × 60.4
National Galleries of Scotland
McTaggart was a student of Robert Scott Lauder at the Trustees' Academy, and his early pictures, not surprisingly, exhibit all the painterly qualities encouraged by his influential teacher. The stylistic evolution which resulted in the dramatically different look of McTaggart's later seascapes did not, however, eliminate all the constituents of the artist's early subject matter; children were to play an important role in his pictures for the duration of his career.

96 WILLIAM McTAGGART
Running for Shelter 1887
Oil on canvas 100.3 × 137.2
City of Edinburgh Art Centre
The raw natural energy conveyed
here make this one of the artist's
most exciting pictures. Such a
truthful rendering of changing
weather effects is rarely found in
the work of the French
Impressionists with whom the
Scottish artist is so frequently and
somewhat misleadingly compared.

Romantic view of the Highlands which McCulloch epitomized in painting and Walter Scott in literature had run its course. McTaggart was part of a new mood, expressing on one occasion the very 'modern' opinion that landscapes were not improved or made more interesting by any literary or historical allusion, either in their titles or in the pictures themselves; his own titles always refer to place or weather conditions. McTaggart could see no advantage in painting 'views' of the sort in which his predecessors specialized.

A wonderfully evocative photograph of McTaggart on the beach at Machrihanish, brush in hand and about to attack a massive canvas (Plate 97), reveals everything one needs to know about his attitude to painting. Nevertheless, the image of the artist presented in the photograph – the fearless painter committing the visual evidence of the seascape before him directly onto the canvas – should not be taken at face value. For the greater part of his career, McTaggart stuck to the traditional practice of either 'working up' a picture begun outdoors or painting the entire thing from sketches and studies made on the spot.

The Storm (Plate 98), probably his finest wholly resolved picture, is

97 *Photograph of William McTaggart* 1898
National Galleries of Scotland
This photograph of McTaggart taken just before the turn of the century is a rare and fascinating image of a nineteenth-century Scottish artist at work. The artist's son steadies the canvas against the breeze on Machrihanish beach.

a case in point. In spite of the remarkable freshness of the painting – the way in which the pigment seems almost to become the turbulent atmosphere it describes – it is very unlikely that McTaggart painted either of the two versions entirely out-of-doors. In this second version the artist achieves the convincingly naturalistic effect by mixing copious amounts of white with an uncommon though scarcely revolutionary palette of colours ranging from a deep Prussian blue in the sky to ochres, greens and black-greys in the sea.

The only precedents for an artist managing to invest nature with such vibrant energy are to be found in the work of Turner and Constable. McTaggart was regularly compared with the latter in particular during his lifetime (probably because of his generous use of white), although his ability to paint the sea allies him more closely with Turner. It is interesting to note that, like Turner, McTaggart too found it difficult to discard the figurative elements which he felt substantiated his land and seascapes. In fact, it was not until his very last days, in a remarkable series of evanescent pictures of the fields around his Midlothian home, that he felt sufficiently confident to abandon them completely.

It is now almost certain that by the time McTaggart was painting works such as *The Storm*, he had already experienced the paintings of the French Impressionists at first hand in the early exhibitions of

98 William McTaggart
The Storm 1890
Oil on canvas 121.9 × 183
National Galleries of Scotland
In McTaggart's masterpiece a
turbulent skein of brushstrokes
unites land, sea, sky and figures
under a furious meteorological
onslaught. The cowering
foreground figures pinned to the
clifftop by the wind, and the almost
imperceptible fishing skiff
relentlessly buffeted in the middle
distance, suggest that the theme of
the picture is man's impotence in
the face of angry nature.

their work in London. Yet resemblances between his method of painting and that most thoroughly developed by an artist such as Monet, for example, remains at best superficial. McTaggart was never seduced by any of the various scientific colour theories which the French Impressionists attempted to employ in an effort to make their painting of light and colour effects more truthful. The impulse behind McTaggart's painting remained to the end spontaneous.

There is no better illustration of the difference in attitude between McTaggart and the French painters with whom he is so often compared than two pictures he painted in the late 1890s which are, in spite of their general appearance as pure seascapes, essentially history pictures. Prompted by the 1300th anniversary of the arrival on the west coast of Scotland of the early Christian missionary St Columba, McTaggart painted a number of canvases purporting to show the event. True to his roots in the High Victorian tradition of accurate reconstruction he went as far as to search out the real location on the Ayrshire coast where Columba was supposed to have first touched land.

In a second, similar group of pictures of which *The Sailing of the Emigrant Ship* (Plate 99) is the best, McTaggart tackled a theme from more recent national experience: the forced depopulation of the Highlands in the early nineteenth century which resulted in large-

scale Scottish emigration. The picture, apart from being a simple, very beautiful seascape, is a poignant reflection on one of the most tragic episodes in Scottish history. No self-respecting Impressionist painter would have allowed one of his pictures to carry with it such a weight of emotional baggage.

It seems that McTaggart was especially attached to these pictures, since they were found in his studio after his death. There were, however, a number of other canvases found along with them which are usually described as 'unfinished'. On these the indications of land and seascape elements are so cursory – almost casual – that the effect is virtually abstract. McTaggart undoubtedly intended to work these pictures up into a more finished state as was his practice. Nevertheless, there are no comparable essays by any other British artist produced before the First World War in which paint is applied in such a free, modern-looking way.

99 WILLIAM MCTAGGART
The Sailing of the Emigrant Ship
1895 Oil on canvas 75.6 × 86.4
National Galleries of Scotland
The mass emigration from Scotland which resulted from the Highland Clearances was a subject which appealed to Victorian sentimental taste, and several Scottish artists (most notably Tom Faed in *The Last of the Clan:* Plate 70) tackled it. Rather than mawkishly dwelling on the distress of the victims, however, McTaggart suggested the poignancy of their predicament by the squally weather effects.

CHAPTER FIVE

Modern
MOVEMENTS

The artistic pulse of Scotland has almost always beaten more vigorously in Edinburgh than in any of her other major cities. This is hardly surprising. In spite of steadily increasing political and social integration with England since the Act of Union of 1707, Scotland's capital has retained its individual cultural identity to a remarkable degree. The over-riding reasons are the city's political status and concomitant professional character: Scotland's capital is home to the prestigious national art collections, the Royal Scottish Academy and the country's oldest art college; Scotland's independent legal and educational systems are, of course, still based there. Every summer since 1949 the annual Festival has been transforming Edinburgh into the world's best-known international showcase for the arts.

The RISE OF *Glasgow*

Towards the end of the nineteenth century, however, there was a swing of the artistic pendulum westward – to the city which, in spite of the decline of its traditional industries, remains Scotland's industrial hub and the largest centre of population. The Gaelic root of the name Glasgow means 'dear green place'; the irony of this poetic appellation is not lost on Glaswegians, who have become weary of their city being used as a byword for urban decay. Little more than two hundred years ago, however, Glasgow was indeed a dear green place. Its metamorphosis from a large town with a rural atmosphere in the 1770s to the Second City of the British Empire which it had become by the end of Queen Victoria's reign was dynamic.

The rise of Glasgow was truly staggering. In 1800 only a twentieth of Scotland's population lived there; by 1900 a fifth. An economy originally based on the milling of grain had by 1850 been replaced by one based on the production of textiles. The tobacco and sugar trade contributed in no small degree to the city's prosperity, and later in the century came carpet weaving and related industries such as dyeing.

All these activities, however, were eventually eclipsed by the heavy industries which were to gain Glasgow her unrivalled international reputation. Rich coal deposits nearby, access to an extensive canal system and the essential asset of the River Clyde itself made Glasgow an ideal location for the building of ships and locomotives. The construction of the world's greatest ocean liner, the *Queen Mary*, on Clydeside in the 1930s was the culminating achievement of a century of increasingly sophisticated industrial expertise – a symbol of the city's mercantile prowess.

The GREAT GLASWEGIAN *collector-patrons*

The concentration of wealth in Glasgow created perfect conditions for art to flourish. A happy and productive alliance of dealers and patrons emerged, which spawned a market first for nineteenth-century European art and very soon after for the local product. Glasgow's art enthusiasts were internationally aware and adventurous in their tastes, and so, in this respect, artists choosing to make their careers in Glasgow were, by the latter part of the nineteenth century, more fortunate than their peers anywhere else in Britain.

Pre-eminent among Glasgow's great patrons was the shipowner Sir William Burrell (1861–1958), whose diverse and fascinating collection is now housed in contemporary splendour in Glasgow's Pollok Park. A multi-millionaire in the mould of the American press magnate William Randolph Hearst, Burrell possessed tastes which ran from Dutch Old Masters to Chinese ceramics; a fine assortment of medieval tapestries and crafts is the glory of the Burrell Collection. But Burrell also bought contemporary painting. Although, in contrast to his American counterparts who were busy acquiring French Impressionist paintings in the 1880s and 1890s, modern French art left him cold, Burrell was keen on the work of the equally progressive American-born artist James Abbott McNeill Whistler and on the significant group of Scottish artists who were influenced by him.

Sir William was, however, only unique in the scale of his collecting. Foremost among his precursors had been the wealthy coachbuilder Archibald McLellan (1797–1854). It was McLellan who gifted the recently renovated galleries on Sauchiehall Street to the city, and whose bequest of Old Masters (including the painting probably by Titian called *The Adulteress*) forms the core of Glasgow's municipal art collection. James Reid of Auchterarder (1823–94), the director of Europe's largest locomotive-manufacturing company, amassed a

100 VINCENT WILLEM VAN GOGH
Portrait of Alexander Reid 1887
Oil on board 43 × 33
Glasgow Museums and Art
  Galleries

Alexander Reid was the doyen of
Glasgow art dealers from 1889
when he founded his first gallery,
the Société des Beaux-Arts, until
he retired in 1926; the London
dealer Lefevre took over his gallery
in 1931. Almost single-handedly
Reid was responsible for cultivating
the taste of Scottish collectors for
French art, but he also supported
and promoted his friends the
Glasgow Boys. This – one of two
portraits made of him by the friend
to whom he bore a remarkable
resemblance, was painted during
Reid's short employment by the
Parisian dealers Boussod and
Valadon.

relatively small but choice collection of pictures including a superb
Corot, *Souvenir d'Italie*, which is now also one of the great treasures
of the Glasgow Art Gallery. The Paisley thread manufacturer William
Allen Coats (1853–1926) collected pictures from both Dutch and
French Schools, and it is thanks to Coats that an extremely rare
early masterpiece by Vermeer, *Christ in the House of Martha and Mary*,
now hangs in the National Gallery of Scotland.

The INFLUENCE OF THE *art dealers*

The taste of such patrons was assiduously cultivated by an equally
enterprising group of dealers. In the 1880s the most influential of
these was Craibe Angus (1830–99) who, through personal contacts
with the Dutch art market, did more than any other individual to
encourage the taste of Glaswegian collectors for Dutch pictures.
Almost all the private collections built up in Glasgow during this
period were rich in pictures by artists of the Hague School such as
Anton Mauve and the Maris brothers. The unpretentious rural
subjects in which these artists specialized particularly appealed to the
taste of the nouveau riche Scottish businessman.

Overshadowing Craibe Angus in retrospect, however, is the more
charismatic personality of Alexander Reid (1854–1928). It was Reid
who was largely responsible for encouraging the enthusiasm for
French painting among patrons and artists which persists in Scotland
to this day. He was peculiarly qualified to do so. In the late 1880s
Reid learned his business first-hand at the Paris dealers Boussod and
Valadon. A friendship with one of the firm's managers, Theo Van
Gogh, led to Reid sharing lodgings with his then struggling artist
brother. The smaller of the two portraits that Vincent Van Gogh
painted of his Scottish dealer friend (Plate 100; Reid, incidentally,
was his only British sitter) has become a symbol of the artistic revival
of the traditional cultural links with France which dominates late
nineteenth- and early twentieth-century Scottish art.

Reid, then, is to be credited with having introduced to Scotland
the painting of the French Impressionists and in particular that of
Degas, Monet and Pissarro; scarcely a decent Impressionist picture
in any of Scotland's public collections today did not pass through his
hands at one time or another. His tastes though were catholic; and,
if French Impressionism was the most significant string to his bow,
an only slightly lesser one was the work of his avant-garde compatriots
and friends the Glasgow Boys.

The GLASGOW *Boys*

Viewed against the urban, industrial background of late nineteenth-
century Glasgow, the work of the most important artists who comprise

Scotland's first modern art movement, the so-called Glasgow School, strikes a surprisingly pastoral note. With the assumption that artists should reflect the world in their immediate vicinity now long since accepted, artists coming from, trained in or at least connected with Glasgow during its industrial heyday might be expected to have produced pictures of huddled masses and billowing chimney stacks. But the Glasgow Boys, as these artists called themselves from the mid-1880s, did no such thing.

James Guthrie (1859–1930), Edward Arthur Walton (1860–1922), William York Macgregor (1855–1923) and Joseph Crawhall (1861–1913), the original key members of the group of 'Young Turks', were consciously rebelling against the tired conventions of what by the last quarter of the nineteenth century had become an entrenched tradition of Scottish academic painting. What the Boys despised most was the kind of painting churned out by the established older generation of Scottish artists: sentimental, anecdotal pictures rooted for the most part in the genre tradition originally established by David Wilkie (see Chapter Three), and which for the Boys might have been typified by a work such as Tom Faed's *The Last of the Clan* (Plate 70). They detested the niggling finish and the concentration on detail which by the 1880s many Scottish artists had developed from the example set by English Pre-Raphaelites. Contemptuously, they dismissed such painters as 'glue pots'.

The art to which the Glasgow Boys aspired in general was the subtle, low-key naturalism of the group of French landscape painters known as the Barbizon School; of artists such as Charles Daubigny, Narcisse Diaz and Théodore Rousseau. While in terms of technique their model was the popular French realist artist Jules Bastien-Lepage (1848–84), the philosophy which informed their work was the 'Art for Art's Sake' approach most meaningfully espoused for them by the innovative James Abbott McNeill Whistler (1834–1903).

At one time or another more than twenty artists have been classed under the umbrella term 'Glasgow School'. They range from E. A. Walton, in whose pictures of Lowland countryside subjects painted in the 1880s is to be found the essence of early Glasgow Boy painting, to Edward Atkinson Hornel (1864–1933), best known for his rich, colourful treatment of the exotic Japanese subjects he painted during the next decade. As with most such late nineteenth-century artistic alliances, however, homogeneity of artistic aim was short-lived. By 1900 most of the Boys had moved on. The career of John Lavery (1856–1941), for example – as Glasgow Boy as any of his *confrères* in the 1880s – was to culminate with his success as the most fashionable of society portrait painters.

If the work of any single artist can be said to typify Glasgow Boy

A Highland Funeral 1882
Oil on canvas 129.5 × 193
Glasgow Museums and Art
   Galleries
The twenty-three-year-old Guthrie
painted this impressive and, in
the context of Scottish painting,
innovative picture after witnessing
such an event in the Perthshire
village of Brig O'Turk. The solidity
with which the artist has described
the scene was inspired by the
French artists Courbet and Bastien-
Lepage. An influential picture,
Guthrie's *Highland Funeral* set the
tone for much subsequent Glasgow
Boy painting.

painting in its original manifestation, however, it is that of James
Guthrie. Unlike almost all of his colleagues, Guthrie never studied
in Paris and therefore his assimilation of the ideals of French
naturalism must either have come from French pictures he saw
exhibited in Glasgow (probably at Alexander Reid's grandly named
Société des Beaux-Arts), or from the reports of his friends.

Although Guthrie's painting in general is as indebted to the
Barbizon School as that of any of the Boys, his first important
picture, *A Highland Funeral* (Plate 101), was directly inspired by a
major work by an earlier French figurative painter. The great sombre
canvas called *The Burial at Ornans* by the doyen of radical French
realist artists, Gustave Courbet, is clearly the model for Guthrie's
Highland funeral service. Yet the skill with which the artist has
composed his figure group was in fact learnt first-hand from the late
Victorian Scottish anecdotal painter John Pettie (see Chapter Three),
with whom he studied in London. Guthrie's work, however, is devoid
of the mawkish sentiment which an artist of Pettie's cast of mind
would undoubtedly have made its overwhelming aspect, and it is this
restraining of the emotional content of the subject which marks the
picture out as a Glasgow School work.

Guthrie's *Highland Funeral* was painted in the studio from sketches
he had made in the Perthshire village of Brig O'Turk, the first of a

102 JAMES GUTHRIE
A Hind's Daughter 1883
Oil on canvas 91.5 × 76.2
National Galleries of Scotland
One of the innovations introduced
into Scottish art by the Glasgow
Boys was the idea that the effect of
the way in which paint is applied –
the 'hand-crafted' quality – is, in
itself, worthy of appreciation. In
this picture, as in all those which
Guthrie produced during the
heyday of the Glasgow Boys,
Guthrie insists that the work be
appreciated first and foremost as a
'painting'; the intrinsic interest of
the subject (in this case the daughter
of a Scottish farmworker) is of only
secondary importance.

number of artist colonies formed by the Boys in the 1880s. More
significant in terms of style are the pictures he painted slightly later
at Cockburnspath, a farming village near the Berwickshire coast and
a further attempt by the Boys to emulate the Barbizon School's
trailblazing community on the edge of the forest of Fontainebleau.
In 1883 Guthrie was joined in this pretty though scarcely spectacular
spot by his close friend E. A. Walton, then by Joseph Crawhall,
George Henry and the older, Edinburgh-based artist Arthur Melville.

A Hind's Daughter (Plate 102), painted by Guthrie in 1883, is without
doubt the most important picture produced at Cockburnspath. In
the bleak grey winter light characteristic of this area of south-east
Scotland, the farm worker's young daughter – an island of childhood
innocence in a sea of cabbages – confronts the spectator with an
emotionless gaze. It is hard to imagine a more anti-picturesque
image, and it is precisely this, the unaffected way in which Guthrie
has realized his subject, which is the point of the picture.

In order to create an unrefined surface texture Guthrie used the square-ended brush and palette knife favoured by Bastien-Lepage (Plate 103), who at this time was immensely highly regarded even outside the Glasgow Boy circle. With these tools the artist has 'hacked out' his picture in an attempt to efface his idiosyncratic artistic personality. The subdued light and subtle harmonies of the picture also reflect the influence of Bastien-Lepage and similar characteristics are likewise uppermost in the picture *A Berwickshire Fieldworker* (Plate 104) painted by Walton in the following year. Guthrie's brighter picture of a young girl herding geese, *To Pastures New* (Plate 105), consolidated his supremacy among the Glasgow Boys when it was exhibited at the Glasgow Institute of Fine Arts in 1885.

103 JULES BASTIEN-LEPAGE
Pas Mêche 1882
Oil on canvas 132.1 × 89.5
National Galleries of Scotland
The over-riding influence on the early work of the Glasgow Boys during their formative years was the French realist painter Jules Bastien-Lepage. Although, even prior to the 1880s, the most prominent future Boys had been tackling 'realist' subjects, it was not until the influence of Bastien-Lepage took hold that their pictures acquired their characteristic Glasgow Boy look.

Right 104 EDWARD ARTHUR
  WALTON
A Berwickshire Fieldworker 1884
Oil on canvas 91.4 × 60.9
Tate Gallery, London
Although Walton's later work often appears to lack conviction, at the outset of his career his pictures were as virile as those of any of his colleagues.

Most of the Glasgow Boys, coming from fairly ordinary backgrounds, needed to make their livings from selling their work and this accounts for much of their later painting appearing depressingly 'comfortable' by comparison with the relatively small group of early ground-breaking pictures. The exception was the oldest of the Boys, W. Y. Macgregor (1855–1923), the scion of a Glasgow shipowning family, whose commodious studio became something of a talking shop during the winters several of the group spent back in Glasgow in the 1880s.

Still-life was not a subject which greatly excited the Glasgow Boys; a large painting by Macgregor called *The Vegetable Stall* (Plate 106), generally agreed to be a masterpiece of Glasgow Boy painting, is a brilliant exception. In this picture the primary qualities of the group's painting are perfectly exemplified, from the down-to-earth, dispassionate way in which the paint has been used to describe the clumpy forms of the subject, to the no-nonsense, confrontational way in which it is presented. 'Hack the subject out as you would were you using an axe, and try to realise it; get its bigness,' Macgregor advised his juniors.

While Guthrie, Walton and Macgregor found inspiration in the Scottish scene, a separate group of the Boys felt the need to work near the geographical source of the French naturalist tradition. The

105 JAMES GUTHRIE
To Pastures New 1883
Oil on canvas 92 × 152.3
Aberdeen Art Gallery and
   Museums
To Pastures New is Guthrie's freshest and most appealing picture. The simplicity of the composition and the high tonality of the colour are indicative of his vehement rebuttal of the values espoused by those Scottish artists who continued to work in the tradition established by Wilkie and Raeburn. It was this painting which convinced John Lavery to settle in Glasgow upon his return from France.

106 WILLIAM YORK MACGREGOR
The Vegetable Stall 1884
Oil on canvas 105.5 × 150.5
National Galleries of Scotland
Macgregor's *Vegetable Stall* displays
all the finest qualities of Glasgow
Boy painting. Originally a coster
counting her earnings was depicted
to the right of the canvas, but
Macgregor, perhaps aware of the
inadequacy of his figure-painting,
painted her out. On seeing
Macgregor's great picture for the
first time, the Austrian Expressionist
painter Oskar Kokoschka declared:
'To think the picture was painted
before I was born – and I never
knew!'

charming village of Grez-sur-Loing on the edge of the forest of Fontainebleau was already something of an artists' colony when John Lavery, William Kennedy, Alexander Roche and Thomas Millie Dow arrived there fresh from their studies in Paris in the mid-1880s.

Not surprisingly, the persuasive artistic personality of Jules Bastien-Lepage was more keenly felt by the Boys who chose to work in France than by their stay-at-home brothers. Several had encountered the famous young man in Paris and Lavery received some advice from him which his subsequent painting shows him to have taken to heart: 'Select a person – watch him – then put down as much as you remember. Never look twice.' In a picture such as *On the Loing: An Afternoon Chat* (Plate 107) Lavery achieves a delicate atmospheric naturalism which suggests an affinity with the Impressionists.

According to Lavery, it was the impact of Guthrie's *To Pastures New* which made him eventually decide to settle in Glasgow rather than London after his return from France. But it was with figurative subjects from middle-class life rather than with the farmyard repertoire of Guthrie and Walton that Lavery made his name. At the outset, sales of the Glasgow Boys' paintings of rural scenes were not encouraging; Lavery calculated the taste of his market and reaped the financial benefits.

The Tennis Party (Plate 108) is the artist's masterpiece from his years as a paid-up member of the Glasgow Boy fraternity. The concept is monumental without being in the least portentous; the tonal control everything Lepage could have wished for; the colouring so fresh that even today there seems nothing fusty or Victorian about the picture. The committee of the Paris Salon acknowledged the quality of the work by awarding it a gold medal when it was exhibited there in 1888.

By the end of the decade, however, the influence of Whistler proved decisive in the course of Lavery's development. 'We recognised in him the greatest artist of the day and thought his Ten O'Clock Lecture as the gospel of art,' he later wrote of the American-born master whom Ruskin had famously accused of 'flinging a pot of paint in the public's face'. Lavery took on board Whistler's musical approach to the 'orchestration' of colour, his preference for suggesting form rather than describing it in detail, and, above all, his insistence that the artist should impose his own formal will on a subject rather than allowing it to dictate the treatment accorded it.

Nowhere is Lavery's wholehearted embracing of Whistler's theories more evident than in the series of fifty small pictures he painted to record the 1888 Glasgow International Exhibition. The night scenes – tonal harmonies with the occasional dissonant colour chord that seems to be casually struck for sparkle – are overtly Whistlerian. (It

Left 107 JOHN LAVERY
On the Loing: An Afternoon Chat
1884 Oil on canvas 150.8 × 150.4
Ulster Museum, Belfast
This delightful picture, painted in the village of Grez-sur-Loing, south of Paris, was one of the first that Lavery exhibited in Scotland. At the Glasgow Institute exhibition of 1885 both Lavery's picture and Guthrie's *To Pastures New* failed to sell, which suggests that the tastes of Glaswegian collectors at this date were still conservative.

The Tennis Party was Lavery's first great success in Scotland; both its middle-class subject matter and overwhelming naturalness appealed to Glasgow's art-conscious public. In common with several French artists of the period – Degas notable among them – Lavery had become fascinated by the problems of painting figures in motion.

was the commission to paint a crowded scene of Queen Victoria's visit to the exhibition which led indirectly to Lavery's eventual success as a portraitist.) Lavery attached one of the poetic musical titles favoured by Whistler to his best-known portrait, that of R. B. Cunninghame Graham, calling it *Harmony in Brown* (GMAG).

Ultimately Lavery in this Whistlerian mode is Lavery at his most typical. A comparison with a characteristic picture by the prolific Edward Atkinson Hornel might reasonably lead the uninitiated to wonder how such dissimilar artists can possibly share membership of the same school. However, E. A. Hornel and his close friend and colleague George Henry (1858–1943) represent a related though very different flowering of the Glasgow School of painting which, perhaps surprisingly, was to have a more widespread and enduring impact on Scottish art in the twentieth century.

In 1889 Henry painted *A Galloway Landscape* (Plate 109), a picture which, even had it been painted by Gauguin or one of his followers of the Pont-Aven School in Brittany, would have been considered 'advanced' at this time. Henry has taken a very ordinary view of a hillside dotted with grazing cattle and transformed it into a magical, even mysterious world. The main elements of the composition have been deliberately flattened, and the use of intense, unnaturalistic colour augments the unreal feeling that pervades the picture. Henry's painting is in fact a precocious essay in Symbolism, the continental movement which, though it never really took root in Scotland, freed Henry to investigate the colour-determined variety of modern painting which most certainly did.

Van Gogh and any number of French Impressionists fell in love with Japanese art during the 1870s, mostly through seeing imported

woodcuts. None of them, however, was actually to make the journey to Japan as Henry and Hornel did in 1893. The flatness of *A Galloway Landscape* already owes something to Japanese influence, and this is even more prominent in two remarkable pictures on which Hornel and Henry collaborated immediately prior to their Oriental journey. The subjects of *The Druids: Bringing in the Mistletoe* (Plate 110) and *The Star in the East* (GMAG) are very much in tune with the Celtic Revival which was increasingly to influence the applied arts in Scotland as the century drew to its close.

Hornel and Henry's sojourn in Japan, sponsored by Alexander Reid, was a productive phase in both their careers, although many

109 GEORGE HENRY
A Galloway Landscape 1889
Oil on canvas 121.9 × 152.4
Glasgow Museums and Art
  Galleries
The decorative impulse which distinguishes the painting of several Glasgow Boys from the late 1880s first proclaims itself in Henry's remarkable picture *A Galloway Landscape.*

110 GEORGE HENRY AND EDWARD
   ATKINSON HORNEL
The Druids: Bringing in the Mistletoe
1890 Oil on canvas 152.4 × 152.4
Glasgow Museums and Art
   Galleries
Henry and Hornel, in collaborating
on a number of pictures in the late
1880s, were responsible for
introducing a new, exotic range of
subject matter into Glasgow Boy
painting.

of the pictures that Henry painted there were damaged during their
return. Over the eighteen-month period they stayed there the two
artists made a series of brightly coloured, decorative paintings in
which the elegant, poised spirit of the Orient is transfused with a
highly charged coloration adapted from French art. In Hornel's
hands, as in pictures such as *Kite Flying, Japan* (Plate 111), this
combination conspires to produce a gay – sometimes frenzied –
effect. Henry, on the other hand, who generally preferred watercolour
to oil, interpreted his less complex subjects in a more culturally
appropriate if less exciting manner. Hornel's admiration for the
exuberant French artist Monticelli which is so much a feature of his

Left 111 Edward Atkinson Hornel

Kite Flying, Japan c. 1894

Oil on canvas 76 × 48

National Galleries of Scotland

Hornel's Japanese paintings are some of the most glorious achievements of Glasgow Boy painting. Ironically, however, their appearance owes far less to the art of the country in which they were painted than it does to the work of the French artist Adolphe Monticelli.

112 George Henry

Japanese Lady with a Fan 1894

Oil on canvas 61 × 40.6

Glasgow Museums and Art Galleries

Although Henry was far less productive than his friend Hornel during their Oriental sojourn, the relative dearth of Japanese pictures by him is more a result of the damage which occurred to most of them in transit from the Far East. The cool beauty of this painting highlights the loss to posterity.

Japanese work is entirely absent from pictures such as Henry's *Japanese Lady with a Fan* (Plate 112).

Hornel's later work marks a sad waning of the originality, if not the energy, which must have been so impressive in the exhibition of his Japanese pictures mounted by Alexander Reid in 1895. Rarely straying from the confines of his studio in the charming Galloway village of Kirkcudbright (the house is now a museum run by the Hornel Trust), the artist turned his energies to a succession of pictures depicting little girls frolicking against flower-strewn backgrounds. Often, it seems, the figures were painted from photographs and superimposed upon the already finished horticultural backdrops. All these works lack the ideological spine which makes the best Glasgow Boy painting so interesting.

After 1900, critical opinion moved swiftly against the Glasgow Boys; it was generally held that the Boys were dogs who had had their day. Without doubt success had, to some extent, gnawed away at their artistic integrity. Guthrie and Lavery, for example, turned to the less adventurous area of portraiture, becoming pillars of the establishment. Both were knighted, the former elevated to the presidency of the Royal Scottish Academy, the latter achieving an even wider fame by immortalizing Shirley Temple among others on a star-studded list of sitters. Hornel died very comfortably rich, though long since inspired.

Only since the Second World War has the reputation of Glasgow Boy painting reached anything like the heights it scaled in the 1890s. During that decade they not only took London by storm in a group exhibition at the Grosvenor Gallery, but went on to great acclaim in Munich where critics were enthusiastic to a degree. The Bavarian government purchased Lavery's *The Tennis Party*. The Boys exhibited widely throughout Europe and the United States. Lavery was for a time a member of almost all the leading avant-garde artists' societies – known as the 'Secessions' – which sprang up across the Continent in the early years of this century.

This international success, achieved independently of the London art world, has provided a touchstone for generations of Scottish artists ever since. The Glasgow Boys, however, were very much followers of various continental avant-garde art movements; only the most chauvinist of commentators would hail them as pioneering artists of European stature.

Charles Rennie Mackintosh AND THE *Glasgow Style*

The other significant art movement to emerge from Scotland's prosperous industrial capital at the end of the last century – the Glasgow Style as epitomized in the work of its most vital originator,

Charles Rennie Mackintosh – is, by contrast, now universally acclaimed as a major contribution to the European traditions of design and decorative art. The fact that much of the work – architecture, furniture, metalwork – produced by Mackintosh and his circle languished unappreciated by the majority in Scotland for so long is as much the fault of Glasgow's now thankfully extinct municipal philistinism as of fashion.

The work produced by Mackintosh (1869–1928), his wife Margaret Macdonald Mackintosh (1864–1933), her sister Frances Macdonald MacNair (1873–1921) and her husband James Herbert MacNair (1868–1955) during the 1890s is essentially a powerful northern flowering of what is known in the French and English-speaking world as Art Nouveau. The Mackintosh clan was – rather surprisingly – unaffected by the continental art movements which were beacons for the Glasgow Boys, but the two groups did have this much in common: both turned their backs on their immediate environment. For them, art was an antidote to the urban squalor for which, by the 1890s, Glasgow was already notorious; apart from its function as therapy it was no mechanism for coping with the situation.

The Mackintosh group was a product of and remains inextricably linked with the Glasgow School of Art. Until the directorship of the school was taken over by Francis Newbery in 1885, Glasgow, although third in the hierarchy of British art schools, had produced relatively few artists or designers of note. Newbery, known to all as 'Fra', changed all that by changing the system.

The charismatic Fra Newbery was at heart a child of the Arts and Crafts movement which had been founded in England in the 1860s by William Morris. In tune with the movement's philosophy, he believed that the fine arts and the crafts should work in tandem, that mechanized production was at root alien to good design, and that for something to be beautiful it had to be made with pleasure. Mackintosh and his circle benefited from a curriculum and a method of instruction geared to instilling these ideals. Consequently, after leaving college, it seemed quite natural to the four leading exponents of the Glasgow Style that they should set up their own workshops and collaborate to produce all manner of objects. These included mirrors, candlesticks, posters and, most important of all, complete interiors.

The two-dimensional work produced by the group in the 1890s is strongly influenced by the Art Nouveau designs of the Dutch artist Jan Toorop and the Belgian Fernand Khnopff which they had seen reproduced in the *Studio* magazine. Aubrey Beardsley's decadent *fin-de-siècle* illustrations to the works of Malory and Oscar Wilde also played a part. Mackintosh himself had, even as a student, delighted in the intricate, convoluted rhythms of flowers and he was ultimately to use

113 CHARLES RENNIE MACKINTOSH
The Harvest Moon 1892
Pencil and watercolour 35.2 × 27.7
Glasgow School of Art
Although primarily an architect and designer, Mackintosh drew and made watercolours throughout his career. This highly symbolic early watercolour is as stylized and enigmatic as any of the more typical productions of his wife and sister-in-law. Mackintosh had become acquainted with continental Symbolist artists primarily through reproductions of their work in magazines.

114 MARGARET MACDONALD
Summer 1897
Pencil and gouache on vellum with
    beaten lead frame 45.4 × 20.3
Glasgow Museums and Art
    Galleries
In the late 1890s the Macdonald
sisters experimented with various
media to achieve rich and
mysterious effects. In this exquisite
panel a metal surround embellished
with a Celtic-looking linear motif
sets off a subtle painting of a female
figure with attendant *putti* who
represent the fertility of summer.

the knowledge he gained from drawing them to create the stylized decorative elements of his architectural designs. But the excessive elongations of forms, the wilful changes in scale and the choice of macabre subject matter which was to earn 'The Four', as they were known during their college days, the nickname of the 'Spook School', are most striking in the work of his wife and her sister.

Looking at their early watercolours, works such as Frances Macdonald's *A Pond* (Glasgow School of Art), it is not hard to understand the derision with which the original work of The Four was greeted when it was exhibited at the London Arts and Crafts Society exhibition in 1886. The androgynous forms are attenuated to the verge of abstraction; and the mood of the works, with their highly charged sexual overtones, is as 'unhealthy' as anything produced by Beardsley. By contrast, the watercolours that Mackintosh himself was painting during the early 1890s, although heavily symbolic (Plate 113), are positively benign.

Some of the loveliest items made by The Four are the beaten metalwork framed mirrors and pictures of the Macdonald sisters (Plate 114). By daringly combining media such as pencil and watercolour they created ethereal images which they set off with equally strange, though more ostentatiously decorative, surrounds. Although the effect is seductive, purist Arts and Crafts Society members cannot have taken kindly to the unpractical, heavy-framed mirrors.

To appreciate the full glory of the Glasgow Style and to understand why it made such an impact, however, one must turn to the famous Glasgow tea rooms conceived by Mackintosh himself in their entirety, but to which other members of the group also contributed major elements. Mackintosh was lucky in his patron, the formidable Miss Catherine Cranston whose several establishments in the city centre were the social hubs of the thriving, turn-of-the-century Scottish metropolis. Miss Cranston allowed her designers a free hand to use every possible fancy of design and decoration.

The *pièce de résistance* of Miss Cranston's emporia was the Willow Tea Rooms in Sauchiehall Street (Plate 115). Taking his theme from the Gaelic root of the name 'sauchiehall', the alley of willows, Mackintosh created a series of surprising, inter-related spaces, decked out with silver-painted furniture and enamelled mirrors. The white and purple glass shapes on the mirrors which are such a feature of the Willow Tea Rooms' Room de Luxe are merely ancillary decoration to a magnificent panel designed by Margaret Mackintosh based on the sonnet by Dante Gabriel Rossetti 'Oh ye, all ye that walk in Willowwood'. The opulent though light effect of the panel results from the Mackintoshes' unusual technique of working string and coloured beads into gesso. 'I had talent, Margaret had genius,'

115 CHARLES RENNIE MACKINTOSH
*Interior of the Room de Luxe, Willow
    Tea Rooms, Sauchiehall Street,
    Glasgow* 1903
Hunterian Art Gallery, University
    of Glasgow
Largely a result of the impact of
the temperance movement on
turn-of-the-century Glasgow, Miss
Catherine Cranston's tea rooms
once blessed all the city's major
thoroughfares. Only the Willow
Tea Rooms, built in 1903 and now
restored, remain. By employing
Mackintosh and his associates
among others Miss Cranston was
directly responsible for making the
Glasgow Style a part of everyday
Glaswegian life.

Mackintosh is supposed to have said; a comment which, in the context of the Willow Tea Rooms, it is tempting to take at face value.

Mackintosh himself painted and drew regularly throughout his life. Indeed, he viewed his graphic work as an activity essential to his primary role as architect. Nevertheless it was as an architect that he made his greatest impact. In the years following 1900, after the MacNairs had moved to Liverpool where Herbert MacNair had taken up a teaching post, Mackintosh's reputation was at its zenith.

Like many of his generation Mackintosh regarded both the Classical and Gothic aspects of the architectural revivals which dominated the Victorian age as exhausted and outmoded. His attitude to the Renaissance was equally unsympathetic; a visit to Florence, for example, left him cold. 'Shake off all the props, the props tradition and authority offer you, and go alone, crawl, stumble, stagger, but go alone,' he urged his audience in the course of a lecture to fellow professionals in 1902. He was not antipathetic to all ancient architecture, however, and greatly admired the medieval architecture of his own country, for example. He saw honesty in the forms of 'Scottish baronial' and appreciated its empathy with its surroundings.

Mackintosh had two aims: to replace the slavish reiteration or reinterpretation of an inherited formal vocabulary with a practical approach based on an honest analysis of architectural needs (an attitude which foreshadows the 'form follows function' philosophy of that post-First World War cradle of all modern architecture, the German Bauhaus), and to involve decoration closely with nature. In Mackintosh's architecture the decoration of a building is derived

116 CHARLES RENNIE MACKINTOSH
Glasgow School of Art 1897–1909
Photograph *c.* 1955 by Bran &
    Shere
Glasgow School of Art
Both as an admirably practical
building and as an exciting
sculpture, the Glasgow School of
Art is Mackintosh's masterpiece.
The harmony of mass and
decorative elements gives rise to a
deeply satisfying architectural
experience.

from natural forms and integrated into the structure to form an expressive sculptural whole.

In spite of the unforgivable destruction over the years of several of Mackintosh's most important buildings in Glasgow, his masterwork, the Glasgow School of Art (Plate 116), remains intact, providing a magnificent contrast to the miserable post-war developments along Sauchiehall Street. The elevations of the building have the massive feel of medieval fortifications about them; while the wire motifs – the railings and window stays – on the exterior are elegant, stylized plant forms which point up the sculptural mass of the whole. But it is inside – and in the art school's library in particular – that a harmony of layout, scale and decoration achieves what the architectural historian Sir Nikolaus Pevsner described as an 'overwhelmingly full polyphony of abstract form'.

The heyday of the Glasgow Style after the turn of the century was paraded abroad to an extraordinary degree. As part of the economic race which gathered pace in the years leading up to the First World War it was thought useful to display the best British design abroad, particularly in Germany. Mackintosh, supported by Francis Newbery, took advantage of the several opportunities which were presented as a result of this climate of opinion, and the Mackintosh style was shown at the Turin International Exhibition of Decorative Art, at the Venice Biennale and in Budapest.

It was, however, the Vienna Secession exhibition of 1900 which firmly established Mackintosh and the Glasgow Style on the Continent. Room X of the exhibition was painted white. Beneath

Margaret Macdonald Mackintosh's gesso panel *The May Queen* stood the classic Mackintosh chair with its pierced oval back rail. The ensemble captivated the Viennese art world, and photographs of the Glasgow Style rooms were published in magazines across Europe. Leading Austrian designers such as Josef Hoffmann and Koloman Moser drew inspiration from the Glaswegian work, and the geometrical shapes which increasingly became a hallmark of Mackintosh's work served as an example to the German designers who evolved the more severe-looking work which later issued from the Bauhaus. In those years it must have seemed to Mackintosh that things could only go from strength to strength.

Sadly, this was not to be. During the very years of his continental success, and while Mackintosh's few but important Scottish commissions were being realized, the vogue for Art Nouveau was already abating. By 1913, partly because there were insufficient artistic-minded patrons in Glasgow and partly because he had earned a reputation of being a difficult architect to work with, Mackintosh had become disenchanted with the country whose architecture he had single-handedly tried to transform.

The Mackintoshes first moved to Walberswick in Suffolk, where, in a bizarre incident which cannot have encouraged them to stay,

117 CHARLES RENNIE MACKINTOSH
Fritillaria, Walberswick 1915
Pencil and watercolour on paper
25.3 × 20.2
Hunterian Art Gallery, University of Glasgow
Mackintosh intended to publish his watercolours of flowers as a book, but the project was never realized. This particular flower – common to the area of Suffolk in which he and his wife spent the First World War years – allowed his natural enthusiasm for abstract pattern full rein.

118 CHARLES RENNIE MACKINTOSH
Palalda, Pyrénées-Orientales c. 1924–7
Watercolour on paper 51.5 × 51.5
Michael Davidson
The control of tone in this superb late watercolour by Mackintosh is breathtaking. The picture is clearly informed by his continued fascination with architectural forms.

Charles Rennie's Scots accent coupled with his ever-present sketch-book led to accusations that he was spying for the Germans! While in Suffolk, however, he reverted to a youthful passion for painting flowers, and his superb watercolours of fritillaries (Plate 117), then a common flower in the area, exude the pleasure Mackintosh obviously found away from the architect's drawing board. If the temptation is to enjoy Mackintosh's flower paintings more on the level of design than of botanical accuracy, then it is worth remembering that at one time these watercolours were used to teach students of botany at Glasgow University.

The failure of an attempt to establish his own architectural practice in London prompted an extremely creative retirement to the South of France in the early 1920s. Here, the draughtsmanship that Mackintosh had perfected over a long career combined with his natural flair for composition to find joyous fulfilment in a series of exquisite water-colours. In the best of them (Plate 118) Mackintosh describes the topography of Pyrénées-Orientales and the characteristically geo-metric physical structure of the hill towns there in a manner which suggests an awareness of the earlier experiments in Cubism made by those other lovers of the South of France, Braque and Picasso.

The Colourists

By coincidence, the Mackintoshes had moved to France on the suggestion of J. D. Fergusson, the most adventurous member of a group of Scottish painters who were the most adept in Britain at absorbing the revolutionary developments made by French avant-garde artists in the wake of Impressionism. The four artists – Samuel John Peploe (1871–1935), John Duncan Fergusson (1874–1961), George Leslie Hunter (1877–1931) and Francis Campbell Boileau Cadell (1883–1937) – came to be known as the Scottish Colourists, a label which, though misleading since it suggests that the four worked as a team which they never did, draws attention to the central concern of their work. What they absorbed first from the two great Impressionist precursors of modern art, Cézanne and Van Gogh, and then from Matisse and the so-called Fauves (wild beasts) who came to be viewed as Post-Impressionists, was less the formal basis of modern art than the fact that a picture is first apprehended in terms of colour. They realized that manipulating colour in a clever way was the most direct means of producing a good painting.

The artistic roots of the Colourists were, with the exception of Hunter, in the east of Scotland. But the independent path to international fame trodden by William McTaggart and the Glasgow Boys was at the outset undoubtedly at the back of their minds. Peploe held W. Y. Macgregor in high esteem and hung one of his

119 SAMUEL JOHN PEPLOE
A Girl in White: Peggy Macrae c. 1907
Oil on canvas 81.28 × 60.96
Fine Art Society, London
Peploe's fluid early style is obviously
indebted to Manet, but the Dutch
master Frans Hals was also an
influence. As a young man, Peploe
apparently ducked under the ropes
at the Rijksmuseum in Amsterdam
in order to get a closer view of the
Dutch painter's technique!

pictures in his studio. Cadell's parents were close friends of Arthur Melville. Unlike the situation perceived by the Glasgow Boys, however, in the Colourists' early years Scotland seemed not only a dreary place to study but also one which offered few subjects worth painting. Nevertheless, both Peploe and Cadell were eventually to base themselves in Edinburgh, filtering Scottish subjects such as Western Isle landscapes and bourgeois Edinburgh sitting rooms through sensibilities honed in France.

Peploe was the eldest of the Colourists and it was he, closely followed by his friend Fergusson, who first shook off the cobwebs of Scotland and immersed himself in the stimulating intellectual life of Paris and in the exciting milieu of Mediterranean France. As early as 1894 Peploe was studying at the famous Académie Julien in Paris, spending some time under the by then elderly academic master Bouguereau. Not that the highly esteemed Bouguereau impressed Peploe much: '. . . damned old fool' he noted down with characteristic Scots bluntness! In 1895 Peploe visited the Rijksmuseum in Amsterdam where he was captivated by the work of Frans Hals, and it is a combination of the influence of Hals and that of the equally 'painterly' Manet which informs his earliest mature work.

There is an attractive, fluid quality about these early pictures by Peploe. In now well-known works such as *The Black Bottle* (NGS) the brushwork displays an astonishingly confident bravura for an artist still only in his twenties; and Peploe's virtuoso handling of paint is even more enjoyable in a series of energetic portraits that he painted in the late 1890s and during the first decade of the new century. *Old Tom Morris* (GMAG) is clearly a homage to the bibulous 'topers' of Dutch seventeenth-century art. *A Girl in White: Peggy Macrae* (Plate 119) is a splendid example of painterly dash and commitment. In 1905 Peploe moved into the Edinburgh house the great Henry Raeburn had vacated some eighty years earlier, so a large number of these pictures were painted in a studio built by Scotland's very greatest portrait painter.

During these years Peploe spent regular painting holidays both in Scotland and Brittany with Fergusson, and in the work of both artists a steady conversion to the kind of colourful, expressive painting practised by Matisse and his fellow Fauves can easily be discerned. Peploe's small-scale French beach scenes are particularly seductive: fresh air and atmospheric sparkle seem to emanate from them and they are entirely devoid of the stodgy quality which is sometimes apparent in Fauvist pictures. The fluidity of pictures like Peploe's spectacular little *Boats at Royan* (Plate 120) is breathtaking and feels true to life, while similar scenes he painted when staying in the village of Comrie in Perthshire, though less immediately appealing, are important because the Scottish landscape was here being viewed through the eyes of a 'modern' artist for the very first time.

Peploe and his wife finally moved to Paris in 1910 with the encouragement of Fergusson, who had been living there since 1907. These were the heady years of the visits by Diaghilev and his sensational Ballets Russes, and of intellectual American expatriates making the most of the city they saw as the Mecca of European culture. The Peploes were part of an especially exotic, bohemian clique which included Fergusson, his American girlfriend Anne Estelle Rice, the writers John Middleton Murry and Katherine Mansfield, the Glasgow artists Jessie King and E. A. Taylor, and the

120 Samuel John Peploe
Boats at Royan 1910
Oil on board 27 × 34.9
National Galleries of Scotland
The Scottish Colourists who went to France in the early years of the twentieth century were overwhelmed by the brilliant colour and spirited technique of Matisse and his fellow Fauves. The stylistic alliance between the Scottish and French avant-gardes was never closer than during this period.

American sculptor Jo Davidson. At this time Van Gogh was the chief influence on a series of small Parisian pictures by Peploe which are imbued with the carefree spirit of this pre-First World War Parisian milieu.

Fergusson's work from these years, even when it is less immediately appealing than Peploe's, contains a strong sense of an artist constantly rethinking his method of painting. It is this dynamic intellectual struggle which lends excitement to Fergusson's early French pictures and identifies him far more closely than Peploe with the great French avant-garde adventure. The most controversial Paris-based artists of this period – Picasso, Othon Friesz, Albert Marquet – were all either friends or acquaintances, and, within a year or two, Fergusson himself was exhibiting at Paris's most important showcase for up-and-coming artists, the Salon d'Automne. It was here that the Fauves he admired had made their debut in 1905; in 1909 Fergusson was made a *sociétaire*.

In common with Peploe, Fergusson's initial guiding lights had been the Fauves and Van Gogh, but around 1910 he began painting his repertoire Parisian subjects in a dramatically simplified fashion, outlining the forms in much the same way as the French artist Albert Marquet was doing. This manner gives an air of what might be described as chic monumentality to his pictures. *The Blue Beads*, a

121 JOHN DUNCAN FERGUSSON
The Blue Hat, Closerie des Lilas
1909 Oil on canvas 76.2 × 76.2
City Art Centre, Edinburgh
No Scottish Colourist immersed himself in Parisian avant-garde artistic currents as thoroughly as J. D. Fergusson. The artist was, however, later to abandon the rich colour and dense impasto which characterize this striking portrait in favour of a more linear approach. The sitter for *The Blue Hat* was the wife of the American sculptor Jo Davidson.

portrait of Anne Estelle Rice, is an essay in drastic simplification which seems designed to produce a provocative 'ugly' image; if *The Blue Hat, Closerie des Lilas* (Plate 121) is marginally less shocking it is only because of the lady's fashionable accoutrements.

Two years later Fergusson painted a far more radical picture than either of these. *Rhythm* (Plate 122) is a stylized, volumetrical rendering of the nude female form which demonstrates that, at this stage of his career, Fergusson was in the thick of the theorizing which lay behind movements such as Cubism and its offshoot Vorticism. If any Scottish painter has been at or near the vanguard of European art at any time in the last hundred years, it was Fergusson in 1911.

The concept of 'rhythm' was very much in vogue in 1911. Under the editorship of John Middleton Murry, Fergusson became art editor of a magazine called *Rhythm*. Inspired by the philosophy of the Frenchman Henri Bergson, Murry had become enamoured of the

122 JOHN DUNCAN FERGUSSON
Rhythm 1911
Oil on canvas 160.6 × 114.3
University of Stirling
From around 1910 the female nude
became Fergusson's constant artistic
preoccupation. Under the influence
of Cubism and other associated
avant-garde movements of the
period he gained the confidence to
manipulate form in quite drastic
ways. In his wife, the voluptuous
dancer Margaret Morris, the artist
found the perfect model.

idea that rhythm governs the progress of healthy existence, and that
art must in some way chime in with it. Dance and music, of course,
are the two creative activities to which rhythm is absolutely vital, and
thanks to his lifelong partnership with the dancer and choreographer
Margaret Morris, Fergusson was, especially during the early part of
his career, in close touch with the world of avant-garde dance. A
vast canvas entitled *Les Eus* (Private Collection), painted around this
time, celebrates the physicality of dance and marks the beginning of
a series of works extolling youthful – usually female – vigour which
punctuate the artist's mature career.

   The First World War brought Peploe and Fergusson back to
Britain; Peploe returned to Edinburgh, while Fergusson set up house
near Charles Rennie and Margaret Mackintosh in Chelsea. During

123 JOHN DUNCAN FERGUSSON
Damaged Destroyer 1918
Oil on canvas 73.6 × 76.2
Glasgow Museums and Art
    Galleries
In general, Scottish artists produced
very few significant paintings as a
result of the experience of the First
World War. Fergusson's
memorable *Damaged Destroyer* – one
of a number of pictures by him of
the naval dockyards at
Portsmouth – is a rare and
powerful example.

these years in London Fergusson came close in a number of pictures of the naval dockyards at Portsmouth (Plate 123) to the drastically stylized paintings of First World War subjects made by Wyndham Lewis.

By contrast, there issued from Peploe's studio in the New Town of Edinburgh a series of still-lifes which, compared with his more spontaneous earlier work, now look somewhat tediously formula-bound. *Still-Life with Roses* (Plate 124) is a fine example of Peploe in this rather pedestrian mode; in an attempt to emulate Cézanne's analytical approach to the painting of still-life, Peploe constructs jigsaws of interlocking tonal planes in which the priority given to the structure of the subject saps any life it may contain. More pleasing than these are a number of paintings of the coastline of the magical little island best known because of its association with St Columba and the early Christian period of Scottish history, Iona. The island became a summer retreat for Cadell, Peploe and a host of lesser talents in the 1920s. In these Peploe admirably captures the distinctive luminous quality of light which is a special feature of Iona.

In common with his close friend Peploe, F. C. B. Cadell came from a comfortable, middle-class Edinburgh background. But, whereas it would be difficult to deduce Peploe's family background or social milieu from his paintings, Cadell's work, especially the series of smart ladies posed in Edinburgh drawing rooms, evokes the respectable Edinburgh forever associated with Muriel Spark's fictional heroine Jean Brodie. Cadell's lifestyle – the perfectly turned out bachelor living with his manservant in one of the most fashionable squares of Edinburgh's New Town – dovetails with this impression. The wit of fun-loving 'Bunty' Cadell, as he was known to his friends, was legendary, and a period feeling of *joie de vivre* is one of the most enjoyable aspects of his painting.

Unconventional for an artist though Cadell's personality and circumstances were, however, to infer from them that there is anything superficial about his art would be a mistake. Cadell the painter knew precisely what he was doing in artistic terms, and at his best his pictures are as rewarding as those of any of his fellow Colourists.

It was Glasgow Boy Arthur Melville, a close friend of Cadell's parents, who suggested that their clearly talented son should study in Paris; so it was thanks to Melville that Cadell found himself in the 1890s in various Paris *ateliers*, including that most frequented by young, foreign artists, Julien's. Like the other Colourists at that time Cadell witnessed at first hand the radical twists and turns of Post-Impressionism. A number of exuberant, sketchy small oils painted during a visit to Venice in 1910 show that by his late twenties Cadell had adopted the bright palette of the Fauves and had achieved a natural-looking competence in the free manner they favoured. Even Venice – that most painted of cities – has rarely been painted with such panache.

In subsequent pictures painted back home in Scotland, however, Cadell drained all the bright colours from his pictures and began to play on a variety of tinted whites which not only describe the marble fireplaces, voile curtains, silverware and mirrors of the Edinburgh drawing rooms he chose as subjects, but also seem to represent the light which illuminated them. Paintings such as *Reflections* (Plate 125) shimmer with light, and the summary treatment Cadell accords a glove, a vase or a china cup intensifies the impression that light is dissolving form. This swift technique, similar to that used by Peploe

124 SAMUEL JOHN PEPLOE
Still-Life with Roses   c. 1924
Oil on canvas 50.8 × 40.6
Aberdeen Art Gallery and
   Museums
Still-life was a favourite subject of the Scottish Colourists and, during the 1920s, Peploe produced an extensive and monumental series. In these brightly coloured pictures the artist explores the geometric relationship between the various forms in his compositions. Unfortunately, the fluid application of paint which is such an attractive feature of Peploe's earlier work is almost entirely absent from them.

Right   125 FRANCIS CAMPBELL
   BOILEAU CADELL
Reflections   Date uncertain
Oil on canvas 116.8 × 101.6
Glasgow Museums and Art
   Galleries
Of the four Scottish Colourists, only Cadell and Hunter remained loyal to the painterly style they had evolved under French influence. The panache with which Cadell describes light suffusing bourgeois interiors is one of the most enjoyable features of his painting.

eminent Glasgow tourist destination, Loch Lomond (Plate 128), the shape of each major element in the composition is indicated with a minimum number of brushstrokes; the colour is bright and luminous. Scotland has never looked more French than in Hunter's last pictures. Hunter died prematurely in 1931; fittingly, his final years had been

127 GEORGE LESLIE HUNTER
Still-Life with Anemones and Fruit
c. 1920–5 Oil on board 40.5 × 35.2
National Galleries of Scotland
Hunter's light touch and economic brushwork are well displayed in this delightful still-life. In spite of the fact that the quality of the artist's production is less even than that of his fellow Colourists, occasionally – as in this picture – a touch of genius can be detected. Hunter is undoubtedly the most exciting of the Scottish Colourists.

spent at St Paul de Vence in the South of France, not far from the home of his hero Matisse.

By the Second World War Fergusson was the only surviving Colourist. Having spent most of his life in France he returned to Glasgow before the outbreak of war, and it was here, in the 1950s, that he assumed the mantle of grandfather of modern art in Scotland. Both he and his wife, Margaret Morris, provided a vital source of inspiration for an entire generation of post-war Scottish artists.

In spite of the impression of bohemian poverty cultivated by Hunter, the Scottish Colourists as a group were immensely successful, exhibiting together during the 1920s to considerable acclaim in both London and Paris. No small part of this success was due to enthusiastic promotion by Alexander Reid and, over a much longer period, by Scotland's oldest commercial gallery, Aitken Dott (now The Scottish Gallery). As early as 1903 Aitken Dott had mounted a show of Colourist paintings.

128 GEORGE LESLIE HUNTER
Reflections, Balloch 1929–30
Oil on canvas 63.5 × 76.2
National Galleries of Scotland
Although in their early years most
of the Scottish Colourists had fled
to France to escape from what they
saw as the greyness of Scotland,
this did not prevent an artist like
Hunter eventually capitalizing on
the range of vivid colour which is
in fact present in the Scottish
landscape. There is a *joie de vivre*
about this and other pictures from
Hunter's Loch Lomond series
which make them some of his most
satisfying.

Considering the quality of their work and the high auction prices
that Colourist paintings have achieved over the past twenty years, it
is perhaps surprising that Peploe, Fergusson, Cadell and Hunter are
not as widely known south of the Border as their near contemporary,
the English artist Walter Sickert. Within Scotland, however, they
remain highly esteemed: in 1992 a gallery dedicated solely to Fergusson was opened in Perth.

One reason for their relatively low profiles elsewhere in Britain
could well be that their work is simply too French for English taste.
The French artist Dunoyer de Segonzac once made an amusing and
significant comment to the Colourists' friend and biographer, the art
dealer T. J. Honeyman: 'You are a strange people, you English.
Hunter is one of your great painters and nobody knows anything
about him.'

CHAPTER SIX

Contemporary TRENDS

129 STANLEY CURSITER
The Sensation of Crossing the Street, West End, Edinburgh 1913
Oil on canvas 50 × 60
Private Collection
Although Scottish artists scarcely signed up *en masse* to the Post-Impressionist avant-garde, the impact of movements such as Cubism and Futurism was felt at a surprisingly early date in Scotland. In 1913 Stanley Cursiter mounted an exhibition of Post-Impressionist painting at the Society of Scottish Artists in Edinburgh. This picture was the artist's own response to the work of the Italian Futurist Severini, which he included in it.

In his treatise *Aesthetics in Scotland*, written in 1950, the poet Hugh MacDiarmid, chief instigator of Scotland's twentieth-century literary 'Renascence', argues passionately for an indigenous contemporary culture which might be achieved by combining traditional values and the ideas which lay behind international modernism. MacDiarmid, who had in effect achieved such a marriage in his own poetry, believed that the visual arts in Scotland possessed similar potential.

The LEGACY OF *Cubism*

By coincidence, it had been the Colourist J. D. Fergusson's dream of incorporating the rhythmic linear quality characteristic of ancient Celtic art into Post-Impressionist painting that had influenced Mac-Diarmid's thesis. Fergusson, however, never really succeeded in fulfilling the ambition MacDiarmid formulated. First and foremost he was his own man. He was never to suppress the subject in an attempt to manufacture an autonomous pictorial reality as those firebrands of Cubism, Braque and Picasso, maintained was the true course for the modern artist; the pictures of Portsmouth Docks he painted during the First World War (Plate 123), for example, and the many later female nudes, with their stylized, curvaceous forms, are inspired by Cubism rather than bona-fide Cubist works.

The Colourist aesthetic was perhaps too firmly anchored in late nineteenth-century French art for the members of the group to embrace our own century's fledgling avant-garde. The Orkney-born artist, Stanley Cursiter (1887–1976), on the other hand, suffered from no such inhibitions.

In the years prior to the First World War Cursiter made what is, in the context of British art, a precocious attempt to emulate the

radical variety of Cubism developed by the group of Italian artists known as the Futurists. In 1913 the artist included Futurist paintings in an exhibition of Post-Impressionist art he staged at the Society of Scottish Artists, and in his own picture, *The Sensation of Crossing the Street, West End, Edinburgh* (Plate 129), the values of Futurism are overwhelmingly apparent. In this work Cursiter has attempted to create a painterly equivalent to movement in a manner remarkably similar to that developed by artists such as Boccioni and Severini.

Unfortunately perhaps, in view of this courageously experimental approach, Cursiter was subsequently seduced by the market for society portraiture and topographical landscape. Today, he is best remembered as a progressive and popular director of the National Gallery of Scotland and for his authorship of one of the most lucid histories of Scottish art.

In 1908 the art school which had succeeded the Trustees' Academy in the 1860s, the school run by the Royal Scottish Academy itself, moved from its premises on Princes Street to the specially designed building on the edge of Edinburgh's Old Town which remains the

130 WILLIAM CROZIER
Edinburgh from Salisbury Crags 1927
Oil on canvas 71.1 × 91.5
National Galleries of Scotland
The only Scottish artist who really appeared qualified by talent and temperament to make an original personal contribution to Cubism was the short-lived William Crozier. In this cityscape Crozier cleverly exploits the Scottish capital's potential for Cubist analysis.

Scottish capital's college of art. The move, however, made very little difference to the conservative, thoroughly Victorian attitude to the training of artists which had prevailed at the Academy. (Even as late as the 1920s apparently, Cézanne – by that time generally accepted as the modern master of 'classicism' he himself had aspired to be – was considered a subversive influence by members of the college staff!)

Students at the new Edinburgh College of Art, however, benefited from the rather generous system of travelling scholarships which had grown up over the years, and it was this that enabled many of them to immerse themselves in the more progressive atmosphere to be found on the Continent. As a result, a number of Scottish artists, if not leaders of European avant-garde painting in the 1920s and 1930s, at least became very closely allied to those who were.

One of the most talented of the early students at Edinburgh's new college was William Crozier (1897–1930) who, like several of his colleagues, made haste to Paris upon graduating and there searched out the atelier of one of the most respected exponents of Cubism, the so-called 'academician' of the movement, André Lhote. In Crozier's *Edinburgh from Salisbury Crags* (Plate 130) the Cubist approach to the treatment of townscape ultimately derived from Cézanne is rendered with the restrained, earthy palette favoured by Lhote in his own depictions of French hilltowns. Sadly, Crozier was not to be allowed time to develop the ambition obvious in this picture; a sufferer from haemophilia, the artist bled to death at the tragically young age of thirty-three.

William Johnstone AND ABSTRACTION

Conceivably, Crozier might have followed a similar path to his exact contemporary, William Johnstone (1897–1981). Like Crozier, Johnstone studied in Paris under Lhote and, again like Crozier, his hitherto provincial notions about painting were dramatically cosmopolitanized by the experience.

Through his cousin, the composer Francis George Scott, Johnstone got to know Hugh MacDiarmid and is, therefore, a rare example of an artist who was directly influenced by the man who is nowadays regarded as the driving force behind Scotland's individualistic modern culture. In Johnstone's mature work sentimentality, the legacy of an artistic tradition which for over a century had derived inspiration from Scotland's romantic, heroic past and her quaint, rural lifestyle, is entirely absent. Like Fergusson, he was to free himself from the conventions of his native tradition by turning to Scotland's Celtic heritage.

In Johnstone's case, however, America also played a strong part

131 WILLIAM JOHNSTONE
Ode to the North Wind 1928–30
Oil on canvas 71.1 × 91.4
Dundee Art Galleries and
  Museums
No twentieth-century Scottish artist
has taken on board international
avant-garde developments with as
much enthusiasm as William
Johnstone. In this work can be
detected an interest in creating
biomorphic – often sexually
inspired – forms which was
common during this period among
Surrealist artists such as Max Ernst.
Even with the perspective of more
than half a century Johnstone's
daring still seems extraordinary.

in internationalizing his outlook and emancipating him from his background. In 1927 he married an American sculptress and emigrated to California, although he was forced to return two years later owing to the lack of sufficiently supportive patrons.

By this time, however, Johnstone had become familiar with the most up-to-date developments in American art which, during this period, was increasingly building upon the advances made by European artists. The paintings Johnstone executed after his return are some of the most sophisticatedly modern produced by any Scottish artist up until this time. *A Point in Time* and *Ode to the North Wind* (Plate 131), works which date from the late 1920s, were inspired by the pictures being made at about the same time by continental Surrealists such as Max Ernst, and bear similarities to those of the Americans Arthur Dove and Georgia O'Keeffe. From O'Keeffe's work in particular, Johnstone learnt how forms derived from nature could be made to evoke a dream-like atmosphere which seems to mirror the subconscious.

When Johnstone exhibited these works, however, they were met with blank incomprehension and not a little derision. Consequently – in spite of the admiration for them expressed by Henry Moore – the artist virtually withdrew from the public stage of exhibitions and galleries for the next thirty years, devoting himself instead to teaching. In 1939 he was unexpectedly appointed principal of Camberwell School of Arts and Crafts and then, in 1947, to one of the most senior posts in British art education, that of principal of London's Central School of Arts and Crafts. As an art educationalist Johnstone

132 WILLIAM JOHNSTONE
Lithograph accompanying poem, 'of william johnstone's exhibition', by Hugh MacDiarmid 1977
55.9 × 38.1
Printmakers' Workshop, Edinburgh

The extremes to which William Johnstone was willing to push abstraction – especially in his later years – can be appreciated in this intriguing print. Coupled as it is with a poem by a writer to whom Scotland's sense of historical identity was of prime importance, the work's uncompromising modernism perhaps strikes an ironic note. A determination to escape the shackles of Scotland's artistic traditions has motivated a whole range of modern Scottish artists; Johnstone was probably the most aggressive of them.

turned out to be something of a visionary, his progressive approach being reflected in the appointments he made while at the Central: Victor Pasmore and the Scots, Alan Davie and Eduardo Paolozzi – all artists who were to make international reputations for themselves in the 1950s and 1960s were all employed by Johnstone.

By 1960, however, Johnstone himself was finding the bureaucratic demands which had always stifled his own activity as a painter too onerous. In that year, having resigned his post at the Central, he returned to Scotland in order to devote himself exclusively to his own painting and, over the next two decades, produced a remarkable body of late work which, in retrospect, seems a logical conclusion of his preoccupations over the previous half-century.

Much of this wholly abstract work shows close affinities to the American Abstract Expressionist painting which dominated the international art scene from the early 1950s until the advent of Pop Art in the 1960s; the similarities between Johnstone's painting and that of the most famous of the Abstract Expressionist painters, Jackson Pollock, are too marked to ignore. Yet, Johnstone's late, abstract paintings are pervaded by a very Scottish sense of place (due in part to the artist's reversion to the earthy palette of his youth), and this

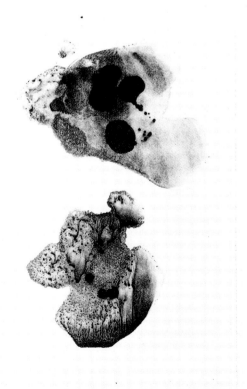

"Any commonplace acceptance of the visible world was due, not to the importunacy of mere occupations, but to sheer grossness of perception, men, women, and children going to the grave in groups, unaware, unawakened."

Llewelyn Powys.

So, now, instead of a world, a Scotland,
Which always and in all its parts remains the same,
Instead of a process of development,
Instead of the idea of transforming
All that is important into the imperceptible,
Which is so imperceptible that it cannot be seen,
We will live like eagles
And grow new forests of humanity:
Now before our eyes arises a Scotland, a world,
Of sudden, wonderful, and mysterious transformations,
Each of which means more than the whole process
Of today and its natural development
(Even as, by becoming collective, poetry in the era of communism,
Will not become less individual but more so,
The world of ideas behind language expanding for poetry
In the same way as it did in the Elizabethan era.)
Such a world, it is true, cannot be "comprehended".
But such a world need not be comprehended.
In such a world comprehension is superfluous.
Comprehension is necessary for the natural world
From man, who came in natural wise into it;
But in a world of wonderful transformations
In an eternally unnatural world,
Comprehension is only a meagre and wretched gift
From the pauper world of limitation.

sets them apart from the work being produced by the New York-based group of painters at the same time. There are, nevertheless, a great number of very free ink drawings and a fine set of lithographs commissioned in 1977 to accompany a suite of poems by MacDiarmid (Plate 132) which are as advanced in their confidence and impulsiveness as anything by artists to whom the label Abstract Expressionist is usually unequivocally applied.

In an age, however, where originality has become a touchstone of an artist's worth, the jury still appears to be out in the case of William Johnstone; his reputation has never scaled the heights achieved by a comparable English painter like Ivon Hitchens, and it is likely that the diffuseness of his work when viewed as an entity – the way it appears to have been tugged hither and thither by the competing charms of Cubism, Surrealism and Abstraction – will continue to consign him to secondary status. Nevertheless, if any twentieth-century Scottish painter has come close to fulfilling MacDiarmid's vision it must be Johnstone. In his poem 'The War with England' MacDiarmid wrote:

> When was anything born in Scotland last,
> Risks taken and triumphs won?

William Johnstone was certainly not afraid of taking risks and, in the process, he won many a triumph.

William Gillies: A NATURAL *talent*

In view of the character of both the man and his work, it comes as something of a surprise to find that William Gillies (1898–1973) was only a year younger than Crozier and Johnstone. In almost every respect he is the antithesis of the latter painter.

Gillies was born in the East Lothian market town of Haddington. He enjoyed a glittering secondary school career at Knox Academy, was the first in his diploma class at Edinburgh College of Art and (in preference to Johnstone) was awarded one of the much sought after travelling scholarships. At the age of thirty-four he was voted a member of the prestigious Society of Eight whose numbers had included Guthrie, Lavery, Peploe and Cadell. Invited to join the college staff soon after graduating, Gillies was eventually to become head of painting there in 1946 and college principal in 1960. He was elected a Royal Scottish Academician in 1947 and President of the Royal Scottish Society of Painters in Watercolour in 1963.

In spite of this illustrious track record, however, Gillies was famed for his unassuming nature. He lived with his mother until her death at the age of one hundred only ten years before his own, and it was not until the 1950s that electricity was installed in their simple cottage

133 WILLIAM GEORGE GILLIES
Skye Hills from near Morar c. 1931
Watercolour and gouache on board
37.6 × 55.8
National Galleries of Scotland
In his masterful watercolours Gillies
succeeded in breathing new life
into the tradition of Scottish
landscape painting; apart from the
Colourists, surprisingly few early
twentieth-century Scottish artists
had taken advantage of what might
be considered Scotland's greatest
attraction from the artist's point of
view. The chief merit of Gillies'
watercolours is the freshness which
results from the artist's spontaneous
response to the visual stimulus.

in the Midlothian village of Temple. Home-made wine and a passion for motor bikes seem to have been his only vices. Vanity certainly was not. Asked how he thought history might judge him, he apparently replied, 'Och, a very good minor Scottish painter'! Like both Crozier and Johnstone, Gillies spent time in André Lhote's Paris *atelier*, but for most of his life he never felt the urge to travel in search of subjects. Venice, he commented, 'looked like Princes Street on a wet day'. Until his dying day he believed he had never produced a decent picture away from Scotland.

Before his early death Crozier had shared a studio with William MacTaggart, grandson of the famous earlier artist, and it was MacTaggart's future wife, the Norwegian journalist Fanny Aavatsmark, who was directly responsible for introducing Gillies to the artist who was to have such a profound effect on his work. In 1931 Aavatsmark mounted an historic exhibition of the paintings of her compatriot artist, the great Norwegian Expressionist Edvard Munch, at the Society of Scottish Artists.

Gillies was overwhelmed by the eerie passion of Munch's landscapes and immediately set about trying to emulate the Norwegian's freedom of handling paint and his emotional response to nature. In the Scot's work the result is far less anguished but equally memorable.

Several of Gillies' watercolours from this period are masterpieces of the medium, informed as they are by the artist's intensely lyrical nature. Works such as *Skye Hills from near Morar* (Plate 133) and *In Ardnamurchan* are richly atmospheric and are distinguished by Gillies'

134 JOHN MAXWELL
View from a Tent 1933
Oil on canvas 76.2 × 91.5
National Galleries of Scotland
Although – like many of his generation – John Maxwell had flirted with Cubism during his early years, he soon abandoned the experiment and opted for a subdued Expressionism more appropriate to the Scottish landscape. In this hugely enjoyable picture there is no hint of the self-consciously primitive approach to picture-making which characterizes so much of the artist's later painting.

ability to maintain a respect for a scene's topography while freely indulging his natural propensity for expressive drawing.

Both these watercolours were produced during regular summer camping trips to the Highlands on which Gillies was frequently accompanied by John Maxwell (1905–62). The younger artist, it seems, preferred to work quietly from within their tent while the prolific Gillies dashed off a dozen or so views before breakfast. Although Maxwell studied with Fernand Léger in Paris (an even better-known modern master than Lhote), his work was never to assume the distinctive look which makes any work by Gillies unmistakable. In *View from a Tent* (Plate 134), however, he undoubtedly produced a very important picture; rarely has an Expressionist technique been applied to a Scottish scene so successfully.

Following an exhibition of the quirky work of the Swiss artist Paul Klee at the Society of Scottish Artists in 1932 Gillies flirted with abstraction, but he was, in truth, too intrigued by the particularities of Scotland's landscape to be diverted long from recording it with respect. His friend, the writer George Scott-Moncrieff, got it about right when he wrote of the artist: 'In his work abstraction retains, and therefore explains, the forms of reality.'

135 WILLIAM GEORGE GILLIES
Still-Life, Blue and Brown
Date uncertain Oil on canvas
96.5 × 45.7
Glasgow Museums and Art
  Galleries
A decorative impulse, ultimately
borrowed from Matisse, informs
the still-life painting of several
Edinburgh-based artists who
achieved their mature styles after
the Second World War. Most of
Gillies' still-lifes in this vein depend
for their success upon clever and
deliberately calculated harmonies
and dissonances of colour: primary
against tertiary, brilliant against
subdued. But Gillies also enjoyed
the rough textures which can be
achieved with oil paint and it is
this which gives his still-lifes their
distinctive character.

During the 1950s Gillies painted an extended series of still-lifes
and it is chiefly upon these that his formidable reputation within
Scotland still rests (Plate 135). Many of them were produced as show-
stoppers for the annual summer exhibition of the Royal Scottish
Academy in which Gillies was for many years the brightest star.
They are, in fact, painted in a semi-abstract manner, or at least in a
way which depends for its impact on the abstract qualities the artist
perceived in the compositions he took such pains to arrange. Several
of the more drastically simplified of them are strongly reminiscent of
still-lifes by Braque, a similarity of which Gillies was fully aware.
When asked what he thought of one of his own still-lifes after seeing
it hanging alongside a number of major pictures by Braque at the
1956 Edinburgh Festival exhibition of the French artist's work, Gillies
replied characteristically: 'It looks awful thin.'

Gillies' greatest achievement, however, grew out of his original
approach to the Scottish landscape. He was equally at home in oils
and watercolour, yet it is in the latter medium that one senses most
forcefully the authenticity of the atmosphere of the Lowland scenes
he mostly chose to paint.

This is especially true of the pictures of Fife fishing villages he

made in the forties where a combination of pen and ink with watercolour manages to give a great deal of information without appearing at all pedantic. Some of Gillies' most satisfying works depict the most prosaic of subjects; the austere flanks of the Moorfoot Hills near his home, for instance (Plate 136), transformed by way of their skein of stone dykes and stunted trees into a perfectly balanced, spare geometry. In literally hundreds of views of his home-village of Temple, the clever pictorial manipulation of commonplace features like broken fences and garden huts elevates this ordinary Lowland hamlet into the realm of the poetic idyll (Plate 137).

The EDINBURGH *School*

Along with their equally talented contemporary Anne Redpath (1895–1965), Gillies, Maxwell and MacTaggart came to be known during the post-Second World War period as the Edinburgh School. Considering their distinct individual artistic personalities the label must always have been something of a misnomer and, moreover, there was an ironic ring to it since commentators on modern art had long since abandoned talking about artists in terms of 'schools'. There is, however, some legitimacy in grouping these artists together apart from the fact that all four of them made their careers in the east of Scotland. In their work there is a general inclination to emphasize the 'painterly' quality of a picture at the expense of the subject, a way of painting inherited more or less directly from the Scottish Colourists.

Nowhere is this more clearly demonstrated than in the work of Anne Redpath. Like most of her generation, Redpath's admiration was cast firmly in the direction of French art. After training at Edinburgh College of Art during the First World War years, she and

138 ANNE REDPATH
The Indian Rug *c.* 1942
Oil on plywood 73.9 × 96.1
National Galleries of Scotland
Anne Redpath took pains with the arrangement of her still-life subjects in order to maximize the decorative impact of her final picture. To judge from the vibrant, singing colours Matisse was clearly at the back of the artist's mind while she was painting this picture, but the asymmetrical composition and variety of paint textures are very much her own.

her husband moved to France, returning to her Borders hometown of Hawick to raise her young family in 1934. Carefully selecting brilliantly coloured objects – painted furniture and patterned cloth – Redpath created during the late thirties and early forties a series of extremely opulent pictures which introduced something fresh and vibrant into Scottish art. *The Indian Rug* (Plate 138), with its echoes of Matisse and even of Cadell, is typical of these, depending as it does for its success on a busy decorative energy. Later, after moving to Edinburgh in 1949, Redpath travelled extensively in the Mediterranean, developing a thickly-painted, exuberant manner with which to record the exotic environments she encountered. In many of her paintings of places as diverse as Brittany and Corsica there is a charming sense of visual excitement which is only rarely found in the work of comparable twentieth-century English artists.

Unfortunately, by the 1960s, the daring which had been evident in the earlier work of the Edinburgh School painters had been replaced by a comfortable approach which is reflected in the repetitiveness of the pictures they produced. This was probably due indirectly to their success in dominating the art scene of the Scottish capital; apart from calling the tune in their capacities as senior members of staff at Edinburgh College of Art, they also controlled the main exhibiting bodies and were tirelessly promoted by Scotland's longest-established commercial art gallery, Aitken Dott. As a consequence of this extended hegemony and a healthy local market for their works, a penchant for 'pretty picture-making' for its own sake (especially among artists reared in the east of the country) crept into Scottish art, and sadly this has persisted, most noticeably in the work of artists of the older generation, until the present day.

Glasgow AND THE *'Two Roberts'*

Significantly, no such situation ever developed in the more diverse cultural milieu of Glasgow. Ever since the heyday of the Glasgow Boys and the Glasgow Style (see Chapter Five) Scotland's great working-class metropolis has always been viewed by artists as a more conducive place in which to develop their talents than middle-class orientated Edinburgh. Despite the city's steady economic decline and the concomitant substantial decrease in its population, especially since the last war, Glasgow has remained a thriving centre of intellectual exchange.

J. D. Fergusson's choice of Glasgow as a suitable place to settle upon his return to Scotland before the Second World War marked a turning point in the development of the city's self-image as a creative hub. Partly, the Colourist father figure's decision was based on the somewhat romantic notion that Glasgow's large immigrant

Highland population made it a suitable venue for the Celtic Revival he was still contemplating. But he must also have realized that the war would inject a fierce energy into a city which would undoubtedly be obliged to play a prominent role in the national industrial effort.

This certainly proved to be the case. A number of distinguished refugee artists, foremost among them the German-Jewish Josef Herman and the Pole Jankel Adler, ended up in Glasgow and there exerted, both directly and indirectly, a crucial influence on several younger Scottish artists upon whose work the experience of the war years was to make a lasting impact. Of these, Robert Colquhoun (1914–62) and Robert MacBryde (1913–66) – the 'Two Roberts' as they were nicknamed – are the most interesting.

Both Colquhoun and MacBryde were from working-class Ayrshire backgrounds but, although they spent their childhoods scarcely twenty miles apart, they were not to meet until they enrolled in Glasgow School of Art in 1933. From that moment, however, the two were inseparable and continued to live and work together for the next thirty years.

In most cases the relevance of an artist's personal life to his work is at best tangential; in that of Colquhoun, however, it is impossible to overestimate the importance of the fiercely introspective and mutually dependent homosexual relationship which developed with MacBryde. From the outset MacBryde tended to manage Colquhoun's career (often at the expense of his own) and, as the years wore on, even after the at one time brilliant reputation of the more widely acclaimed younger artist had dimmed, he became increasingly resentful about having (as he saw it) compromised his own talent for the sake of his partner.

Colquhoun's facility as a draughtsman – for many years legendary in Glasgow – earned for him the drawing prize at Glasgow School of Art and, after graduating, both he and MacBryde were awarded a further postgraduate year at the college. In 1937 the two spent several months at Hospitalfield House, the Victorian mansion near Arbroath still used as a summer school for postgraduate students from Scotland's art colleges.

It was while at Hospitalfield that Colquhoun and MacBryde came into close contact with the artist James Cowie (1886–1956) who was at that time the college outpost's warden and tutor. The encounter was important for both the younger artists. Cowie was a confident and assured draughtsman, as can be judged from the large number of figure drawings of schoolchildren he made during his twenty years' teaching at Bellshill Academy near Glasgow (Plate 139). This clear, firm drawing style, which bears a close resemblance to that of the English artist Wyndham Lewis, helped to strengthen the line in both

139 JAMES COWIE
Student with Plaster Cast
Date uncertain Black chalk on
    paper 50.5 × 36.8
National Galleries of Scotland
Although perhaps alien to the free painterly approach which has prevailed in most twentieth-century Scottish art, Cowie's controlled draughtsmanship was a determining influence upon two of the most talked about Scottish painters of the 1940s and 1950s, Robert Colquhoun and Robert MacBryde. Cowie's cool fastidious technique is well illustrated in this fine study.

Colquhoun's and MacBryde's drawing. The portraits they made of one another while on a travelling scholarship to the Continent in 1939 (Plates 140 and 141) bear witness to Cowie's quality as a teacher.

Having been obliged to cut short the trip during which these fine drawings were made owing to the imminent outbreak of war, both Colquhoun and MacBryde anticipated the imposed hiatus in their careers which was to be the fate of so many other British artists of the period. Luckily, they were both to escape (MacBryde was deemed medically unfit for service and Colquhoun was invalided out of the army after only a year) and subsequently spent the remainder of the war years as linchpins of the bohemian fraternity which grew up in the Soho district of London. The 'Two Roberts' Notting Hill flat became one of the more famous rendezvous for the capital's literati; Dylan Thomas was a regular visitor.

Colquhoun and MacBryde's introduction to wartime London had been facilitated by the well-known publisher and art collector Peter Watson, and it was Watson who also introduced his protégés to the leading lights of what became known as the Neo-Romantic movement, the artists John Minton, Lucian Freud and John Craxton. Looking back somewhat nostalgically to the peaceful life of eight-

Left 140 ROBERT COLQUHOUN
Robert MacBryde 1939
Pen and sepia on paper 28.5 × 22.5
National Galleries of Scotland

Above 141 ROBERT MACBRYDE
Robert Colquhoun 1939
Black chalk on paper 27.3 × 15.7
National Galleries of Scotland
The bohemian lifestyle of the 'Two Roberts' and their fiercely inter-dependent personal relationship set a standard of behaviour for Scottish artists which, even thirty years after their deaths, aspiring young Scottish artists seek to emulate. In 1992 a play about these two painters, *Colquhoun and MacBryde*, by the Glaswegian artist and writer John Byrne, breathed new life into their legend.

eenth-century rural England as interpreted by the artist Samuel Palmer, these artists had rapidly developed an introspective style of painting which, both in its subject matter and style seemed to shun the horrors of war. In 1942 Colquhoun exhibited several landscapes with a Neo-Romantic flavour alongside pictures by Johnstone and Gillies at the Lefevre Gallery and it was this critically acclaimed début which led to his first one-man show of figure paintings at the same gallery the following year.

It was, however, the arrival in London from Glasgow of Jankel Adler in 1943 which really fired Colquhoun to do something original. Before the war Adler had lived both in Germany, where he had taught the Swiss artist Paul Klee, and in Paris, where he had become familiar with the recent work of Picasso. Within a year Colquhoun had completely absorbed these influences transmitted to him by Adler and soon embarked upon a moving series of expressive paintings depicting grieving spinsters and deformed beggars.

Woman with Leaping Cat (Plate 142) is one of Colquhoun's most

142 ROBERT COLQUHOUN
Woman with Leaping Cat 1945
Oil on canvas 76.2 × 61
Tate Gallery, London
The angular distortions imposed upon the figure by Colquhoun and the mysterious hieratic quality which is particularly striking in this picture were both new to British art in the 1940s. The colour range favoured by the artist during this period, however, is similar to that employed by English Neo-Romantic artists such as John Minton and John Craxton.

memorably monumental pictures of this period in spite of its relatively small scale. The combination of the rich amber and wine colouring and the subject's gloomy expression creates an elegiac mood which is violently shattered by the diagonal thrust across the composition of the rapacious cat. In this and similar pictures, the artist handles his medium with great dexterity, setting off the smoothly painted backgrounds against the striated faces of his tragic victims.

Even as early as this in his career, Colquhoun had dispensed with the model; yet, no matter how schematic the invented forms he chose to impose upon his figures, his subjects continued to be drawn from personal experience. *The Whistle Seller* (Edinburgh City Art Centre), for example, was based upon a one-legged peddler he used to encounter in Oxford Street.

With this kind of work it is clear that Colquhoun touched a nerve in post-war Britain, perhaps because there is something intensely humanistic lurking behind the pessimism inherent in the subjects he chose to paint. In a review of Colquhoun's work in *The Listener*, Wyndham Lewis alluded to this when he wrote: 'There is a grave dug behind all his canvases of a certain kind.' In Colquhoun's pictures of the forties the compassion which all those who had experienced the trauma of the war needed is conveyed in a way which appears modern and optimistic.

Compared with that of his partner, MacBryde's output during these years was undoubtedly inferior. The still-lifes upon which he was concentrating appear too flat and calculated as designs, and the overtly decorative pictures he produced are devoid of the psychological depth which make Colquhoun's similar works so powerful. Occasionally, however, as in his lithograph *Woman at a Table* (Plate 143), his natural sense of rhythm could unite a figure and a still-life to convincing and highly enjoyable effect.

Throughout the immediate post-war period Colquhoun was regularly hailed as the leading British artist of his day. The British Council toured exhibitions of his work through Europe and the United States and, in 1947, New York's prestigious Museum of Modern Art acquired his picture *Two Scotswomen*, the first picture by a British artist of his generation to enter the collection. His popularity, however, turned out to be short-lived. The renewed international interest in abstraction in the fifties made Colquhoun's figurative concerns seem old-fashioned, and the artist's own obsession with Picasso – largely resulting from his experience of the Tate Gallery's 1946 Picasso retrospective – merely served to undermine the authenticity of his own artistic personality.

In 1949 Duncan MacDonald, Colquhoun and MacBryde's keenly supportive dealer at the Lefevre Gallery, died and, in the following

143 ROBERT MACBRYDE
Woman at a Table 1946
Lithograph 381. × 30.48
Private Collection
In contrast to Colquhoun, who in general preferred the more mysterious atmosphere varying the texture of his paint evoked in his pictures, MacBryde enjoyed creating hard edges and a smooth finish. His figure compositions, nevertheless, possess a similar unworldly character.

Right 144 ROBERT COLQUHOUN
Figures in a Farmyard 1953
Oil on canvas 185.4 × 143.5
National Galleries of Scotland
In this, one of Colquhoun's most ambitious compositions, the artist was attempting a picture on the larger scale which eventually became the norm for artists during the 1960s. The anguish that Colquhoun manages to convey by dramatically distorting form did much to encourage the most admired English artist of recent times, Francis Bacon, who knew the 'Two Roberts' well.

145 ROBERT COLQUHOUN
Man with Goat 1962
Monotype 71.12 × 76.2
Private Collection
Both Colquhoun and MacBryde
discovered in print-making a
medium of expression which
particularly suited their artistic
temperaments. The post-war
tradition of print-making in
Scotland remains extremely
healthy, and few contemporary
Scottish painters of note do not
make prints alongside their
primary activity.

year, what turned out to be Colquhoun's final show in the gallery
signalled the end of his successful professional career; sales were poor
and the reviews scathing. By the early fifties both artists had descended
into an unproductive round of alcoholism and compulsive socializing.
In a retrospective of Colquhoun's work generously mounted at the
Whitechapel Art Gallery in 1958 by its then director, Brian Robertson,
only four of the pictures had been produced after 1951 and these
painted more or less to order for exhibitions organized by the Arts
Council and the Contemporary Art Society.

It is clear, however, from a picture such as *Figures in a Farmyard*
(Plate 144), that Colquhoun's ability to paint had not entirely left
him. This important picture painted for the 1953 Contemporary Art
Society exhibition, *Figures in Their Setting*, is a romantic view of a
tortured peasantry rooted in the earth like trees; the pig is a
masterpiece of bristly ferocity rendered in the rich colours and varied
textures the artist had favoured during the war years.

In 1962, Robert Colquhoun collapsed and died of a heart attack
while working on an exhibition of prints: these final sad images
(Plate 145) prove that his graphic abilities at least had survived.
MacBryde was to die in a car accident in Dublin some four years
later.

The meteoric careers of Colquhoun and MacBryde have over the
years acquired a legendary status among Scottish artists; but although
the myth has remained strong their contribution to modern art in
Britain has been underestimated. Francis Bacon once said that

Colquhoun had taught him everything he knew about painting, and certainly, in searching for the roots of the most recent figurative art in Britain, Colquhoun cannot be ignored.

Alan Davie and ABSTRACT EXPRESSIONISM

On the back cover of the catalogue for Robert Colquhoun's final exhibition at the Lefevre Gallery there was an advertisement for a forthcoming show by the American abstract sculptor, Alexander Calder. In retrospect it looks ominous: the ascendancy of American abstraction in the fifties eclipsed the very personal, European kind of art Colquhoun had so bravely evolved. In that same year, 1950, however, another young Scottish painter, Alan Davie (born 1920), showed a number of distinctive, abstract canvases at London's Gimpel Fils Gallery. Davie, who had come into contact with the work of the great exponents of Abstract Expressionism, Jackson Pollock, Mark Rothko and Robert Motherwell, in Peggy Guggenheim's famous collection in Venice, was the first British artist to take on board the revolutionary principles of the American movement. Born in Grangemouth, Davie entered Edinburgh College of Art in 1939 but was called up before he could take advantage of the travelling scholarship he was awarded. During military service he played the saxophone in a jazz group and, for a short time afterwards, actually succeeded in earning his living as a professional jazz musician. In 1948, however, he was able to take up his scholarship and it was during this trip that he made his way to Venice.

Davie had always intuitively felt that painting should aim to approximate to music and be totally free of narrative content and so, not surprisingly, the experience of seeing the American Abstract Expressionist pictures in Peggy Guggenheim's collection was very important for him: the American work confirmed him in his belief. Guggenheim herself purchased one of the pictures Davie had taken to Venice and this support also encouraged him to search for his own new pictorial language. Davie, however, has never considered himself an action painter even though for a time he followed Pollock's example of painting on the floor and dribbling pigment onto the canvas. In Davie's work composition and design – however loose – are always present.

In recent years Davie has become a devotee of Zen Buddhism, believing in the primacy of intuition over the intellect; yet even in the fifties his disconcertingly anthropomorphic pictures seem to reflect the unresolved struggle between the conscious and subconscious self. During this period he was teaching jewellery design at the Central School of Arts and Crafts in London under William Johnstone, to whose own work Davie's is not unrelated.

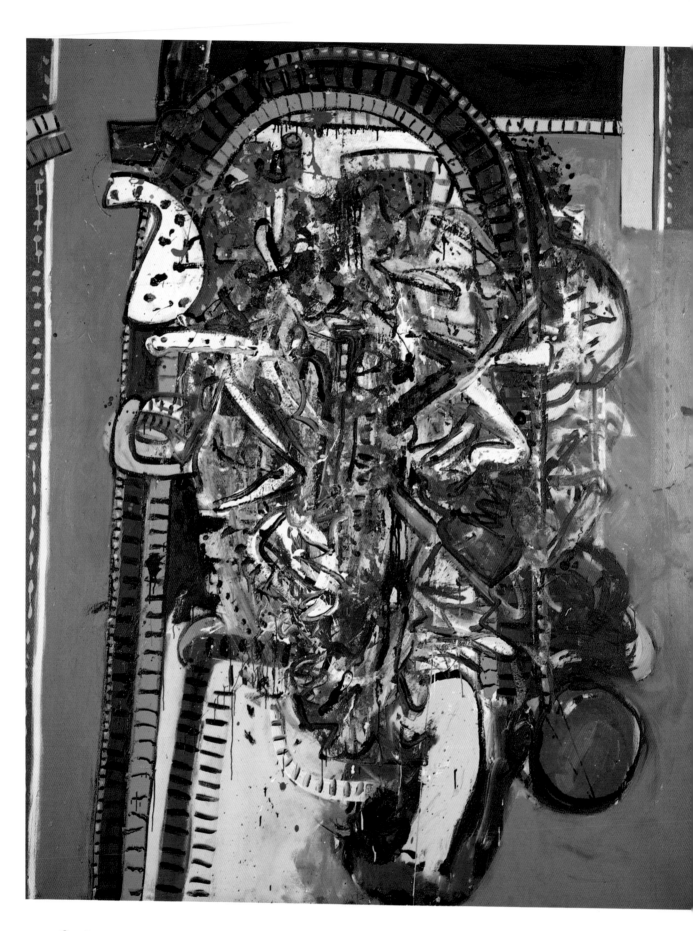

The Horse that has Visions of
Immortality, No. 2   1963
Oil on canvas 213.3 × 172.7
National Galleries of Scotland
The brilliant colour, busy textures
and cryptic title of this work are all
typical of Davie's most ebullient
creative period. His confidence was
bolstered by the extrovert nature of
post-war American Abstract
Expressionist painting.

Oh to be a Serpent that I might love
you longer   1962
Oil on two canvases 182.9 × 304.8
Gimpel Fils, London
A clever use of the 'painterly
accident' and spontaneous
calligraphy combine in this
memorable picture to create an
image which, while rich in
anthropomorphic allusions, makes
its immediate impact by virtue of
its strong abstract qualities.

In 1956 Davie's paintings were shown for the first time in New York, and it was there that his international success was stamped by the purchase of a work by the Museum of Modern Art. Although he met all the leading Abstract Expressionists based in New York, he now claims to have been more interested in American Indian art than in their work. Nevertheless, from this moment onwards his work became increasingly abstract, his handling of paint broader and his colour brighter. Davie, now at the hub of the international avant-garde, attempted, over the course of the next decade, to suppress his conscious self and to produce an art that '... just happens, like falling in love'. Paintings like *The Horse that has Visions of Immortality* (Plate 146) and *Oh to be a Serpent that I might love you longer* (Plate 147) might be viewed as visual equivalents of jazz improvisation.

In Davie's work of the seventies there is a very definite change of character. During this period he came to rely upon a highly personal vocabulary of mysterious hieroglyphics, fantastic creatures and ritualistic-looking emblems; illusory perspective and landscape details crept back into the pictures. Several critics have expressed dismay at the tighter drawing and seeming lack of spontaneity which is especially evident in his most recent pictures, yet Davie is unrepentant. For him the process of making art is more important than individual works. He insists that he is painting in order to find personal enlightenment and not to manufacture art for the market.

Joan Eardley: A TALENT *cut short*

In 1948, while Davie was looking at the works of Pollock in Peggy Guggenheim's palazzo, another recipient of a Scottish art college travelling scholarship was contemplating Giotto's frescos in Assisi.

Joan Eardley (1921–63) is one of the most enigmatic figures in modern Scottish art, although on the surface her work appears quite straightforward. Eardley studied at the Glasgow School of Art some years after Colquhoun and MacBryde, and, like Colquhoun, won prizes for her draughtsmanship. After a short hiatus in her career due to the Second World War she studied under James Cowie at Hospitalfield before taking up her travelling scholarship in 1948. After her return she set up a studio in the Gorbals district of Glasgow and it was here that she made her celebrated pictures of Glaswegian street children, constantly varying her media between oil, pastel and chalk (Plate 148). In Scotland so much sentiment surrounds these works that it is hard to appreciate them on a purely artistic level. In the best examples, however, Eardley takes an austerely objective attitude towards her subjects; heads can appear like scarred turnips and graffiti-splattered tenement walls like the restless stormy seas in which she was later to specialize.

In 1956 Eardley moved permanently to the dramatically situated east coast village of Catterline where she painted what are undoubtedly her finest works: an inspired series of powerful seascapes which seem to capture the violent weather effects of this part of Scotland.

Above left 148 JOAN EARDLEY
Children with Chalked Wall 3 1962–3
Oil and collage on canvas 61 × 68.6
National Galleries of Scotland
The drawing evident in this picture from Eardley's maturity is a reminder of the years of discipline imposed by the drawing class.

149 JOAN EARDLEY
The Wave 1961
Oil and grit on hardboard
  121.9 × 188
National Galleries of Scotland
In spite of Eardley's refusal to
acknowledge the influence of other
artists or movements, such a work
as this is scarcely conceivable
without the precedent of American
'action painting'.

In pictures such as *The Wave* (Plate 149), however, the abstract qualities of which the artist was surely conscious are as vivid as the naturalness of her transcription of nature. There is a rampant, almost sexual energy about many of these pictures and it is not too fanciful to suggest that something of Eardley's smouldering, emotional nature is reflected in them; perhaps the anger she must have felt at the oppression to which she and other lesbians were subject during those less emancipated times found an outlet in her painting.

In view of the years in which she was producing these pictures it is scarcely surprising that critics have noted the influence of one of the boldest of the American Abstract Expressionists, Willem de Kooning, in her work, but when questioned on the matter Eardley would claim that 'as a matter of fact my greatest influence is just looking at nature. I never look at painting at all.' It was a somewhat disingenuous assertion since she had always paid close attention to the work of Turner, and Constable, whose technique so obviously influenced her own, was something of a hero for her. She had also admired works by Jackson Pollock and de Kooning (at least in reproduction) and was, apparently, impressed by the 1956 de Stael exhibition at the Society of Scottish Artists.

150 JOAN EARDLEY
Catterline in Winter   *c.* 1963
Oil on board 120.7 × 130.8
National Galleries of Scotland
The painterly bravura of Eardley's paintings of her home village should not lead those unacquainted with the area to suspect that they are in any way untruthful. On the contrary, the way in which the tiny cottages (the artist lived in one of them) huddle together as if to protect themselves from the icy blasts of winter is vividly realistic.

Eardley died of breast cancer at Catterline aged only forty-two. She had been unaware of the seriousness of her illness and had in fact been motivated to paint with a renewed vigour – extreme even by her standards – by a recent love affair with a young student she had met at Hospitalfield. *Catterline in Winter* (Plate 150) was one of the happy results of this last creative burst. How Eardley's work might have developed had she lived longer it is hard to say. The many superbly confident pictures she did manage to produce in her comparatively short life, however, have been more than sufficient to guarantee her a place of honour in the history of post-Second World War Scottish art.

John Bellany: A NORTHERN *Expressionist*

In the summer of 1963, as Eardley lay on her deathbed requesting books 'full of bloodshed, desire and death', two students were busy hanging an open air protest exhibition on the railings of an Edinburgh city centre street. John Bellany (born 1942) and Alexander Moffat (born 1943) had been viewed as troublemakers ever since arriving at Edinburgh Art College. Initially, having angered the college authorities by turning their backs on the academic disciplines of life-drawing, anatomy, still-life and composition, they had begun painting abstracts in the manner of Alan Davie. From this, however, they had progressed to a political awareness which they expressed by painting in a Socialist Realist style of the variety favoured in Communist countries. The exhibition on the railings outside the Royal Scottish Academy was meant to cock a snook both at the academy's stuffy annual summer show and at the then unchallenged orthodoxy of

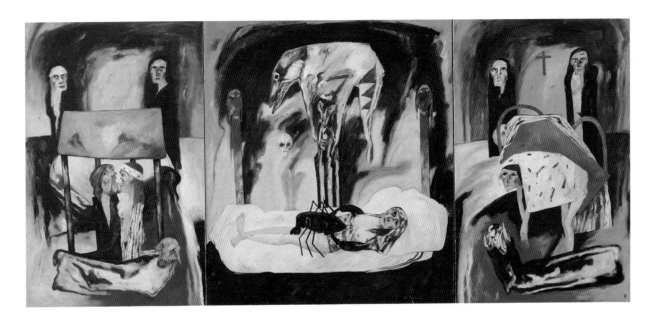

151 JOHN BELLANY
Journey to the End of the Night
1972 Oil on canvas 209.5 × 462.3
Glasgow Museums and Art
 Galleries
The disturbing iconography of Bellany's pictures of the 1970s has its roots in the artist's childhood spent in the fishing village of Port Seton. In his hands both sea creatures and the debris of the port – benign in themselves – take on a mysteriously menacing quality as if transformed by nightmares.

international abstraction. Looking at the works that caused the uproar now, they seem tame; but the stark realism of Bellany's fisherfolk and Moffat's workers was nothing less than an assault on the art world status quo.

In 1965 Bellany left Scotland to take up a postgraduate scholarship at the Royal College of Art in London and subsequently made England his home for the next twenty years. An exhibition of painting by the German Expressionist Max Beckmann at the Tate Gallery, and a few years later, a trip to the site of the Buchenwald death camp in East Germany had a dramatic impact on Bellany's work; the stoic-looking fishermen who dominate in his early pictures (Bellany's childhood had been spent in the East Lothian fishing community of Port Seton) were gradually replaced by nightmarish, totemic creatures, often dressed in the striped uniforms of the death camp inmates. In later work giant grinning fish invade dry land and equally huge crustaceans copulate with impotent women. The most ambitious of these compositions is *Journey to the End of the Night* (Plate 151) where Bellany uses the triptych format favoured by Beckmann to monumental and disturbing effect.

During the seventies, as alcoholism led to a disintegration of Bellany's personal life, a pathetic desperation entered his painting and his compositions became more and more chaotic; carcasses and predatory birds grapple with one another, seemingly reflecting the artist's inner torment. The tortured expressions of his self-portraits, decomposing flesh and an omnipresent ticking clock, are signs that he suspected his days were numbered.

In 1984 Bellany's liver finally collapsed and doctors gave little hope for his survival. After a successful liver transplant operation in 1988, however, the artist went on to make an extraordinary and dramatic recovery. Within days of the operation Bellany was demanding paint and brushes and began to record his physical progress in a harrowing series of self-portraits. For these Bellany no longer needed to communicate his personal drama through the use of symbols. *Self-portrait* (Plate 152) is a painfully honest rendition of the ignominy of hospitalization.

152 JOHN BELLANY
Self-portrait (from Addenbrooke's
 Series) 14 May 1988
Red chalk on paper 57 × 38.5
National Galleries of Scotland
Bellany's close brush with death at the end of the 1980s inspired a period of intense creativity. In an extended series of self-portraits the artist catalogued his recovery at Addenbrooke's Hospital in Cambridge. Very few artists since Van Gogh have probed their personal mental condition with such honesty.

153 JOHN BELLANY
Sunset Song 1991
Oil on canvas 203.2 × 218.44
Collection of the Artist
There is an exuberant, life-
affirming spirit present in the
paintings Bellany made after his
successful liver transplant
operation which is generally lacking
in his previous work. Using bright
colours and rapid brushwork, the
artist reflects in this work upon his
origins, family background and
present relationships.

Since his miraculous recovery – the artist himself views it as a
kind of resurrection – Bellany has begun to celebrate life again. The
demons who had taken over his pictures have been exorcized and in
their place Bellany now paints exotic flower arrangements, sensuous
female nudes and contented family groups. *Sunset Song* (Plate 153) is
a poignant reaffirmation of life; gone forever is the morbidity which
overwhelmed in the earlier work. In this picture Bellany has depicted
his own relatives, living and dead, against a glorious golden sunset.

Pop Art AND ITS *avant-garde successors*

Until the international acceptance of a new brand of figurative art
in the 1980s, Bellany was never considered a mainstream artist; his
Expressionist treatment of figurative subjects had been perpetually
at odds with the abstract and later minimalist orthodoxies of the

avant-garde. Meanwhile, however, the Pop Art movement had found in the Italo-Scots sculptor, Eduardo Paolozzi (born 1924), an original and innovative talent. Paolozzi was a friend and colleague of Alan Davie in the design department at the Central School of Arts and Crafts. Having begun his career as a Surrealist in Paris, by 1960 he had become a central figure in British Pop Art. Originally Paolozzi made collages using cuttings from magazines and science fiction comics, but he soon progressed to making sculptures into which he incorporated casts of 'found objects' and machine parts. Later he produced popular screen prints made up of impressions of electronic circuit-like components. *Calcium Light Night* (Plate 154), a series of prints inspired by the symphonies of the American composer Charles Ives, gives a good idea of the way Paolozzi employs a visual vocabulary suggested by the computer age. According to the artist 'there is nothing new in art, just new combinations'.

The sixties and early seventies saw a succession of short-lived, fashionable avant-garde art movements which swept through Western culture. After Pop Art, Minimalism and then Conceptual Art held sway for brief periods and in Scotland these all benefited from the energy and enthusiasm of another remarkable Italo-Scot, the impresario Richard Demarco.

Demarco founded his first gallery in a three-storey house in Edinburgh's New Town in 1966. His aim was to bring challenging contemporary foreign artists to Scotland and exhibit them alongside native talent and in doing so, he instigated a kind of cultural devolution. Leap-frogging London, he made a series of cultural exchanges directly with continental countries, many with eastern Europe. His most important collaboration was with the German Conceptual artist and intellectual guru, Joseph Beuys.

Part of Demarco's motivation was due to his dislike of the cultural hegemony America held over the international art scene, and so, with the help of Beuys and Karl Ruhrberg, the director of the Düsseldorf Kunsthalle, he organized an exhibition of work by twenty-five Düsseldorf artists called *Strategy-get-Arts* for the 1970 Edinburgh Festival. This single art event shook Scotland's art establishment to its foundations. Nothing like this wide-ranging exhibition of installations, performance art and video had ever been seen anywhere else in Britain, let alone Scotland.

In spite of the praise heaped on Demarco for his courage, however, Edinburgh College of Art, where ironically much of the extravaganza was staged, was outraged (the governors decided to mount an exhibition of Edinburgh School work the following year as a riposte). The damage, however, was done; Scotland's attitude towards contemporary art was never to be quite the same again.

154 EDUARDO PAOLOZZI
Central Park in the Dark some 40 years ago from *Calcium Light Night* 1974–6
Screenprint 99 × 69
Collection of the Artist
Paolozzi's annexation of the imagery of the technological and computer ages has permitted him to evolve an entirely original visual vocabulary which he uses in an often complex way to produce exciting works in both two and three dimensions. The artist currently holds the position of Queen's official sculptor in Scotland.

Although Richard Demarco's art operation received funding from the Scottish Arts Council for many years, it was never sufficient to finance the ambitious international programmes Demarco wished to run from Scotland. In 1974 the Scottish Arts Council re-allocated the lion's share of its funds in favour of its own prestige public galleries, the Fruitmarket in Edinburgh and the Third Eye Centre in Glasgow. The Fruitmarket at first was run directly by the Scottish Arts Council though it was later given pseudo-autonomous status along with the Third Eye. Yet the purse strings were always tightly controlled by the Scottish Arts Council and, to some extent, both galleries followed the Council's line by exhibiting the work of well known contemporary artists tried and tested on the international gallery circuits. Unable to compete, Demarco was obliged to operate from various unsuitable temporary premises until the total withdrawal of his Scottish Arts Council grant forced him to close down his gallery in 1992. Ironically, however, both his Arts Council-supported competitors, the Edinburgh Fruitmarket and the Glasgow Third Eye Centre, had already ceased to operate.

The 369 Gallery AND THE Edinburgh Girls

By the late seventies, in spite of the generally healthier climate for contemporary art than had hitherto prevailed in Scotland, there was still no commercial gallery offering international exposure to young Scottish artists who wished to remain working in their homeland. It was in response to this need that, in 1978, a group of graduates fresh from Edinburgh College of Art, set up the 369 Gallery in the Scottish capital's Old Town. Demarco's example convinced them that the only way of making a mark within Scotland was by gaining a reputation abroad. The 369 Gallery pursued a policy of forging links with artists' groups and galleries abroad, both in Europe and the United States. At the 1987 Edinburgh Festival the gallery mounted the first contemporary Russian exhibition in Britain, following it up in 1989 by an exhibition of Scottish art in Moscow.

Unlike most other commercial art galleries in Britain, the 369 Gallery in Edinburgh had from the outset a policy of actively promoting women artists and, by the early 1980s, a group of female artists had become closely identified with it. Most had studied at Edinburgh College of Art and in the work of the more prominent members of the group – June Redfern, Fionna Carlisle and Caroline McNairn – a definite attempt to revitalize Scotland's east coast tradition of the painterly treatment of highly personalized subject matter can be discerned.

The earlier work of June Redfern (born 1950), the oldest of the trio, was infused with the spirit of Pop Art, but by the late seventies she had discarded the tight, almost graphic style with which she had depicted scenes of hectic night-life, for example, in favour of a vigorous Expressionism, applying paint in a broad and energetic fashion usually on a vast scale. The lead provided by new German Expressionists – most notably that of Rainer Fetting in the case of Redfern – was certainly important in freeing the artist's approach to painting, but Redfern had always had a profound admiration for her compatriot John Bellany, with whose personal angst-ridden vision her own has much in common.

Redfern is a committed feminist, and in her pictures she frequently tackles women's issues such as the importance of sisterly bonding

155 JUNE REDFERN
On the Edge of the World *c.* 1984
Oil on canvas 231 × 308
City Art Centre, Edinburgh
Some of the most spirited painting to come out of Scotland during the 1980s was produced by Redfern, applying broad swathes of colour across often very large canvases. Increasingly generalized though the artist's indication of the human presence may be, the figure continues to provide the basis for almost all Redfern's work.

and childbirth; in a work entitled *On the Edge of the World* (Plate 155) she draws a parallel between her relationship with her mother and that with her lover. Redfern was appointed Artist in Residence at the National Gallery in London in 1985 and subsequently settled in the south.

Fionna Carlisle (born 1954) is the member of this Edinburgh group of female artists whose work is most obviously related to the kind of painting produced by members of the Edinburgh School in the post-war period. There is even an element of Colourist bravura in the way in which the artist handles her usually brightly coloured paint, although the speciality she has made of still-life subjects recalls the enthusiasm for this genre of William Gillies. Nevertheless, several years of constant travel have broadened Carlisle's stylistic horizons considerably.

Since moving permanently to the island of Crete in 1984, Carlisle's pictures have increasingly reflected – in their opulent colour as much as in their subject matter – the Greek life and culture in which she has immersed herself. A series of large works painted in acrylic on paper amount to a commentary on unrequited love (Plate 156). There is also a certain classical monumentality about her most recent pictures which is undoubtedly inspired by her present house.

The burden of Scotland's artistic tradition weighs even more

156 FIONNA CARLISLE
Anterastes I 1986
Acrylic on paper 200 × 203
Private Collection
The tradition of Scottish artists travelling to the Mediterranean and the Near East in search of exotic subject matter goes back to the nineteenth century, when artists such as William Allan and David Roberts made some of their most memorable pictures out of foreign subject matter. Although Carlisle's themes are almost invariably introspective, they remain flavoured by the everyday life she experiences in Crete.

heavily on Caroline McNairn (born 1955) than it does on either Redfern or Carlisle. McNairn's father, the artist John McNairn, studied at Edinburgh College of Art in the twenties alongside William Gillies and William Johnstone and became a close friend of the latter. Johnstone apparently told his friend's daughter to avoid any involvement whatsoever with the Edinburgh college, but – not having heeded the great man's advice – McNairn graduated from Edinburgh College of Art in 1978.

McNairn takes a more consciously formal approach to composition than most artists of her generation, having tended to cold-shoulder the persuasive Expressionist figuration which held sway for most of the 1980s, and looks instead for inspiration to the work of pioneers of early modernism such as Matisse. In *The Fall* (Plate 157), a picture painted like much of her most recent work in Russia, McNairn avoids the dramatic visual elements of the scene which must have

presented themselves – St Basil's Cathedral for example – preferring to concentrate on its more ordinary features. William Gillies (had he had a taste for travel) might have done much the same.

The NEW *Glasgow Boys*

By the mid-1980s, some years after these 'Edinburgh Girls' (as they have occasionally been called) had come to public attention, a loose grouping of male graduates of Glasgow School of Art made an even more powerful impression on the Scottish art scene and – perhaps more unexpectedly – on the wider international world of contemporary painting.

All of these students had come under the influence of the artist Alexander Moffat (born 1943) while at college and, to some extent, can be viewed as his protégés. Moffat (John Bellany's fellow *enfant terrible* in his Edinburgh days) had progressed by the seventies from painting in an Expressionist manner not dissimilar to that of Bellany and largely inspired by the German artist Max Beckmann, to a smooth, academic-looking form of realism. His major achievement had been a series of portraits of Scotland's leading literary figures made in a conscious tribute to the creators of Scotland's post-war cultural renaissance (Plate 158).

It was, however, Moffat's conviction that the most fruitful path that young Glasgow artists could follow was one in the direction of a socially-conscious realism that was to have the most profound effect

157 CAROLINE McNAIRN
The Fall 1992
Oil on canvas 139.7 × 238.8
369 Gallery, Edinburgh
The art of Matisse, having played a dominant role in the formation of the styles of Scottish painters during the 1930s and 1940s, continues to exert its influence on the younger generation. A passion for the electrifying effect of dramatic colour juxtapositions and an apparently naive approach to drawing ensure that McNairn's strikingly individualistic artistic personality pervades all her work.

on the group which, not surprisingly, was very soon christened the 'New Glasgow Boys'. (Moffat has at times wryly referred to them as his 'Frankenstein's monsters'!) In 1982 Moffat organized an exhibition of the work of several of his protégés at Edinburgh's New 57 Gallery, following it up three years later with a larger one at Glasgow's Third Eye Centre called *New Image Glasgow*. It was here that all the major figures in the group – Steven Campbell, Adrian Wiszniewski, Ken Currie and Peter Howson – came together for the first time.

The sheer imaginative power of the work on show by Steven Campbell (born 1953) meant that he was immediately seen as the leader of the pack. Campbell had been an engineering apprentice before entering Glasgow Art School as a mature student, and his initial interest lay in performance art. By the time he graduated in 1982, however, he had caught on to the figurative revival which was sweeping Europe and the United States. The award of a Fulbright Scholarship enabled him to spend a postgraduate year at New York's Pratt Institute and it was there that he consciously decided to forge a figurative style full of allusions to his Scottish background; Hollywood clichés like *Brigadoon* mountainous land-

158 ALEXANDER MOFFAT
Hugh MacDiarmid 1978
Charcoal and pastel on tinted paper
  38.1 × 50.8
Collection of the Artist
Just as in the nineteenth century, when so much Scottish painting depended for its inspiration on the writing of Walter Scott, post-war Scottish art has been helped by the sense of cultural identity championed by the poet Hugh MacDiarmid. This drawing of the one-time Communist and founder-member of the Scottish Nationalist Party is by the influential Glasgow School of Art tutor Alexander Moffat. It was Moffat who was chiefly responsible for encouraging the figurative interests of the group of students who have in recent times become known as the New Glasgow Boys.

scapes, thatched cottages and tweedy lairds were incorporated into his pictures.

Campbell subsequently produced a great many pictures which dramatize both real and imaginary scenes from the novels of P. G. Wodehouse. In these a cast of grossly exaggerated – almost cari-catured – English gents enact often unfathomable scenes which have a strongly surrealist flavour about them. The atmosphere evoked is

Two Humeians Preaching on Causality
1984 Oil on canvas 292.1 × 238.44
Walker Art Center, Minneapolis
Inspired initially by Surrealism,
Campbell constructs bizarre and
often perplexing narratives by
depicting with a consciously
prosaic technique imagined
incidents in the lives of a personal
cast of heroes. Unknowingly
perhaps, his art reclaims the
literary territory abandoned by
Scottish artists almost a century
ago.

frequently threatening and always intriguing. Some critics have seen
in them a scathing analysis by an artist from a predominantly
working-class Scottish city of the disintegration of the English class
system and of the rural myth England has succeeded in spinning
around itself. *Two Humeians Preaching on Causality* (Plate 159) is Campbell
at his most ebullient and fascinating; the picture's ironically pre-
tentious title pertaining to the Scottish philosopher about whom
Campbell blatantly professes to know little. Such pictures, marketed
with vigour and ingenuity first by one of New York's best-known
commercial galleries and subsequently by Marlborough Fine Art,
have assured Campbell of a reputation unsurpassed by any other
Scottish artist in recent times.

Adrian Wiszniewski (born 1958), a fellow student of Campbell at
Glasgow, followed a very similar imaginative figurative path but has
mapped out a territory of subject matter which is less imbued with
aggressive machismo than that of the older artist. Although a picture
by Wiszniewski was sold to the Museum of Modern Art in New
York, the younger artist has never succeeded in breaking into
the American market as significantly as Campbell. Nevertheless
Wiszniewski's lyrical treatment of other subjects struck a chord among
English collectors in particular and he has been widely acclaimed
throughout Britain during the 1980s. Pictures of dreamy youths such
as *Poet* (Plate 160) are typical of the romantic tenor of his work,
recalling as they do the wartime works of English Neo-Romantics
such as John Minton and John Craxton.

Ken Currie (born 1960), the most politically orientated of the
group, is the sole one among them whose work draws most clearly

160 ADRIAN WISZNIEWSKI
Poet 1986
Screenprint 139.5 × 106.5
Glasgow Print Studio
Little of the masculine aggression
which characterizes so much recent
Scottish figurative art is present in
the work of Wiszniewski, whose
painting is more intuitive in
character than that of his
Glaswegian contemporaries. In his
pictures, forms are delineated with
a softness which is ingratiating
rather than combative.

on his Glaswegian background. Moffat, Currie claims, prevented him from 'wallowing in nihilism' and encouraged him to develop the Socialist Realist style to which he was temperamentally inclined. He set out to produce a contemporary equivalent of the socialist art of the thirties, finding a role model in the Mexican muralist Diego Rivera. The materialist values of the yuppie culture which dominated Britain in the 1980s were grist to his mill. Following Léger's advice that mural painting was the best way of using art to reach the people Currie embarked on a project which culminated in 1987 with a series of murals celebrating Scottish labour history for Glasgow's People's Palace Museum (Plate 161). Since the worldwide collapse of Communism, however, Currie has become more sceptical, and now that he sees no radical alternative to capitalism the heroic optimism of his impressive murals has been replaced in his most recent work by a degree of pessimism.

161 KEN CURRIE
The People's Palace Murals – Panel 7
1986–7 Oil on canvas 218 × 251
Glasgow Museums and Art
    Galleries
In view of the highly politicized nature of Glasgow and the city's strong left-wing traditions, it is surprising that so few Glaswegian artists have taken advantage of this rich theme. Almost single-handedly, however, Currie has invented an iconography with which he is able to tackle the many political issues which confront him in Glasgow.

If anything, Peter Howson (born 1958) has enjoyed even greater commercial success than Currie, and Howson's pictures now grace the walls of glamorous collectors such as Madonna and Sylvester Stallone. Like Campbell, Howson was a mature student with a determination to make a living as a professional artist. Time taken out of art school to endure the rigours of army training not only made him keener to pursue the career of an artist, but provided him with a fruitful source of macho subject matter. Paintings of 'squaddies', bruisers and thugs have become his stock in trade, but although their titles suggest a degree of social concern, works such as *Heroic Dosser* (Plate 162) might also be read as a gratuitous glorification of violence and ugliness.

The scale of the international success of the New Glasgow Boys in the 1980s leaves a major question mark hanging over the future of Scottish art. This is primarily because the relationship between so much of their work and the traditions established in Scottish art over the past two centuries is in truth rather slight.

What then would help promote the conditions in which a more authentic indigenous culture of contemporary art might flourish in Scotland? Firstly, the support of institutions such as the Scottish Arts Council and the National Galleries of Scotland must be more vital; this, of course, depends to some extent on funds available, but it also depends on the enthusiasm and dedication of those working in these bodies; they should lead the way for business sponsors and private patrons. Secondly, the establishment of a National Gallery of Scottish Art, which is at present one of the main aims of the National Galleries of Scotland but which in some quarters is viewed as a narrow, provincial concept, should be eagerly pursued. Only in such an institution where, if the exhibits are sensitively selected and arranged, and the fascinating history of the visual arts north of the Border made explicit, will young Scottish artists be able to fully comprehend the value of the artistic tradition on which by birth they are qualified to build.

162 PETER HOWSON
Heroic Dosser 1986
Monotype with oil and crayon on
   paper 104.5 × 75.7
National Galleries of Scotland
By focusing on the underbelly of
life in Glasgow, over the past
decade Howson has created a
pointed commentary on the city's
social ills. Much of the artist's work
has been inspired by the brutish
aggression which he experienced
during a spell in the British army.
In 1993 Howson was appointed
Britain's official war artist in Bosnia.

Further Reading

General Publications

BRYDALL, ROBERT, *Art in Scotland: Its Origin and Progress*, W. Blackwood, London, 1889

CAW, JAMES L, *Scottish Painting Past and Present 1620–1908*, T.C. & E.C. Jack, London, 1908

CURSITER, STANLEY, *Scottish Art to the Close of the Nineteenth Century*, George G. Harrap and Co., London, 1949

DAICHES, DAVID, JONES, PETER AND JONES, JEAN, *A Hotbed of Genius: The Scottish Enlightenment 1730–1790* (Exhibition at the Scottish National Portrait Gallery Annex 1986), Edinburgh University Press, Edinburgh, 1986

ERRINGTON, LINDSAY AND HOLLOWAY, JAMES, *The Discovery of Scotland* (Exhibition at the National Gallery of Scotland 1978). The Trustees of the National Galleries of Scotland, Edinburgh, 1978.

GAGE, EDWARD, *The Eye in the Wind: Scottish Painting since 1945*, Collins, London, 1975

GORDON, ESMÉ, *The Making of The Royal Scottish Academy*, The Royal Scottish Academy, Edinburgh, 1988

HARDIE, WILLIAM, *Scottish Painting 1837 to the Present*, Studio Vista, London, 1990

HARTLEY, KEITH AND OTHERS, *The Vigorous Imagination: New Scottish Art* (Exhibition at the Scottish National Gallery of Modern Art 1987), The Trustees of the National Galleries of Scotland, Edinburgh, 1987

HARTLEY, KEITH, *Scottish Art since 1900* (Exhibition at the Scottish National Gallery of Modern Art and the Barbican Art Centre, London 1989 & 1990). The Trustees of the National Galleries of Scotland, Edinburgh, 1989

HOLLOWAY, JAMES, *Patrons and Painters: Art in Scotland 1650–1760* (Exhibition at the Scottish National Portrait Gallery 1989), The Trustees of the National Galleries of Scotland, Edinburgh, 1989

IRWIN, DAVID AND FRANCINA, *Scottish Painters at Home and Abroad 1700–1900*, Faber & Faber, London, 1975

MACKAY, W.D., *The Scottish School of Painting*, Duckworth, London, 1906

MACLEAN, FITZROY, *A Concise History of Scotland*, Thames & Hudson, London, 1970

MACMILLAN, DUNCAN, *Scottish Art 1460–1990*, Mainstream Publishing Co, Edinburgh, 1990

MACMILLAN, DUNCAN, *Painting in Scotland: The Golden Age* (Exhibition at the Talbot Rice Art Centre, University of Edinburgh and the Tate Gallery, London) Phaidon Press, Oxford, 1986

MARTIN, DAVID, *The Glasgow School of Painting*, George Bell & Sons, London, 1897

SKINNER, BASIL, *The Scots in Italy in the 18th Century*, Trustees of the National Galleries of Scotland, Edinburgh, 1966

SMOUT, T.C., *A History of the Scottish People 1560–1830*, William Collins Sons & Co. Ltd., Glasgow, 1969

THOMSON, DUNCAN, *Painting in Scotland 1570–1650* (Exhibition at the Scottish National Portrait Gallery 1975), The Trustees of the National Galleries of Scotland, Edinburgh, 1975

Publications Relating to Individual Artists

ARMSTRONG, SIR WALTER AND CAW, JAMES L., *Sir Henry Raeburn*, London and New York, 1901

BILLCLIFFE, ROGER, *Charles Rennie Mackintosh: the Complete Furniture, Furniture Drawings and Interior Designs*, John Murray (3rd edition), London, 1886

ERRINGTON, LINDSAY, *Master Class: Robert Scott Lauder and his pupils* (Exhibition at the National Gallery of Scotland and Aberdeen Art Gallery 1983), The Trustees of the National Galleries of Scotland, Edinburgh, 1983

ERRINGTON, LINDSAY, *Tribute to Wilkie* (Exhibition at the National Gallery of Scotland 1985), The Trustees of the National Galleries of Scotland, Edinburgh, 1985

ERRINGTON, LINDSAY, *William McTaggart 1835–1910* (Exhibition at the Royal Scottish Academy 1989), The Trustees of the National Galleries of Scotland, Edinburgh, 1989

HALL, DOUGLAS, AND TUCKER, MICHAEL, *Alan Davie*, Lund Humphreys, London, 1992

HONEYMAN, T.J., *Three Scottish Colourists: S.J. Peploe, F.C.B. Cadell, Leslie Hunter*, London, 1950

MORRIS, MARGARET, *The Art of J.D. Fergusson*, Blackie, Glasgow and London, 1974

SMART, ALASTAIR, *Allan Ramsay: Painter, Essayist and Man of the Enlightenment*, Yale University Press, New Haven and London, 1992

SMITH, SHEENAH, *Horatio McCulloch 1805–1867* (Exhibition at the Glasgow Art Gallery and Museum and elsewhere 1988), Glasgow Museums and Art Galleries, Glasgow, 1988

STEVENSON, SARA, *Hill & Adamson's The Fishermen and Women of the Firth of Forth* (Exhibition at the Scottish National Portrait Gallery 1991–2), The Trustees of the National Galleries of Scotland, Edinburgh, 1991

THOMSON, DUNCAN, *The Life and Art of George Jamesone*, Clarendon Press, Oxford, 1974

Picture Credits

Index

Numbers in bold refer to plate numbers

Aavatsmark, Fanny, 187
Abstract Expressionism, 185–6, 199–201, 203–4
Académie Julien, Paris, 169, 174
Academy of St Luke, Edinburgh, 29, 72, 120
Accademia di San Luca, 21, 73
Act of Union, 15, 26, 54–6, 119, 136, 147
Adam, James, 54
Adam, Robert, 34, 54, 65
Adam, William, 120
Adamson, Robert, 49–51
Addison, Joseph, 62
Adler, Jankel, 193, 195
Agnew's, 140
Aikman, William, 25–7, 29, 36, 65
    Allan Ramsay, 27; **11**
    Self-portrait, 25; **10**
Aitken Dott, 178–9, 192
Albert, Prince Consort, 83–4, 102–3, 136
Alexander, Cosmo, 65, 70
Alexander, John, 70, 93
    The Rape of Proserpine, 71; **38**
Allan, David
    early career, 65, 71–5, 77, 122
    later career, 84–8
    Mary, Queen of Scots subject, 93
    works:
    The Connoisseurs, 61; **32**
    The Continence of Scipio, 74; **41**
    The Cotter's Saturday Night, 86, 99
    The 4th Duke of Atholl and Family, 85; **50**
    Glaud and Peggy, 86; **52**
    Hector's Farewell to Andromache, 73; **40**
    The Origin of Painting, 64, 74
    The Penny Wedding, 85, 86, 90; **51**
    View of the Foulis Academy, 72; **39**
Allan, William, 92–5, 109, 110, 115, 129
    The Murder of Rizzio, 93, 94; **59**
    Slave Market, Constantinople, 92, 93; **58**
Anderson, John, 17
Angus, Craibe, 149
Anne, Queen, 26, 55
Argyll, 2nd Duke of, 26
Argyll, 3rd Duke of, 31
Argyll, 7th Duke of, 126
Art Nouveau, 162, 166
Arts and Crafts movement, 162, 163
Arts Council, 198
Atholl, 4th Duke of, 85

Bacon, Francis, 198
Baird, Sir David, 99
Balmoral, 84
Barbizon School, 150, 151
Barry, James, 79
Bastien-Lepage, Jules, 150, 153
    Pas Mèche, 153; **103**
Batoni, Pompeo, 47, 65
    Colonel William Gordon of Fyvie, 66; **35**
Bauhaus, 164, 166
Beardsley, Aubrey, 162
Beaumont, Sir George, 89
Beckmann, Max, 205, 206, 212
Bell, Charles, 89
Bellany, John, 204–7, 210, 212
    Journey to the End of the Night, 205, 206; **151**
    Self-Portrait, 206; **152**
    Sunset Song, 207; **153**
Bergson, Henri, 171
Beuys, Joseph, 208
Binning, Lord, 31
Black, Joseph, 54
Blair, Hugh, 45, 79
Boccioni, Umberto, 182
Bouguereau, William Adolphe, 169
Boyd, Alice, 106
Braque, Georges, 181, 189
Breadalbane, Earl and Countess of, 83
Bruce, Sir William, 22
Buccleuch, Duke of, 45
Burnet, James, 34
Burns, Robert, 86, 99, 126
Burrell, Sir William, 148
Burrell Collection, 148–9
Bute, 3rd Earl of, 36–9
Bute family, 31
Byres, James, 43, 64

Cadell, Francis Campbell Boileau ('Bunty'), 167–9, 174–6, 179, 192
    Reflections, 175; **125**
    Still-Life with Grey Fan, 176; **126**
Calder, Alexander, 199
Camberwell School of Arts and Crafts, 184
Campbell, Steven, 213–15
    Two Humeians Preaching on Causality, 214, 215; **159**
Carlisle, Fionna, 209–11
    Anterastes I, 211; **156**
Carse, Alexander, 88

Caylus, Anne Claude Philippe de Tubières, Comte de, 68
Celtic Revival, 158, 181, 183, 193
Central School of Arts and Crafts, 184–5, 199, 208
Cézanne, Paul, 167, 173, 177, 183
Chalmers, George Paul, 116
    The Legend, 116; **76**
Chardin, Jean Baptiste Siméon, 177
Charles I, King, 19, 119
Charles II, King, 19, 54, 94
Charles Edward Stuart, Prince (the Young Pretender), 63, 64, 113
Charlotte, Queen, 39
Clark, Sir Kenneth, 129
Claude Lorraine, 21, 117, 123, 127, 132, 134
Clerk, John, of Eldin, 45
Clerk, Sir John, of Penicuik, 26, 29, 43, 79, 118
Clerk family, 26, 29
Coats, William Allen, 149
Cockburn, Lord, 135
Colone, Adam de, 17
Colourists, the, 167–79
Colquhoun, Robert, 193–9
    Figures in a Farmyard, 197; **144**
    Man with Goat, 198; **145**
    Robert MacBryde, 194; **141**
    Two Scotswomen, 196
    The Whistle Seller, 196
    Woman with Leaping Cat, 195; **142**
Conceptual Art, 208
Constable, John, 144, 204
Contemporary Art Society, 198
Coram, Thomas, 33
Cornelius, Peter von, 102
Corot, Jean Baptiste Camille, 149
Correggio, Antonio Allegri da, 96, 97
Courbet, Gustave, 151
Cowie, James, 193–4, 202
    Student with Plaster Cast, 193; **139**
Craig, James
    Plan of the Edinburgh New Town, 59; **31**
Cranston, Catherine, 163
Crawhall, Joseph, 150, 152
Craxton, John, 194, 215
Crozier, William, 183, 186, 187
    Edinburgh from Salisbury Crags, 182, 183; **130**
Cubism, 167, 171, 181–2
Cunego, Domenico, 69
Cunyngham, Alexander Dick, 29

Currie, Ken, 213, 215–17
  The People's Palace Murals – Panel 7, 216; **161**
Cursiter, Stanley, 181–2
  The Sensation of Crossing the Street, West End, Edinburgh, 180, 182; **129**

Dadd, Richard, 103, 104
Daubigny, Charles, 150
David, Antonio, 70
David, Jacques-Louis, 65, 70, 97
Davidson, Jo, 170
Davie, Alan, 185, 199–201, 205, 208
  The Horse that has Visions of Immortality, No. 2, 200; **146**
  Oh to be a Serpent that I might love you longer, 201; **147**
Defoe, Daniel, 118
Degas, Edgar, 115
De Kooning, Willem, 203, 204
Delacour, William, 120
  Decorative Paintings in the Great Saloon, Yester House, 120; **78**
Delacroix, Eugène, 96–7
Demarco, Richard, 208–9
Diaz, Narcisse, 150
Domenichino, 34
Dott, McOmish, 142
Douglas, William Fettes, 106
  The Recusant's Concealment Discovered: Persecution in Scotland, 106, 107; **69**
Dove, Arthur, 184
Dow, Thomas Millie, 155
Drummond, James, 95, 113
  The Porteous Mob, 95, 96; **61**
Drummore, Lord, 33
Düsseldorf Kunsthalle, 208
Dyce, William, 102–4, 139
  The Baptism of King Ethelbert, 102
  Christ as the Man of Sorrows, 139; **93**
  Pegwell Bay: A Recollection of October 5th, 1858, 103; **66**

Eardley, Joan, 202–4
  Catterline in Winter, 204; **150**
  Children with Chalked Wall 3, 202; **148**
  The Wave, 203; **149**
Edinburgh College of Art, 183, 186, 191, 192, 199, 205, 209, 211
Edinburgh Festival, 147, 189, 208, 209
Edinburgh Girls, 209–12
Edinburgh New Town, 58, 59, 129, 174, 208
Edinburgh School, the, 191–2, 208
Eglinton, 10th Earl of, 36
Ernst, Max, 184
Erskine, Lady Mary, 19

Faed, John, 107
Faed, Thomas, 107–8
  The Last of the Clan, 107, 150; **70**
  The Mitherless Bairn, 107
  The Visit of the Patron and Patroness to the Village School, 107
Fauves, 167, 169, 170–1, 174
Ferguson, Adam, 34, 45, 54

Fergusson, John Duncan, 167–73, 177–9, 181, 183, 192–3
  The Blue Beads, 171
  The Blue Hat, Closerie des Lilas, 171; **121**
  Damaged Destroyer, 173; **123**
  Les Eus, 172
  Rhythm, 171, 172; **122**
Fetting, Rainer, 210
Foulis, Andrew, 72
Foulis, Robert, 71–2
Foulis Academy, 71–3, 77, 122
Franklin, Benjamin, 59
French Impressionists, 141, 145, 158
French Revolution, 60
Freud, Lucian, 194
Friesz, Othon, 170
Fruitmarket, Edinburgh, 209
Fuseli, Henry, 76
Futurism, 182

Gainsborough, Thomas, 43, 49
Gama, Vasco da, 101
George I, King, 27
George III, King, 28, 31, 36, 47
George IV, King, 42, 49, 53–4, 89, 92
Géricault, Théodore, 97, 101
German Expressionism, 205, 210
Gibbon, Edward, 64
Gillies, William George, 186–91, 195, 210, 211–12
  Fields and River, 190; **136**
  In Ardnamurchan, 188
  Skye Hills from near Morar, 187; **133**
  Still-Life, Blue and Brown, 189; **135**
  Winter, Temple: Backs of Houses, 190; **137**
Gilliland, James, 42
Gimpel Fils Gallery, 199
Glasgow, 147–67, 192–8
Glasgow Boys, 149–61, 192
Glasgow Boys, New, 212–17
Glasgow International Exhibition (1888), 156–7
Glasgow School, 150–1
Glasgow School of Art, 162, 165, 193, 202, 213
Glasgow Style, 161–7, 192
Gordon, 2nd Duke of, 70
Gordon, John Watson, 50
Gow, Neil, 90
Graham, Peter, 140
  A Spate in the Highlands, 140; **94**
Graham, R.B. Cunninghame, 157
Graham, Tom, 112
Grand Tour, 26, 47, 63, 65
Grant, Sir James, 69
Gros, Antoine Jean, Baron, 97
Grosvenor Gallery, 161
Guggenheim, Peggy, 199, 202
Gunning, Elizabeth, Duchess of Hamilton, 65, 67
Guthrie, Sir James, 150, 151–5, 161
  A Highland Funeral, 151, **101**
  A Hind's Daughter, 152; **102**
  To Pastures New, 153, 154, 155; **105**

Hague School, 149

Hals, Frans, 44, 47, 169, 176
Hamilton, 6th Duke of, 120
Hamilton, Gavin
  career, 65–71, 75, 78, 93
  influence, 69–70, 73, 74, 77, 86
  works:
  Achilles Lamenting the Death of Patroclus, 69; **37**
  Elizabeth Gunning, Duchess of Hamilton, 65, 67; **36**
Hamilton, Sir William, 64
Harvey, Sir George, 94–5
  The Covenanters' Preaching, 94, 95; **60**
Haydon, Benjamin Robert, 103
Henry, George, 152, 157–61
  The Druids: Bringing in the Mistletoe, 158, 159; **110**
  A Galloway Landscape, 157, 158; **109**
  Japanese Lady with a Fan, 159, 161; **112**
  The Star in the East, 158
Herman, Josef, 193
Highlands, the, 135–8, 143
Hill, David Octavius, 49–51
  Newhaven Fishwives, 50; **26**
  Willie Liston, Redding the Line, 51; **27**
Hilliard, Nicholas, 17
Hitchens, Ivon, 187
Hoffmann, Josef, 166
Hogarth, William, 31–2, 33
Holbein, Hans, 29
Homer, 67, 68, 73
Honeyman, T.J., 179
Hoppner, John, 44
Horace, 40, 61, 126
Hornel, Edward Atkinson, 150, 157–61
  The Druids: Bringing in the Mistletoe, 158, 159; **110**
  Kite Flying, Japan, 159, 160; **111**
  The Star in the East, 158
Hospitalfield House, 193, 202
Howson, Peter, 213, 217
  Heroic Dosser, 217; **162**
Hume, David, 34, 39, 54, 59–61, 78, 215
Hunt, William Holman, 100, 139
Hunter, George Leslie, 167, 176–9
  Reflections, Balloch, 179; **128**
  Still-Life with Anemones and Fruit, 178; **127**
Hutton, James, 42, 54

Imperiali, 29–30
Ives, Charles, 208

James I of Scotland, King, 106
James VI of Scotland, I of England, King, 16, 17, 55, 56
James II, King, 22, 55
James Francis Edward Stuart, Prince (the Old Pretender), 26, 55, 63, 64
Jamesone, George, 16–19
  Lady Mary Erskine, 18; **5**
  Self-portrait, 17; **4**
Japanese influences, 158–61
Jenkins, Thomas, 64
Johnson, Samuel, 28, 118
Johnstone, William, 183–6, 187, 195, 199, 211

Lithograph accompanying poem by
  Hugh MacDiarmid, 185; **132**
Ode to the North Wind, 184; **131**
A Point in Time, 184

Kames, Lord, 34, 58
Keirincx, Alexander, 118–19
Falkland Palace and the Howe of Fife, 119;
  77
Kennedy, Sir Thomas, 70
Kennedy, William, 155
Kent, William, 26
Khnopff, Fernand, 162
King, Jessie, 170
Klee, Paul, 188, 195
Kneller, Sir Godfrey, 24, 25, 26, 29
Knox, John (artist), 137
Knox, John (religious reformer), 95

Landseer, Sir Edwin, 83, 85, 92, 109
The Monarch of the Glen, 82, 83; **49**
La Tour, Quentin de, 36
Lauder, Robert Scott, 108, 109–12,
  115–16
Christ Teacheth Humility, 111; **72**
Lavery, John, 150, 155–7, 161
Harmony in Brown, 157
On the Loing, 156; **107**
The Tennis Party, 156–7, 161; **108**
Lawrence, Sir Thomas, 44, 45, 49
Lefevre Gallery, 149, 195, 196, 199
Léger, Fernand, 188, 216
Lely, Sir Peter, 16, 19, 22, 29
Leven, 3rd Earl of, 22–4
Lewis, Wyndham, 173, 193, 196
Lhote, André, 183, 187, 188
Lindsay, Margaret, 34
Lumisden, Andrew, 64–5

MacBryde, Robert, 193–4, 196, 198
Robert Colquhoun, 194; **140**
Woman at a Table, 196; **143**
McCulloch, Horatio, 136–8, 143
Glencoe, 136, 137, 141; **91**
Loch Katrine, 137–8; **92**
MacDiarmid, Hugh, 181, 183, 186
MacDonald, Duncan, 196
Macdonald, Margaret, *see* Mackintosh
Macdonnell of Glengarry, Col. Alastair,
  47–9
Macgregor, William York, 150, 154, 167
The Vegetable Stall, 154, 155; **106**
Mackintosh, Charles Rennie, 161–7, 172
Fritillaria, Walberswick, 166; **117**
Glasgow School of Art, 165; **116**
The Harvest Moon, 162; **113**
Palalda, Pyrénées-Orientales, 166; **118**
Willow Tea Rooms, 163, 164; **115**
Mackintosh, Margaret Macdonald,
  162–7, 172
The May Queen, 166
Summer, 163; **114**
McLellan, Archibald, 148
MacNair, Frances Macdonald, 162–4
MacNair, James Herbert, 162–4
McNairn, Caroline, 209, 211–12

The Fall, 211, 212; **157**
McNairn, John, 211
Macnee, Daniel, 50
Macpherson, James, 79
McTaggart, William 106, 116, 141–6, 167
Photograph on Beach, 143–4; **97**
Running for Shelter, 142, 143; **96**
The Sailing of the Emigrant Ship, 146; **99**
Spring, 141, 142; **95**
The Storm, 143–4, 145; **98**
MacTaggart, William (grandson of
  above), 187, 191
MacWhirter, John, 112
Manet, Edouard, 169, 176
Mansfield, Katherine, 170
Maratta, Carlo, 26
Maris brothers, 149
Marlborough Fine Art, 215
Marquet, Albert, 170, 171
Martin, David, 42
Martin, John, 125
Mary, Queen of Scots, 17, 55, 93
Mary II, Queen, 22, 55
Masucci, Agostino, 65
*The Marriage of Prince James Francis
  Edward Stewart to Princess Maria
  Clementina Sobieska*, 63; **33**
Matisse, Henri, 167, 169, 177–8, 192, 211
Mauve, Anton, 149
Maxwell, John, 188, 191
View from a Tent, 188; **134**
Mead, Dr Richard, 32–3
Medina, Sir John Baptiste de, 22–5, 26,
  29, 36
David Melville, 3rd Earl of Leven, 23; **8**
Portrait of a Boy, 24; **9**
Melville, Arthur, 152, 169, 174
Michelangelo, 75, 76, 78, 100
Millais, Sir John Everett, 104, 106, 141
Minton, John, 194, 215
Moffat, Alexander, 205, 212–13
Hugh MacDiarmid, 213; **158**
Monet, Claude, 145
Monticelli, Adolphe Joseph Thomas, 159
Moore, Henry, 184
More, Jacob, 122–3, 126, 127, 134
The Falls of Clyde – Cora Linn, 123–4; **81**
*Mount Vesuvius in Eruption: The Last Days
  of Pompeii*, 125; **82**
Morris, Margaret, 172, 178
Morris, William, 162
Moser, Koloman, 166
Mosman, William, 70
Motherwell, Robert, 199
Munch, Edvard, 187
Murillo, Bartolomé Esteban, 96
Murray, Sir Mungo, 22
Murry, John Middleton, 170, 171
Mytens, Daniel, 16

Nasmyth, Alexander, 125–8, 130, 134, 137
Edinburgh from Calton Hill, 129; **85**
Edinburgh from Dean Village, 129; **86**
*Princes Street Showing the Building of the
  Royal Institution*, 127; **84**
Robert Burns, 126; **83**

Six designs for stage sets with views of
  Old Edinburgh for *The Heart of
  Midlothian*, 128; **87**
View of Culzean From the Sea, 57; **30**
Nasmyth, Patrick, 129
National Galleries of Scotland, 110, 111,
  149, 182, 217
Nattier, Jean Marc, 30
Nazarenes, 102
Neo-Classicism, 65–71, 77–8, 81, 84, 127
Neo-Romantic movement, 194–5, 215
Netherlands influence, 16–17
Newbery, Francis ('Fra'), 162, 165
New 57 Gallery, 213
New Glasgow Boys, 212–17
New Image Glasgow exhibition, 213
Newton, Lord, 47
Norie, James, 120
Norie, James Junior, 120
Norie, Robert, 120
Landscape with a View of Ben Lawers, 121;
  79
Norie family, 29, 77, 120–2
Northcote, James, 39

O'Keeffe, Georgia, 184
Orchardson, Sir William Quiller, 112,
  113–15
The Last Dance, 115
Le Mariage de Convenance, 113, 115; **75**
Master Baby, 115
Ossian, 79–81, 130

Palmer, Samuel, 195
Panini, Giovanni, 120
Paolozzi, Eduardo, 185, 208
Calcium Light Night, 208; **154**
Paris Salon, 156
Pasmore, Victor, 185
Paton, Joseph Noel, 104–5, 106
The Reconciliation of Oberon and Titania,
  104–5, 111; **67**
Penicuik House, 79–81; **46**
Penkill Castle, 106
People's Palace Museum, Glasgow, 216
Peploe, Samuel John, 167–70, 172, 173–4,
  179
The Black Bottle, 169
Boats at Royan, 169, 170; **120**
A Girl in White: Peggy Macrae, 168, 169;
  119
Old Tom Morris, 169
Still-Life with Roses, 174; **124**
Perronneau, Jean Baptiste, 30
Pettie, John, 112–13, 151
Bonnie Prince Charlie at Holyrood, 113, 114;
  74
The Drumhead Court Martial, 112, 113; **73**
Pevsner, Sir Nikolaus, 165
Phillip, John, 108–9
La Gloria – A Spanish Wake, 108; **71**
A Presbyterian Catechizing, 108
Picasso, Pablo, 170, 181, 195, 196
Piranesi, Giovanni Battista, 122
Playfair, William Henry, 110
Pollock, Jackson, 185, 199, 204

222 · *Index*

Pop Art, 185, 207–9
Pope, Alexander, 26
Post-Impressionists, 167, 177
Poussin, Gaspard, 134
Poussin, Nicolas, 21, 64
Pratt Institute, New York, 213
Pre-Raphaelites, 102, 104–7, 138–41, 150

Raeburn, Henry
  career, 41–9
  copies, 90, 99
  Father of the Scottish School, 16, 139
  friendships, 126–7, 132
  portraiture, 39, 58, 64, 90, 136
  Scott's opinion, 92
  Scottish Enlightenment, 54, 58
  studio, 27, 126–7, 169
  visit to Rome, 40, 126
  works:
    Col. Alastair Macdonnell of Glengarry, 46,
      47, 113; **24**
    Dr Nathaniel Spens, 43
    James Hutton, 42
    John, 2nd Marquess of Bute, 49
    John Sinclair of Ulbster, 43
    Lord Newton, 45, 47; **23**
    Mrs Ferguson of Raith with her Children, 43
    Mrs James Campbell, 49
    Mrs Scott Moncrieff, 48, 49; **25**
    Sir John and Lady Clerk of Penicuik, 43;
      22
    Sir Walter Scott, 8; **1**
    The MacNab, 49
Ramsay, Allan
  career, 28–40, 70, 120
  Dialogue on Taste, 60
  influence on Nasmyth, 125–6
  portraiture, 15–16, 44, 58
  Scottish Enlightenment, 16, 54, 58–61,
    78
  search for Horace's villa, 40, 61, 126
  works:
    David Hume, 40; **20**
    Dr Richard Mead, 32; **15**
    Hew Dalrymple, Lord Drummore, 33, 47;
      16
    *The Hon. Rachel Hamilton and the Hon.
      Charles Hamilton*, 31; **14**
    Jean-Jacques Rousseau, 41; **21**
    John Stuart, 3rd Earl of Bute, 37; **18**
    Margaret Lindsay, the Artist's Wife, 35, 36;
      17
    Queen Charlotte with a Fan, 38; **19**
    Self-portrait, 30; **13**
Ramsay, Allan (poet, father of above), 27,
  29, 32, 62, 72, 74, 86
Raphael, 42, 68, 72, 101
Redfern, June, 209–11
  On the Edge of the World, 210; **155**
Redpath, Anne, 191–2
  The Indian Rug, 191, 192; **138**
Reid, Alexander, 149, 151, 158, 161, 178
Reid, James, of Auchterarder, 148
Reid, Thomas, 45, 54
Reinagle, Philip, 39
Rembrandt, 29, 49, 87, 99

Reynolds, Sir Joshua, 31, 35, 36, 42–3, 49,
  60, 62
Rice, Anne Estelle, 170, 171
Richardson, Jonathan, 62
Rigby, Elizabeth, Lady Eastlake, 51
Rivera, Diego, 216
Robert the Bruce, 130
Roberts, David, 93, 129, 133
Robertson, Brian, 198
Robertson, William, 45, 54
Roche, Alexander, 155
Romanticism, 16, 128–34, 143
Rome, Scottish community, 62–81, 123
Rosa, Salvator, 134
Rossetti, Dante Gabriel, 106, 163
Rothko, Mark, 199
Rousseau, Jean-Jacques, 39, 59
Rousseau, Théodore, 150
Royal Academy, London, 81, 91
Royal Academy Schools, 89, 102, 104
Royal College of Art, London, 205
Royal Institution, 109–10
Royal Scottish Academy, 50, 109–10, 147,
  161, 182–3, 186, 189, 205
Royal Scottish Society of Painters in
  Watercolour, 186
Rubens, Peter Paul, 17, 29, 69, 72, 75–6,
  91
Ruhrberg, Karl, 208
Ruisdael, Jacob van, 132
Runciman, Alexander, 75, 77–81, 101, 118,
  125, 135
  Agrippina Landing at Brundisium, 77, 78,
    81; **44**
  *The Blind Ossian Singing and Accompanying
    Himself on the Harp*, 80; **47**
  The Landing of St Margaret, 81; **48**
  Orestes Pursued by the Furies, 78; **45**
  The Origin of Painting, 78
  The Tomb of the Horatii on the Appian Way,
    122; **80**
  Ulysses Surprising Nausicaa, 77
Runciman, John, 75–7, 79
  King Lear in the Storm, 76; **43**
  Self-portrait, 75; **42**
Ruskin, Effie (later Millais), 104
Ruskin, John, 102, 104, 106, 138, 139, 142,
  156
Ruskin, John James (father of above), 128
Rutland, 4th Duke of, 64

Salon d'Automne, Paris, 170
Sandby, Paul, 123
Scott, David, 81, 100–1, 111
  *The Discoverer of the Passage to India
    Passing the Cape of Good Hope*, 101, 102;
    65
Scott, Francis George, 183
Scott, Sir Walter
  George IV's visit to Edinburgh, 53
  illustrations, 92, 129, 131, 137
  influence, 41, 84, 92, 93–5
  Romantic view of Scottish landscape,
    129–33, 143
  Waverley novels, 47, 92, 128
Scott, William Bell, 100, 105–6

The King's Quair, 106; **68**
Scott-Moncrieff, George, 188
Scottish Arts Council, 209, 217
Scottish Enlightenment, 16, 28, 34, 53–4,
  56, 57–62, 78, 125
Scottish Gallery, 178
Scougal, John, 28
'Secessions', 161
Segonzac, André Dunoyer de, 179
Select Society, 34
Severini, Gino, 182
Shaftesbury, 3rd Earl of, 27, 68, 72, 73
Shakespeare, William, 78, 104
Sharpe, James, 94
Sickert, Walter Richard, 115, 179
Smith, Adam, 34, 54
Socialist Realist style, 205, 216
Société des Beaux-Arts, 151
Society of Arts, 69, 79
Society of Eight, 186
Society of Scottish Artists, 182, 187, 188,
  204
Solimena, Francesco, 30
Sophia, Electress of Hanover, 55
Spencer, Lord, 64
Stael, Nicolas de, 204
Stair, 1st Viscount, 57
Stewart, Dugald, 54
Strategy-get-Arts exhibition, 208

Talbot, William Henry Fox, 51
Tassie, James
  Portrait medallion of James Byres of Tunley,
    64; **34**
Taylor, E.A., 170
Telford, Thomas, 135
Third Eye Centre, Glasgow, 209, 213
Thomas, Dylan, 194
Thomson, George, 86
Thomson, Rev. John of Duddingston, 110,
  132–3, 134, 137
  *Fast Castle from Below, St Abb's Head in
    the Distance*, 133; **89**
369 Gallery, 209
Titian, 148
Toorop, Jan, 162
Townley, Charles, 64
Trustees' Academy, 88, 95, 100, 101, 109–
  11, 125, 139, 140, 141, 182
Turin International Exhibition of
  Decorative Art, 165
Turnbull, George, 68
Turner, Joseph Mallord William
  influence, 104, 204
  landscapes and seascapes, 125, 144
  Scott illustrations, 129–32, 137
  Scottish landscapes, 118, 130–2, 135
  Loch Coruisk, Skye, 131–2; **88**
  Peace, Burial at Sea, 99–100

Van Aken, Joseph, 31
Van der Goes, Hugo
  Trinity Altarpiece, 12, 13; **2**
Van de Velde, Willem, 132
Van Dyck, Sir Anthony, 16, 29
Van Gogh, Theo, 149

Van Gogh, Vincent, 149, 158, 167, 170–1, 177

Portrait of Alexander Reid, 149; **100**

Vanson, Adrian, 16–17

James VI and I, 16; **3**

Velasquez, Diego de Silva y, 21, 96

Venice Biennale, 165

Vienna Secession exhibition (1900), 165–6

Vermeer, Jan, 149

Vernet, Claude-Joseph, 123–4

Vertue, George, 31

Victoria, Queen, 83–5, 135–6, 157

Vleughels, Nicholas, 30

Voltaire, 59

Wade, George, 56, 135

Waitt, Richard, 27–8

The Henwife of Grant, 28; **12**

Wallace, William, 123, 130

Walpole, Horace, 19, 36

Walpole, Sir Robert, 26–7

Walton, Edward Arthur, 150, 153–5

A Berwickshire Fieldworker, 153; **104**

Watson, Peter, 194

Watt, James, 58

Wellington, 1st Duke of, 91

Westminster Hall competition, 100–1, 106, 111

Whistler, James Abbott McNeill, 115, 148, 150, 156–7

Whitechapel Art Gallery, 198

Wilkie, David

  career, 88–92, 95–9

  genre tradition, 88–92, 108, 136, 150

  late style, 96–9, 110, 115

  opinion of Nasmyth, 129

  portraiture, 50

  Raeburn letter, 44

  works:

  The Chelsea Pensioners Receiving the Waterloo Despatch, 91, 95; **57**

  The Cotter's Saturday Night, 87, 99; **53**

  The Defence of Saragossa, 96, 97; **62**

  General Sir David Baird Discovering the Body of Sultan Tippoo Sahib, 99

  George IV Entering the Palace of Holyroodhouse, 52, 92; **28**

  Josephine and the Fortune Teller, 97, 98; **63**

  The Letter of Introduction, 89; **55**

  The Penny Wedding, 86, 90; **56**

  A Persian Prince, his Slave bringing him Sherbet, 99; **64**

  Pitlessie Fair, 88, 89; **54**

  The Village Politicians, 89

William III, King, 22, 28, 55

Williams, Hugh William ('Grecian'), 129, 134, 137

The Temple of Poseidon, Cape Sunion, 134, 135; **90**

Willison, George, 65

Winckelmann, Johann Joachim, 68, 75

Wiszniewski, Adrian, 213, 215

Poet, 215; **160**

Wodehouse, P.G., 213

Wordsworth, William, 84, 118

Wright, John Michael, 19–22

Sir Mungo Murray, 21; **7**

Sir William Bruce, 20; **6**